Zeitschrift für Kanada-Studien

Im Auftrag der
Gesellschaft für Kanada-Studien
herausgegeben von

Ingrid Neumann-Holzschuh
Wilfried von Bredow
H. Peter Dörrenbächer

29. Jahrgang 2009 / Heft 1

GESELLSCHAFT FÜR KANADA-STUDIEN

Vorstand

Univ.- Prof. Dr. Klaus-Dieter Ertler, Präsident, Zentrum für Kanadastudien, Institut für Romanistik, Merangasse 70, A-8010 Graz, Österreich

Prof. Dr. Hartmut Lutz, Vizepräsident, Universität Greifswald, Department of English and American Studies, Steinbeckerstr. 15, Raum 25a, D-17487 Greifswald

Prof. Dr. Bernhard Metz, Schatzmeister, Albrecht-Dürer-Str. 12, D-79331 Teningen

Wissenschaftlicher Beirat

Englisch-Kanadische Sprache und Literatur: Prof. Dr. Martin Kuester, Institut für Anglistik und Amerikanistik, Philipps-Universität Marburg, Wilhelm-Röpke-Straße 6, D-35032 Marburg

Französisch-Kanadische Sprache und Literatur: Dr. Peter G. Klaus, Institut für Romanische Philologie, Freie Universität Berlin, Habelschwerdter Allee 45, D-14195 Berlin

Frauen- und Geschlechterstudien: PD Dr. Caroline Rosenthal, Universität Konstanz, Fachbereich Literaturwissenschaft, Fach D 166, D-78457 Konstanz

Geographie und Wirtschaftswissenschaften: PD Dr. Ulrike Gerhard, Julius-Maximilians-Universität Würzburg, Institut für Geographie, Am Hubland, D- 97074 Würzburg

Geschichtswissenschaften: Dr. Petra Dolata-Kreutzkamp, John F. Kennedy-Institut für Nordamerikastudien, Abteilung Geschichte, Freie Universität Berlin, Lansstraße 7-9, D-14195 Berlin

Politikwissenschaft und Soziologie: Prof. Dr. Martin Thunert, Zentrum für Nordamerika-Forschung (ZENAF), Johann Wolfgang Goethe-Universität Frankfurt, Robert-Mayer-Straße 1, D-60325 Frankfurt am Main

Andere Disziplinen (u. a. Native Studies): Dr. Kerstin Knopf, Ernst-Moritz-Arndt-Universität Greifswald, Institut für Anglistik/Amerikanistik, Steinbäckerstraße 15, D-17487 Greifswald

Herausgeber

Prof. Dr. Ingrid Neumann-Holzschuh, Institut für Romanistik, Universität Regensburg, Postfach, D-93040 Regensburg *(verantwortlich für den Aufsatzteil)* ingrid.neumann-holzschuh@sprachlit.uni-regensburg.de

Prof. Dr. Wilfried von Bredow, Institut für Politikwissenschaft, Philipps-Universität Marburg, Wilhelm-Röpke-Str. 6, G 23, D-35032 Marburg *(verantwortlich für den Aufsatzteil, Schwerpunkt Sozialwissenschaften)* wvb@staff.uni-marburg.de

Prof. Dr. H. Peter Dörrenbächer, Fachrichtung Geographie, Universität des Saarlandes, Im Stadtwald, Gebäude 11, D-66041 Saarbrücken *(verantwortlich für den Rezensionsteil)* p.doerren@mx.uni-saarland.de

Articles appearing in this Journal are abstracted and indexed in
HISTORICAL ABSTRACTS and AMERICA: HISTORY AND LIFE.

Einzelpreis 14.- €

Gedruckt mit Unterstützung der GKS und der Kanadischen Regierung

Bibliografische Information der Deutschen Nationalbibliothek
Die Deutsche Nationalbibliothek verzeichnet diese Publikation in der Deutschen Nationalbibliografie; detaillierte bibliografische Daten sind im Internet über http://dnb.d-nb.de abrufbar.

Bibliographic information published by the Deutsche Nationalbibliothek
The Deutsche Nationalbibliothek lists this publication in the Deutsche Nationalbibliografie; detailed bibliographic data are available in the Internet at http://dnb.d-nb.de.

ISBN 978-3-89639-690-7

Alle Rechte, auch die des auszugsweisen Nachdrucks, der fotomechanischen Wiedergabe und der Übersetzung, vorbehalten. © Wißner-Verlag, Augsburg 2009.
Redaktion und Lektorat: Dr. Michael Friedrichs. Lektorat Französisch: Catherine Gagnon.

EDITORIAL

In den Geistes- und Sozialwissenschaften werden Interdisziplinarität und die Methodiken des Vergleichs mehr denn je nachgefragt. Das hat mit wissenschaftsinternen Diskursen, aber ebenso mit wissenschafts- und forschungspolitischen Anreizsystemen zu tun. Über letztere kann man sehr unterschiedlicher Meinung sein. Aber unbezweifelbar haben Interdisziplinarität und komparatistische Ansätze verschiedenster Art in Regionalstudien wie den Kanada-Studien nicht nur ihren Platz unter anderem. Sie gehören gewissermaßen zu den Konstitutionsbedingungen von Regionalstudien. Dieser theoretisch-methodische Bonus hat in der Regel eine besonders stimulierende Wirkung für Forschung und Lehre. Und so wäre es paradox, wenn gerade in einem Moment, in dem sich Kanada-Studien und andere Regionalstudien als vorbildlich innovativ erweisen, universitäre Reformen und Studiengangs-Änderungen großen Stils sie mittelfristig zu schwächen drohten.

Noch kann von einer solchen Schwächung keine Rede sein, wofür gerade dieses Heft einmal mehr den Beleg abgibt – stammt doch eine ganze Reihe der Aufsätze aus der Feder jüngerer Wissenschaftlerinnen und Wissenschaftlern. Auch ist die Vielzahl der fachlichen Perspektiven und der Themen bemerkenswert. Aber eben auch, dass sie sich trotz aller thematischen und fachlichen Unterschiede immer erkennbar in einen gemeinsamen Erkenntnishorizont eingliedern.

Mit dem Aufsatz „Could North American Monetary Integration be an Optimum?" steigt *Armin J. Kammel* tief in die wirtschaftswissenschaftliche Debatte über die Theorie optimaler Währungsräume ein. Das hört sich an, als ginge es um sehr abstrakte Dinge. Jedoch ist es nicht so, denn Antworten auf die Frage nach der Stabilität von Währungen unter Stress haben enorme praktische Auswirkungen. In Nordamerika, geprägt von einer engen Wirtschaftskooperation zwischen Kanada und den Vereinigten Staaten, sind Überlegungen über eine nordamerikanische Währungsunion jedenfalls alles andere als Glasperlenspiele. Der Autor nimmt neben wirtschaftlichen Aspekten auch politische in den Blick, was seinen Beitrag besonders aufschlussreich macht.

Falko Brede untersucht die rechtlichen Voraussetzungen und Verfahrensregeln kanadischer *Royal Commissions* und deutscher Expertenkommissionen. Im einen wie im anderen Fall handelt es sich um Einrichtungen der Politikberatung mit dem Ruf, besonders sorgfältig und kreativ zu arbeiten. Die nicht unbeträchtlichen Unterschiede zwischen diesen Einrichtungen führt Brede auf die Andersartigkeiten in den politischen Kulturen beider Länder zurück.

Die folgenden beiden Aufsätze stammen aus der Literaturwissenschaft, aber ihre politischen und gesellschaftlichen Konnotationen sind unübersehbar:

Miriam Richter beschäftigt sich in ihrem Beitrag mit der neueren anglo-kanadischen Jugendbuchliteratur. Um eine Antwort auf die Frage zu finden, welche Rolle den historischen Jugendromanen bei der Herausbildung der nationalen Identität Kanadas zukommt, untersucht sie, wie die Kontakte zwischen Engländern und Franzosen im Akadien des 18. Jahrhunderts, also zur Zeit der Deportation, in ausgewählten Jugendromanen dargestellt werden.

Christian J. Krampe untersucht den aktuellen Roman von Lawrence Hill, *The Book of Negroes*, das 2008 den *Commonwealth Writers' Prize* gewonnen hat. Diesem Roman kommt eine Schlüsselposition innerhalb der afro-kanadischen Literatur zu, deren erklärtes Ziel es nach Krampe ist, das als einseitig empfundene, stereotype Bild von Kanada als einem Refugium für Schwarze und einem multikulturellen Paradies kritisch zu hinterfragen.

Der einzige sprachwissenschaftliche Beitrag in diesem Heft stammt von *Isabelle Mensel*. In ihrer soziolinguistisch ausgerichteten Untersuchung geht es um das Verhältnis von Englisch und Französisch in Ontario, genauer gesagt um die Einstellungen und Argumentationsmuster anglo- und frankophoner Sprecher, so wie sie sich in virtuellen Diskussionsforen manifestieren. Es wird deutlich, dass die Sprachensituation in Ontario nach wie vor Gegenstand der öffentlichen Diskussion ist: Zwar spricht sich eine beachtliche Mehrheit der Bewohner dieser dominant anglophonen Provinz für die offizielle Zweisprachigkeit aus, der Wille zum Erlernen der jeweils anderen Sprache ist allerdings wenig ausgeprägt.

Die folgenden Aufsätze schließen thematisch an das vorige Heft an, denn sie befassen sich mit Québec.

Zunächst beschreibt *Marion Stange* die komplexen Kooperations-Strukturen der Krankenhäuser in den nordamerikanischen Kolonien Frankreichs ab der Mitte des 17. Jahrhunderts beispielhaft anhand von Krankenhäusern in Québec Stadt und New Orleans. Der Kolonialismus beruhte zu dieser Zeit ja vielfach auf einem Prinzip, das man heute *Public Private Partnership* nennt. Wie dies damals auf dem Gebiet der Gesundheitspolitik funktionierte, ist erhellend.

Paul Villeneuve verfolgt in seinem Beitrag die „Konkurrenz" zwischen den beiden Städten Québec und Montréal. Aus beiden Städten sind nachhaltige Impulse für die Entwicklung von Politik, Kultur und Wirtschaft in der Provinz Québec gekommen, und besonders folgenreich ist das Wechselspiel zwischen dem turbulenten Montréal und dem ruhigen Québec.

Das *Forum* enthält zwei hochaktuelle Texte zu Québec, die beide um das Thema Migration kreisen. Der Beitrag von *Peter Klaus* ist der Literatur der Migranten gewidmet: Dank der vor allem aus Haiti sowie verschiedenen südamerikanischen Ländern stammenden Autoren wie Dany Laferrière oder Sergio Kokis hat die quebecer Literatur in den vergangenen beiden Jahrzehnten eine Öffnung hin zu Lateinamerika erfahren, was als klarer Bruch mit der Vergangenheit interpretiert wird. Anhand einer Betrachtung neuester Werke zeigt Klaus, dass sich das lebhafte literarische Leben speziell in Montréal durch eine neue „schöpferische Polyphonie" auszeichnet, die innerhalb der frankophonen Literaturszene einzigartig ist.

Helga Bories-Sawala beschreibt anlässlich der politischen Debatte um die *accommodements raisonnables* in Québec den Umgang mit kulturell und religiös motivierten Konflikten zwischen Minderheiten, speziell Migranten, und der jeweiligen Mehrheitsgesellschaft in Québec, Frankreich und Deutschland. Während sich die drei Länder hinsichtlich des juristischen und politischen Rahmens zum Teil erheblich unterscheiden – das deutlichste Beispiel ist das Verhältnis von Staat und Kirche –, ähneln sich die Konflikte und Problemlösungsstrategien dennoch in gewisser Weise. In jedem Fall fördert kulturelle Vielfalt überall die Diskussion um gesellschaftliche Werte und Normen.

In der Sparte Rezensionen erscheint dieses Mal auch eine längere Sammelbesprechung zur kanadischen Außenpolitik von *David Bosold*, die nicht nur für die Politologinnen und Politologen in der Kanadistik aufschlussreich ist.

Ingrid Neumann-Holzschuh   Wilfried von Bredow   Peter Dörrenbächer

Inhalt

Artikel/Articles/Articles

Armin J. Kammel	Could North American Monetary Integration be an Optimum?	9
Falko Brede	Politikberatung im Vergleich: *Royal Commissions* und deutsche Expertenkommissionen	31
Miriam Richter	Constitutional 'Equality of Status' – From Political Program to Fictional Reality: The Relationship between Anglo- and Franco-Canadians in Anglo-Canadian Children's Literature	47
Christian J. Krampe	Inserting Trauma into the Canadian Collective Memory: Lawrence Hill's *The Book of Negroes* and Selected African-Canadian Poetry	62
Isabelle Mensel	Le débat autour du bilinguisme dans la province canadienne de l'Ontario : la relation de l'anglais et du français commentée par les locuteurs dans les forums virtuels de discussion	84
Marion Stange	Urban Governance in French Colonial North America: Hospital Care in Québec City and New Orleans in the 17th and 18th Centuries	108
Paul Villeneuve	Societal Change in Quebec and Canada: The Roles of Quebec City and Montreal	120

Forum

Peter Klaus	Une certaine latino-américanité de la littérature québécoise	136
Helga Elisabeth Bories-Sawala	Accommodements raisonnables, laïcité républicaine ou mosaïque fédérale: les défis de l'interculturalité au Québec, en France et en Allemagne	151

Besprechungen/Reviews/Comptes rendus — 166

David Bosold	Sammelrezension: Michael Byers, *Intent for a Nation: What is Canada For?* Vancouver/Toronto: Douglas & McIntyre, 2007; Roy Rempel, *Dreamland: How Canada's Pretend Foreign Policy Has Undermined Sovereignty*, Montreal / Kingston: McGill-Queen's University Press, 2006; Patrick James / Nelson Michaud / Marc J. O'Reilly (eds.), *Handbook of Canadian Foreign Policy*, Lanham, MD: Lexington	166

	Books, 2006; Steven Kendall Holloway, *Canadian Foreign Policy: Defining the National Interest*. Peterborough: Broadview Press, 2006; Duane Bratt / Christopher J. Kukucha (eds.), *Readings in Canadian Foreign Policy. Classic Debates and New Ideas*, Don Mills, ON: Oxford University Press 2006; Fen O. Hampson/Brian Tomlin/Norman Hillmer, *Canadian International Policies - Agendas, Alternatives, and Politics*, Don Mills, ON: Oxford University Press 2008; John Kirton, *Canadian Foreign Policy in a Changing World*, Scarborough: Nelson-Thomson 2007	
MARTIN THUNERT	Patrick James / Mark Kasoff (eds.), *Canadian Studies in the New Millennium*, Toronto, Buffalo, London: University of Toronto Press, 2008	175
FRITZ PETER KIRSCH	Rosmarin Heidenreich, *Paysages de désir. J. R. Léveillé : réflexions critiques*, Ottawa: L'Interligne, 2005	176
FRITZ PETER KIRSCH	Gilles Dupuis / Klaus-Dieter Ertler (éds.), *À la carte. Le roman québécois (2000-2005)*, Frankfurt am Main usw.: Peter Lang, 2007	178
AUTOREN UND REZENSENTEN		181
HINWEISE FÜR AUTOREN		182

ARMIN J. KAMMEL

Could North American Monetary Integration be an Optimum?

Zusammenfassung
Spätestens seit der Einführung des Euro als europäische Einheitswährung entstand eine nachhaltige Diskussion über ein ähnliches nordamerikanisches Pendant. Eine wichtige Erkenntnis dieser Debatte ist, dass die Theory of Optimum Currency Areas (OCA) eine politische Dimension gänzlich vermissen lässt. Dieser Aufsatz versteht sich als Beitrag zu dieser breiten und mehrschichtigen Debatte und stellt einen neuen multidimensionalen Ansatz zu OCA vor, der jedoch auf der herkömmlichen OCA basiert. Der Beitrag konzentriert sich vor allem auf die Auswirkungen der politischen Begleiterscheinungen und Konsequenzen, welche mit der Errichtung einer Währungsunion verbunden wären. Das erweitert die Diskussion über eine mögliche nordamerikanische Währungsintegration mit dem Endziel einer nordamerikanischen Währungsunion, weil neben den ökonomischen auch die politischen Aspekte einer solchen Entwicklung in den Blick kommen.

Résumé
L'idée d'un pendant nord-américain de l'Euro fait l'objet d'une discussion de longue haleine et ce, depuis du moins l'introduction d'une monnaie commune européenne. Une conclusion importante de ce débat est que la théorie de l'Optimum Currency Areas (OCA) omet toute dimension politique. Le texte se veut une contribution à ce vaste et complexe débat et propose une nouvelle approche multidimensionnelle de l'OCA, tout en se basant sur la théorie traditionnelle de l'OCA. L'article traite principalement des répercussions sur le plan politique et des conséquences qui seraient liées à l'introduction d'une union monétaire. En tenant compte non seulement des aspects économiques mais aussi des aspects politiques, on élargit la discussion quant à la possibilité d'une intégration monétaire en Amérique du Nord visant une union monétaire nord-américaine.

Introduction

> The link between language and currency has often been noted. Language is a medium of communication and currency is a medium of exchange. National, ethic and liturgical languages are here to stay, but a common world language, understood as a second language everywhere would obviously facilitate international understanding.[1]

This meaningful quote by Canada's 1999 Nobel Laureate in Economic Sciences *Robert A. Mundell* is definitely a perfect starting point to reconsider the Theory of Optimum Currency Areas (OCA) as well as a possible future monetary integration in North America. Latest in the advent of the introduction of the Euro as a single currency in the majority of EU member states, the OCA theory experienced a kind of renaissance after its first introduction by *Robert Mundell* (1961) in his famous seminal paper on OCA theory, which had an extraordinary influence on the subsequent developments of this theory as *Kenen* (2002) points out.

OCA theory basically looks at the advantages and disadvantages of different regions (*Sarno / Taylor*, 2002, 171-177) adopting the same currency and thereby in the light of a single currency making transactions across regions simpler by guaranteeing a fixed rate of exchange (see *Bayoumi*, 1997, 77). In seems to be that particularly the heavy debate on exchange rate policies, with *Friedman* (1953, 157-203) arguing that exchange rates should be allowed to float against other currencies, significantly influenced *Mundell's* work.

By discussing the costs of losing monetary flexibility, *Mundell* emphasized that the similarity of the underlying economic disturbances primarily determines the costs of a currency union. In case two regions face similar economic disturbances, their desired monetary response will also be similar, and therefore the costs of being forced to set the same nominal interest rate will be small (*Bayoumi*, 1997, 78). In contrast to this, he argues that if regions face dissimilar disturbances – like in his example the Eastern and Western halves of the United States and Canada – a single monetary policy will then cause larger costs. However, according to *Mundell*, this intractable problem can be resolved by perfect factor mobility across the regions.

Nevertheless, *Mundell's* model is characterized by a so-called mirror-image asymmetry meaning that due to the nature of his proposed two-country union, the expenditure-switching shock would not be true in a union with more than two member countries (see *Kenen* 2002, 82). Furthermore, this mirror-image asymmetry is the best example for the tendency in literature to focus only on a single criterion in order to define whether a region constitutes an optimum currency area or not. In

---

[1] Robert Mundell (2000), "Currency Areas, Exchange Rate Systems and International Monetary Reform" on www.columbia.edu/~ram15/cema2000.html (last paragraph).

order to challenge the existing, rather specifically focussed literature on OCA theory, this paper comes up with *multi-dimensional approach* of OCA theory in order to define an OCA in a complete manner, as well as to connect the ideas of *Mundell* & the others with the political and social dimensions nowadays. The best argument for such a *multi-dimensional approach* comes from microeconomics, in which the world constitutes an OCA. However, this should not lead to the misleading conclusion that the discussion will be in favour of a world currency. However, in the light of this newly proposed *multi-dimensional approach* it shall be pointed out that a currency union can have outrageous effects for certain regions, if the participants firstly experience a similarity in the underlying economic disturbances which is basically reflecting standard OCA theory and secondly – as new extension to current theory – can incorporate their political views into the empirical and economic suggestions being in favour of monetary integration.

In addition to *Mundell's* article, two other papers representing pillars of early OCA theory should be mentioned as well:

The first by *McKinnon* (1963, 717-725) introduced the degree of openness and the importance of the size of the economy as additional criteria. He argued that, typically, in an open economy, changes in the exchange rate would not alter the ratio of prices between traded and non-traded goods while in a relatively closed economy, the assumption exists that labour does not immediately notice the inflationary effect of devaluation. Two logical reasons for this phenomenon are first, that in a closed economy the traded goods sector contributes just a minimal amount to the consumer price index and therefore the devaluation may have a less-than-obvious effect on the rate of inflation, and second, that the large non-traded goods sector may be able to absorb the change in demand without a corresponding rise in prices. In other words, *McKinnon* tries to show that only relatively closed economies can effectively use the exchange rate instrument. This is a main argument for monetary union in the EU because all member countries are open economies as measured by the share of imports in GDP.

The second by *Kenen* (1969, 41-60) primarily stresses the importance of product diversification in the economy because within a diversified economy the microeconomic shocks can effectively be balanced between the different sectors. According to *Kenen*, an OCA is made up of highly diversified economies, which is interesting because this is already a kind of pre-condition for *Mundell's* approach of the mobility of labour because a highly diversified economy maximizes the amount of employment opportunities for each single worker. *Kenen* (2002, 83-84) also points out that a fiscal system spanning several regions can help to maintain internal balance and thus compensate in part for the macroeconomic disadvantage of having a currency area that spans many labour markets, which however is not optimal in the Mundellian sense.

Three Different Approaches of OCA Theory in Literature

Mundell, *McKinnon* and *Kenen* are representatives of the so-called *traditional approach* of OCA theory, which is characterized by the attempt of several authors to single out different criteria to delimit the domain of an OCA. Within this approach, there are as *Kammel* (2003, 7-9) points out, already some rare attempts to add the degree of financial integration, the similarity in the rate of inflation as well as the degree of policy integration to the original criteria.

Gandolfo (2001, 332-340) nicely describes the so-called *cost-benefit approach*, which simply tries to point out the costs and benefits of a participation in a currency area. However, it has generally be kept in mind that it is necessary to weigh the costs and benefits of such a participation through some kind of social preference function, so that the final decision will then depend on the set of weights chosen and furthermore that it can easily vary from country to country or even from period to period within the same country. This explains why no general rule for weighing the following costs and benefits can be given:

The main benefits of participating in a currency area are first that a permanently fixed exchange rate eliminates speculative capital flows between the partner countries, second, that there is – in case the credibility of the fixed exchange rates is established – no need to keep international reserves for transactions and third that monetary integration can stimulate the integration of economic policies and even economic integration and fourth advantages of a political type, in the sense that a currency area carries more weight than individual countries in negotiating as a whole with outside parties. Moreover, another major advantage is the larger capital market created through the currency area.

In contrast to this, the main costs of participating in a currency area are first the loss of autonomy in monetary and exchange policy of the individual members, second, constraints on national monetary policy in the sense that a member country might be harmed due to the fact that the joint management of the single member's monetary policies is carried out in the interest of the majority, third, a possible increase in unemployment if the currency area includes a country with low inflation and an external surplus, which might become dominant and compel the other members with greater inflation and an external deficit to adjust because the deficit countries will have to take restrictive measurements which will probably lead to a decrease in employment and fourth, a possible deterioration of previous regional disequilibria.

In addition to this, it is important to mention two other models by *Melitz* (1995) and *Bayoumi* (1994). *Melitz's* theory is basically based on a direct relationship between the size of this optimal share and the number of countries wishing to join a given monetary union. In this context it is also has to be stressed that the size of the OCA increases with its openness.

One of the most interesting models within OCA literature is *Bayoumi's* attempt to incorporate the three "single-criteria-models" by *Mundell*, *McKinnon* and *Kenen* in his so-called general equilibrium model of an OCA. See *Bayoumi* (1994, 537-554). In this regard the key assumptions are that each of the two respective countries, call them j and k, are fully specialized in the production of a single differentiated good which they trade with each other. *Bayoumi* argues that the benefits of a currency union between the countries j and k depend directly on the proportions of trade between them, on Bjk and Bkk as well as on the level of transaction costs on this trade. It is important to note that whether or not a currency union is welfare-increasing, depends on the balance of costs and benefits. Therefore, the net benefit of joining a currency union for country k, under the assumption of a negative shock, is greater the larger the cost of transacting currencies, the greater the share of good j in country k's consumption, the lower the share of good k in country k's consumption and the smaller these shocks are. Resulting from that, the openness (defined as a high level of cross or so-called diversified consumption) favours a currency union. Interestingly enough, this is exactly *McKinnon's* criterion, but just reached from a different argument. Further, in support of *Kenen's* use of this criterion is a diversified industrial structure, which would tend to reduce the size of aggregate shocks. Moreover, if labour is mobile between regions, a part of country k's unemployed workers will move to country j where there is excess demand for labour. Thus, while country k's output is still lower, country j's output rises by cutting the cost of forming a currency union. By recalling *Mundell*, one will notice a similar approach with the difference that *Mundell* focuses on the alleviation of asymmetric shocks whereas *Kenen* argues that asymmetric shocks are less likely to occur in well-diversified economies.

Contrary to this, the third country outside the union, m, suffers a welfare loss from the currency union between the other two countries because it does not share the lower transaction costs, and also suffers the lower availability of good k. However, it seems to be obvious that the result would be different, if other benefits, such as economies of scale in the currency union, materialize. This goes hand in hand with the view expressed by the *Commission of the European Communities* (1990) as well as more recently *Franke / Rose* (1998, 1009-1025) whereas *Krugman* (1991) and *Eichengreen* (1992) stress that an increased trade leads to more specialization which will then work against the common currency area. It has to be stated that this school, going back to *Kenen* (1969), does not make clear the assumptions and mechanisms under which its conclusions are reached (see *Demopoulos / Yannacopoulos* 2000). Contrary to this, the opposite view is entirely based on empiricism.

To complete the dogmatic distinction of the different approaches, the so-called *New Theory* has to be added, which is primarily dominated by two issues: the effects of shocks and reputational considerations. Even though this *New Theory* brings up interesting aspects (*Tavlas*, 1993, 663-685), recent theoretical and empirical work has produced ambiguous results (*Gandolfo*, 2001, 339-340).

The Origins of Money and Central Banking

Without money, OCA theory would be useless, so therefore in order to suggest a *multi-dimensional approach* of OCA theory, one has to go back to the roots reflecting the on-going debate between those arguing that the use of currency was based essentially on the power of the issuing authority (the so-called *Cartalists*) and those who argue that the value of currency depends primarily (or solely) on the intrinsic value of the backing of that currency (the so-called *Metallists*)[2]. Besides this, another debate exists between those arguing that money evolved as a private sector, market-oriented response to overcome the transactions costs inherent in barter (the so-called *Mengerians*), and the already mentioned *Cartalists*, who argue that state authorities have generally played a central role in the evolution and the use of money (*Goodhart*, 1998, 408). The on-going debate on how the private sector could evolve towards a monetary economy with the main duty to search for cost minimisation procedures within this system, which a government does not necessarily have to enter at all, is based on *Menger's* early paper and the constructed models vary in many aspects. However, most (if not all) of these models lack the historical fact that money frequently played an initial means-of-payment role in inter-personal social and governmental roles before it played a major role as a medium-of-exchange in market transactions (*Goodhart*, 1998, 418). In addition to this, the governing body played a crucial role for the currency in almost any society, which however does not mean that the private sector would not be able to develop various monetary systems without any state influence.

As *Goodhart* (1998, 409) correctly points out, there seems to be a tendency among economists to have a normative preference for systems determined by private sector cost minimisation rather than the not as transparent political factors. It is correct that the European Monetary Union (EMU) does not show the desired link between political sovereignty and fiscal authority on the one hand and money creation, the mint and the central bank, on the other hand. However, it is important to stress the independence of the European Central Bank (ECB) (see Art 107 EC) and its primary objective being the maintenance of price stability (see Art 105 EC). It has to be kept in mind that the Euro system reflects more or less the existing national sensitivities among the member states and the desire of national banks to keep some power in the formulation and the implementation of monetary policies. However, from a structural point of view, it is worth mentioning that the ECB has some shortcomings: The ECB incorporates to a certain extent two models of central banking which have evolved in the post-war period, the so-called Anglo-French model and the so-called German model. As *DeGrauwe* (2000, 150-174) correctly distinguishes, these two models basically differ from each other on two counts, the first

---

[2] *Goodhart* (1998, 407-432) nicely divides the two schools into the "C-team" and the "M-team". He kind of ironically lists the economists of both "teams" such as *Aristotle, Locke, Menger*, or *Kiyotaki and Wright* for the "M-team" and *Knapp, Mireaux* and most post-Keynesians for the "C-team".

one being concerned with the objectives a central bank should pursue and the other being related to the institutional design of the central bank. Regarding the objectives of the central bank, a central bank in the Anglo-French model has to pursue a few objectives such as price stability, stabilization of the business cycle, the maintenance of high employment or financial stability, whereas in the German model, price stability is its primary objective in the sense that any other objective pursued by the central bank always has to be conditional on the requirement that its pursuit does not endanger price stability. Regarding the institutional design of the central bank, the Anglo-French model favours the political dependence of the central bank, meaning that monetary policy decisions have to be approved by the government, whereas the German model is characterized by the political independence as the leading principle. In *DeGrauwe*'s words, the Anglo-French model was discarded as a guide for the design of the ECB, and the German model prevailed due to the German Bundesbank's appearance representing the new monetarist paradigm of price stability being the primary objective and political independence as the instrument to achieve that and the dominant position of Germany, during the negotiations for a monetary union.

These elaborations show that the lack of clear accountability is a serious shortcoming of the ECB because its strong degree of independence, a feature of utmost importance, is not equally matched by a strong procedure to control its performance. One might consider the general failure to centralize the supervision of the banking system at the supranational level as another shortcoming of the ECB. However, due to the *Lamfalussy* committees on the supranational level and the increased supervisory cooperation in Europe, such a centralized approach is currently not necessary. Nevertheless, a separate institutional approach analogously to the ESCB might be an option in the future.

Reasons for a Multi-dimensional Approach of OCA Theory

Why are all these fairly detailed elaborations necessary in a paper that primarily tries to outline various perspectives of a possible North American Monetary Integration (NAMI)? Why is OCA theory so crucial for monetary integration? What would a *multi-dimensional approach* of the OCA theory mean?

Pure OCA theory basically compares the advantages and disadvantages of having a single currency in a wider region. As already pointed out above, the main factors affecting an OCA are its size, openness, labour market flexibility, product diversity and the nature of either symmetric or asymmetric shocks. It is a substantial shortcoming of standard OCA theory that the functions and role of a government do not enter these models. Theoretically speaking, there is no need that currency domains have to be co-incident and a co-terminus to sovereign states. This means in other words that it is easily possible that a sovereign state has any number of currencies as from one to n and that furthermore an OCA should be able to include as many separate and sovereign countries as from one to n. However, even in case of basic agreement with this theory, there is a substantial need to extend these approaches to a *multi-dimensional* level. Even though models, as reproductions of the real world, can never include every detail of reality, they shall be constructed as "real" as possible. Before this background, the development of the *multi-dimensional approach* of OCA theory shown in terms of a possible monetary integration in North America, tries to reflect also the political realities.

The *multi-dimensional approach* consists of two main dimensions with various sub-dimensions, depending on the specific case. The first and traditional dimension in OCA theory is the economic dimension constituting the fundament of the model, which also includes the proposed new political dimension as well as a new semi-dimension, being the monetary institutions dimension.

North American Economic Integration in General

Before going into details of the model, a few words have to be said in general on specific issues of North American economic integration (see *Harris*, 2001), a broader term than NAMI. Especially since the 1980s it can be said that a fairly high level of trade integration between Canada and the U.S.A. has been developed. Economic integration can e.g. take the forms of FDI, trade flows in general, mergers and acquisitions, labour movements across borders, cross-border transportation flows as well as political interactions at the federal, state-province and local level, different networks or cultural exchanges.

By observing these forms of integration in North America, one observes a tendency towards a North-South Integration rather than an East-West Integration, although this trend seems to have shifted recently due to the increase of interregional trade in Canada and the strength of the Canadian dollar. However, according to *Harris* (2001, 4), five potential drivers for the until recently rather prevailing North-South Integration can be indicated: technology in all its various forms, geopolitical events such as the emergence of the EU or the political reform in Mexico, certain demographic trends like the baby boom and bust, economic policy namely the Canada-U.S. free trade agreement (FTA) as well as NAFTA and geography due to the unique nature of the long Canada-U.S. border and the proximity of most Canadians to the U.S. border.

Despite the questionable success of NAFTA and the bilateral FTA between Canada and the U.S.A., numerous – in particular Canadian – concerns emerged. Especially the 1990s showed a significant gap between Canadian and U.S. living standards, mainly resulting from a weaker Canadian productivity (see *Courchene*, 2001, 3-11) and employment performance. Therefore certain worries that future Canadian economic prosperity is at risk emerged. Additionally, the failure of the OECD Multilateral Agreement on Investment (MAI) and the troubles at the WTO meetings from Seattle 1999 onwards bolstered the anti-globalization movement as well as concerns that the multilateral system might not turn out as expected. Canada's increased export dependency on the U.S.A. as well as substantial declines in global commodity prices

– here it is important to stress that commodity prices are traditionally a source of Canada's comparative advantage due to its enormous resources – at the same time as U.S. growth in knowledge-intensive sectors increased, raised serious concerns in Canada, whether special economic policies would be necessary to implement and whether Canada is already substantially behind in the developments towards a new knowledge-based economy. Furthermore, Canada's decline in the share of total North American FDI during the last 20 years led to the negative development that foreign investors "forget" Canada more and more.

Despite the recent economic turbulences and the comparable weakness of the US economy, Canada has to do something in order to improve its current situation. A few policy options have to be taken into consideration in this regard. As *Harris* (2001, 6) correctly points out, there are basically four of them:
- strengthening and improving NAFTA in certain areas,
- pursuing policy convergence, and in some areas policy harmonization with the U.S.,
- making radical changes in specific domestic policy areas such as tax policy or
- trying to create a common market network (if not within NAFTA, then at least on a bilateral basis)

The last policy option is the most controversial one and has caused lots of literature. In the following, the paper focuses on a possible monetary integration as part of this option and discusses it in the light of OCA theory.

North American Monetary Integration and OCA Theory
Basics

The advent of the Euro during 1998-99, raised a heavy debate in Canada on the merits of the current floating exchange rate system as well as on the merits of a certain form of monetary integration with the U.S.A. As suggested in various papers, it shall be argued that a North American Monetary Union (NAMU) could make sense in particular for Canada but only by adapting a new *multi-dimensional approach* of the existing OCA theory. However, NAMU is considered as the final stage of NAMI and until today there is no support for any kind of currency integration from Canadian authorities, a phenomenon that also seems to be widespread among academics, economists and financial analysts (see e.g. *Courchene*, 2001) who all tend to remain in favour of the current situation of flexible exchange rates.

Nevertheless, from a European point of view, one supports fixed exchange rates and thereby the arguments of *Courchene / Harris* (1999). However, as an extension of their arguments the newly constructed model reflecting the *multi-dimensional approach* of OCA theory shall now be examined in more detail.

The Economic Dimension

Like standard OCA theory, the model is based on strong and dominating economic arguments that make sure the region[3] fulfils the necessary economic preconditions before moving to the upper political dimension. When elaborating on the economic dimension, three interrelated arguments have to be discussed:
- Canada suffers more from its existing floating exchange rate system than it gains from it and therefore experiences a significant welfare loss.
- Economic analysis suggests persuasively that greater exchange rate stability between Canada and the U.S.A. will have positive impacts in particular for Canada.
- The long-term objective for this exchange rate fixity could be a NAMU.

The already traditional argument to defend the floating Canadian dollar is that Canadian monetary independence and a floating dollar create policy sovereignty and economic flexibility, particularly in the sense of being able to implement "home-made"-inflation and nominal interest policy as well as that a flexible exchange rate constitutes a potential buffer role of accommodating asymmetric shocks that hit the Canadian economy, which is actually the classic Keynesian argument defending flexible exchange rates. Despite the argument being valid, following *Courchene / Harris (1999)*, it can under certain circumstances be the case that the presumed advantages associated with this exchange rate buffering may also turn out to be illusory.

In the following it should be shown that the traditional approach to exchange rates and dealing with asymmetric shocks is not appropriate for the changing geopolitical realities and Canada-U.S. economic integration. The best example to illustrate this is Ontario's inter-provincial exports on the one hand and its international exports on the other. In the early 1980s, both domains of Ontario's exports were in the range of around CDN-$ 40 billion, while already during the 1990s Ontario's international exports increased to a three times higher level than its exports to other provinces. In 2001, the market value of Ontario's international exports being a percentage of Ontario's GDP exceeds 50% and since just over 90% of Ontario's international exports are to the U.S., the value of Ontario's north-south exports is running at roughly 45% of its GDP. These facts underline the first rather obvious aspect of the model, being the necessity of a geographical proximity in order to be able to have a high trade volume in terms of exports and imports. As we will see later on, this geographical proximity will constitute the necessary link between the economic and political dimension of the model.

---

3 At this stage, when arguing in the economic dimension, a region does not necessarily have to be identical with the borders of a sovereign state but as we will see later in the political dimension, it would not make much sense to split a sovereign state in order that two or more provinces of one or more states can constitute an OCA. Besides that, it would probably not be possible to find the necessary political consensus for that.

Ontario is not the only example experiencing by trend a shift rather from east-west to north-south trade because already in 1996 all but two of Canada's ten provinces exported more to the rest of the world (being the international exports) than they did to the rest of Canada (being the inter-provincial exports). Nevertheless, as indicated above, the recent economic developments and the increasing strength of the Canadian Dollar might lead to a reversal in this regard. Anyhow, contrary to the situation in the 1980s, in 1996 at the aggregate (meaning all-province) level, for each CDN-$ of inter-provincial exports, international exports were running at CDN-$ 1.83 with a strong tendency to even increase that, since over 80% of Canada's international exports are destined to the U.S.A.

What are the implications that can be drawn from these numbers? First of all, that comparing to the on average 63% of the exports of the EU-15 countries that are destined to the other member states of the union, around 80% of Canada's exports are to the U.S.A. Therefore, as *Courchene* (2001, 12) correctly points out, the argument for monetary integration or even for a common currency based on economic integration is at least as compelling as for the monetary integration and monetary union in Europe. Second and stressing the geographical argument again, Canada seems to become more and more a series of north-south (and here implying cross-border) economies instead of being a single east-west economy – a tendency that should make Canadians worry and rethink their position concerning economic integration. Third, these newly emerging east-west series of cross-border economies are causing different effects regarding their business cycles.

These recent geo-economic developments lead to a new perspective – not extensively reflected in literature – on the issue of external shocks that supposedly have an asymmetrical impact on Canada and the U.S.A.:

Suppose that B.C. gears to match its policies with those of the American Northwest and the Pacific Rim. Similar to this, Alberta, Saskatchewan and Manitoba align their policies to compete with Montana, North Dakota and Minnesota, like Ontario and Quebec adapt their policies to match those of the U.S. Great Lakes States. The same happens in Canada's Atlantic Provinces in order to become competitive with the New England States and the Atlantic Rim. This scenario is characterised by the fact that each Canadian province has adapted its policies in order to be competitive with its cross-border counterpart.

When assuming that a commodity price shock such as an increase in commodity prices occurs, it has to be kept in mind that this kind of shock will typically be of an asymmetric nature due to the fact that Canada is a larger commodity producer in terms of share of GDP than the U.S.A. Nevertheless, initially, this shock affects each side of every regional cross-border economy similarly in the sense that there is no regional cross-border asymmetry because e.g. B.C. lumber faces the same price changes as lumber in the American Northwest, or Windsor, Ontario is still similar with Mo'town Detroit in terms of car industry. If an appreciation of the Canadian exchange rate now "buffers" this commodity price shock, then – as *Courchene* (2001) convincingly states – all of the Canadian provincial or regional economics are offside with respect to their American counterparts. Not only due to the certain danger of an exchange rate overshooting or misalignment, this "buffering" function of the exchange rate is more than inappropriate because it is pretty obvious that each Canadian trading region would rather prefer to maintain exchange rate and transactions with both east-west as well as with north-south trading partners. The conclusion that can be drawn is, that in such a case it is necessary that the Canadian exchange rate has to be fixed relatively to the US-$, a variant of an argument that was first introduced by *Mundell* (1961), who stressed already the asymmetries being rather east-west than north-south.

Along the lines with *Courchene*, it is convincing that in addition to this "regional" aspect of supply or demand shocks, a "national" aspect has to be stressed as well, especially because commodities represent a much larger percentage of overall output in Canada than in the U.S.A. Therefore, the commodity-based goods and services are a much larger component of Canadian-GDP than U.S.-GDP. Furthermore, the example showed that the important asymmetries are east-west. Nevertheless, the "national" aspect requires a certain kind of "buffering" as well, which however does not necessarily have to be one of the exchange rate variety. After pointing out the inappropriate policy of flexible exchange rates, now the question arises how this "buffering" is accomplished in case of fixed exchange rates.

The answer is fairly complex but can be divided into three main mechanisms:

The first one, being the internal adjustment of prices, is basically characterized by the similarity of the terms-of-trade shocks that affect the Canadian as well as the American side. As the example above indicates, it is not the commodity shock that causes the disequilibrium for the Canadian provincial economies, but the exchange rate response! Therefore, in case of a fixed exchange rate, the Canadian provinces can adapt in the same way their regional U.S. counterparts are able to.

The second mechanism deals with fiscal stabilization, which is dogmatically part of the philosophy underpinning fixed exchange rates. From a theoretical perspective, an individual region is involved in the fiscal stabilization of the exchange rate, no matter if an economy would be positively affected by a trade shock. In such a case – underpinned by *Courchene / Harris* (1999) who refer to} the example of Ontario in the late 1980s, the region makes use of its fiscal levers in order to temper a boom. As the mentioned example of Ontario indicates, the results of such policy would have been more transparent and efficient if Canada had been under fixed exchange rates. However, this example should not suggest different exchange rates for each province in Canada but underscores the usefulness of having one fixed exchange rate for the whole country.

The third mechanism being the most important one reflects the typical east-west asymmetry within Canada. In this regard, it underscores the importance of national policy mechanisms such as e.g. the national tax-transfer system, unemployment insurance or federal-provincial equalization payments that are automatically triggered, especially in case of regional-specific shocks.

It can easily be derived from the analysis that these economic arguments support the deepening of North America's economic integration. However, they also indicate that a floating Canadian exchange rate is not necessary and might sometimes even be inappropriate for an efficient adjustment to external (commodity) price shocks. Nevertheless, the deep economic integration makes the case for Canada-U.S. currency integration much stronger than most economists and politicians realize. Moreover, a closer Canada-U.S. exchange rate link would even strengthen such a process.

In addition to this, the advanced stage of the previous elaborations, the so-called monetary integration also has to be mentioned within the discussions of the economic dimension of the model: Especially *Courchene* and *Harris* but also *Grubel* (1999) regularly express their confidence that Canada would successfully be able to maintain a sustainable fixed exchange rate and would also benefit from a monetary union with the U.S.A.

However, when talking about a single currency in North America, two basic considerations and routes have to be taken into account:

Dollarization

The route of dollarization is two-dimensional. The first conception is the so-called "policy dollarization" which is defined to refer to an official decision by policy authorities to proclaim the US-$ as legal tender. However, it seems to be more than unlikely that Canada would ever follow this route. Nevertheless, the economic advantage would be that Canada would be able to act unilaterally and it would ultimately constitute exchange rate fixity. Nevertheless, its economic disadvantages significantly outrange these benefits. The main disadvantage would be Canada's loss of its existing seigniorage. Furthermore, adopting dollarization being triggered by an unstable floating Canadian exchange dollar would cause enormous additional costs for the country.

The second conception of dollarization is the so-called "market dollarization", a scenario in which Canada's private sector progressively conducts its affairs in US-$. There is already a certain tendency into this direction by just considering high-tech firms, banks and other large corporations doing their financial accounting in US-$, or that the Montreal Stock Exchange established a NASDAQ satellite which trades in Canada in US-$. This tendency will sooner or later lead to the danger that the Bank of Canada's ability to conduct monetary policy will be extremely limited.

Concluding from these elaborations, dollarization does not seem to be beneficial for Canada due to its wide variety of negative economical side-effects. The recent rise of the Canadian-$ is simply a strong argument supporting this view.

North American Monetary Union

The preferable alternative to dollarization would be the so-called North American Monetary Union (NAMU)[4], which is the final stage of NAMI and also constitutes an ultimate exchange rate fixing. NAMU basically means the North American equivalent of the European Monetary Union. Typical characteristics of NAMU would be the following:

- In analogy to the European Central Bank (ECB), a supranational bank would have to be established. Let us name this new overarching central bank North American Central Bank (NACB). This NACB would have a board of directors, in which the 12 existing Federal Reserve Banks would have a seat as well as the Bank of Canada and the 7 newly founded Canadian Reserve Banks. In order to create a balance of power and control in terms of monetary policy of NACB, 7 new "Canadian Reserve Banks" should be established, one in B.C (Vancouver), one in Alberta (Edmonton), one in Saskatchewan (Regina), one in Manitoba (Winnipeg), one in Ontario (Toronto), one in Quebec (Montreal) and the last one in Atlantic Canada (Halifax). These newly created banks would have a similar structure like the Bank of Canada but being on a provincial (state) level. They would be the Canadian counterparts of the Federal Reserve Banks in the United States. Such an organization would give the U.S. the possibility to retain majority control and Canada – contrary to other suggestions[5] – a kind of balanced power and control. In contrast to the ECB, NACB would have a different structure in order to retain some political control regarding monetary policy. In this context *Grubel* (1999) is completely wrong when suggesting that the NACB would only be responsible for the maintenance of price stability and not for full employment because as we have see above, this is exactly the situation we have in Europe due to the strong former influence of the Deutsche Bundesbank. In order to avoid this non-existing political control over monetary policy as in Europe, the constitution of the NACB would have to include provisions that certain actions need the approval of supranational bodies. However, to underline the importance of this aspect, the central bank (the NACB) would constitute the second link between the economic and the political dimension. Anyhow, this link is not as strong as the geographical link and includes a certain control function of the political dimension with regard to the economic one.

---

4 In this context NAMU includes Canada and the U.S.A. and therefore all these suggestions have to be seen in this context. However, it would be possible for Mexico to join NAMU (maybe later) as well.

5 Especially *Courchene* and *Harris* regularly suggest that just the Bank of Canada should have a seat in the FRBNA as well as the 12 existing Federal Reserve Banks. It is likely that such an imbalance would always be to the detriment of Canada as a whole because the 12 Federal Reserve Banks can not be compared with the national/central banks in Europe representing each country. 12 Federal Reserve Banks and just the Bank of Canada would regularly mean 12:1 U.S. votes within the board.

- NAMU would also lead to an ultimate exchange rate fixing in North America, meaning that there would no longer be a Canadian-U.S. exchange rate.
- In order to further stimulate trade between Canada and the U.S.A. due to the elimination of the costs of currency trading and risk, a new currency would have to be issued similar to the Euro. It makes sense to a certain extent, when *Courchene* (2001, 18) argues that the US-$ would continue to be the U.S. currency, however it seems – especially from a political point of view – to make more sense to introduce a new currency in both countries. As the European experience shows, flexibility in terms of currency symbolism has to be given, meaning that – similar to the Euro – one side of the coins would state that the currency is North American legal tender, while the other side is the so-called "landscape" side for each country[6]. The common currency bills would all show the same symbols and have the same two sides in Canada as well as in the U.S.A.
- In order to know the value of one unit of this new currency, central rates R defined in terms of the so-called North American Currency Unit (NACU), which is a weighted basket of specific amounts or units, U, of the two – in case Mexico would join NAMU, the three – currencies. NACU can be seen analogously to the ECU in Europe. The weight, W, of each currency in this basket is determined collectively by precise criteria[7] based on the relative economic strength of the member state. According to these criteria the central rates for each currency can be determined by $R = U/W$. Nevertheless, the bilateral exchange rate between any two currencies (in case Mexico would also join NAMU) is the quotient of their central rates. The just above mentioned weights then have to be frozen in, in order to avoid periodic re-weighting which creates uncertainty and would therefore be counterproductive when having fixed exchange rates.
- The name of the new currency could – as *Grubel* (1999) strongly suggested – either be "Amero" or as it is suggested here "Noam" (the "*Northamerican*").
- NAMU could only come into existence if its later member countries (Canada, U.S.A. and probably Mexico as well) fulfil certain convergence criteria regarding the inflation rate, the long-term interest rate, the government budget as well as the government debt. There is a similarity to the so-called convergence criteria in Europe. For further details on the European situation, see e.g. *Gandolfo* (2001, 360-363), *DeGrauwe* (2000, 130-136), or *Krugman / Obstfeld* (2000, 618-619).
- Each member state of NAMU, in particular Canada, would be free to maintain its policies and its regulatory approach towards financial institutions and the financial sector in the sense that e.g. the Bank of Canada or one of the seven

---

6 This "landscape" side of the Canadian coins could e.g. show the maple leaf, the CN Tower, maybe a hockey player, the prairies or the Rockies, in other words typical Canadian symbols.
7 Such criteria are for example each country's shares in NAMU-GDP, intra-NAMU trade or similar to the European Monetary System (EMS), a North American Monetary System (NAMS) financial support system.

newly created Canadian Reserve Banks could conduct clearings on a national or provincial basis and then clear with the other members of NAMU.

After elaborating on the dominating economic dimension of the model and before adding the political dimension, the model shall in the following be presented graphically in order to better point out the suggested *multi-dimensional approach*. The following graph shows the two main dimensions, the thicker line above being the political dimension and the thicker, longer line below being the economic one. These two main dimensions are connected via the geographical dimension to the left and the central bank, strongly influenced by the economic dimension and controlled by the political one.

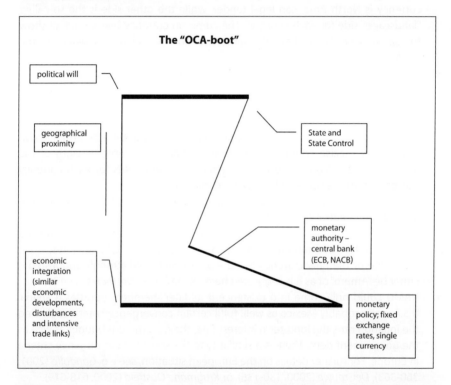

The "OCA-boot": The "OCA-boot" consists of two dominating dimensions, the lower and largest one being the economic dimension, constituting the basis for the entire construction and being linked with the second dominating domain, the political dimension through the dimension of geographical proximity which is actually already a pre-condition of an OCA besides being as well a "connecting dimension" within this model. The other "connecting dimension" is the monetary authority (the central bank, or in the particular cases the ECB or the NACB). The inside buckling shows that the monetary authority is strongly influenced by the economic dimension but should – to a certain extent – be controlled by the political dimension.

The Political Dimension

After having focussed primarily on the dominating economic dimension representing standard OCA theory, pointing out the importance of geographical proximity between (potential) members of a monetary union and/or an OCA and stressing the role of the supranational central bank on the European example, the emphasis of the analysis will now be shifted to an issue basically ignored by standard OCA theory: the political dimension of this model.

Probably the biggest shortcoming of standard OCA theory is its failure to reflect any political component. Therefore it shall be argued here that even the greatest economic theory on monetary integration is basically useless, if there is no political will of potential member states to make it reality. The best example for this is actually North America itself because *Mundell* stressed already in 1961 the possibility of an OCA on this continent due its similar economic developments, disturbances and structures. However, it was Europe, the war-plagued continent, which became the first example of a monetary union[8]. This happened not due to the perfect economic preconditions – which actually seem to be much better in North America – but due to the political will with various charismatic political leaders seeing such integration as a possibility to prevent the emergence of further wars and conflicts on the continent. This necessary political will exists not only in the foundation members of the European Community (EC), which became the European Union (EU) during its transformation process introduced by the Maastricht treaty, but can also be found in every country that joined the EU afterwards. Even now, with the EMU[9] already in existence and the entry criteria being much higher and more difficult to reach, ten additional countries[10] joined the EU on May 1st 2004, of which three[11] already joined

---

8 There have already been some relatively similar examples during history but on a much smaller scale such as the Zollverein of 1834, a customs union between Prussia and Hesse-Darmstadt that laid down the economic foundation for the political unification of Germany, the Moldovian-Wallachian Customs Union of 1847 that led to the foundation of Romania in 1878 or the Swiss Confederation of 1848 that led to the economic and political unification of Switzerland. Aside from that it has to be kept in mind that probably East Asia, commonly defined as the ten economies of China, Hong Kong, Indonesia, Japan, Korea, Malaysia, the Philippines, Singapore, Taiwan and Thailand could – besides a possible monetary integration in North America – probably constitute the next example of a monetary union or even an OCA. For further details on this, it is referred to *Zhang/Sato/McAleer* (2002) or *Trivisvavet* (2001).

9 Fifteen out of the 25 EU member states joined already the EMU: Austria, Belgium, Cyprus, Finland, France, Germany, Greece, Ireland, Italy, Luxembourg, Malta, The Netherlands, Portugal, Slovenia and Spain, while Denmark, Sweden and the UK decided to stay out of the monetary union even though they satisfied the convergence criteria. Denmark obtained the right to subject its entry to a national referendum, the UK obtained the right to opt out and Sweden decided not to join the monetary union by using a loophole in the Treaty by refusing to enter the third stage being the irrevocable fixing of the exchange rates between the national currencies.

10 These ten countries were the Czech Republic, Cyprus, Estonia, Hungary, Latvia, Lithuania, Malta, Poland, Slovakia and Slovenia.

11 These countries are Cyprus, Malta and Slovenia.

the EMU, due to their political will and commitment. As the model clearly shows, the political will is on the one side the main triggering point besides geographical proximity and economic integration and on the other side responsible for state action and state control after the people expressed their will to follow the route of monetary integration until achieving the stage of a complete monetary union. Fifteen countries in Europe have already followed exactly this route but it seems that in North America the political will for monetary integration is not (yet) extant. What are the possible reasons for this lack of political will?

The prevailing view among Canadians seems to be that they will object to the political consequences in terms of loss of sovereignty in areas other than monetary policy despite maybe favouring the economic benefits of a single currency and/or fixed exchange rates. The visual side of these fears seems to be the Canadian dislike of losing currency symbolism. However, the key word associated with these fears is "sovereignty". Fact is, that when joining whatever supranational organization or construction, a sovereign state has to give up quite a substantial part of its sovereign power because otherwise, such a supranational organization would not be able to fulfil its typical characteristics of executing formerly specific functions of a nation-state on a higher level, namely above national state authorities. Therefore, citizens need to perceive the supranational union as "their" place to live, as "their" home. Being part of the union must be a part of the citizens' identity: they must identify themselves with the union without ceasing to identify with their own nation-state. This means that multiple identification homogeneity is a prerequisite for a union's individual charisma, and is thus a prerequisite for the union's ability to secure not only rational allegiance, but also emotional loyalty. Each supranational union must, therefore, evolve specific characteristics which make it interesting and attractive for its own citizens. However, philosophical and political fundamental values and ideals will not be sufficient for this because since they are universal, they are realised elsewhere. What matters are, instead, cultural factors in the widest sense and thus homogeneity of cultures within a supranational commitment such as the EU. Furthermore, as *Courchene* (2001, 24) correctly states, 21st century sovereignty will have much less to do with having one's own currency than had heretofore been appreciated.

In the North American context, and particularly from a Canadian point of view, there is the widespread fear that a move to a common currency will also mean to become more "Americanized" regarding a broad range of policy areas. These fears are understandable – however, the situation can be compared in a certain sense to the Austrian one. Austria, being a small country in the heart of Europe, has always been in the shadow of its "bigger brother" Germany. Its previous currency, the Austrian Schilling, was informally pegged to the Deutschmark and similar to the Canadian situation, Germany has by far been Austria's most important trading partner. Aside from this, the same language is spoken in both countries, as well as culture and history is closely connected with each other. However, Austria has – at least in modern Austrian history after World War II never become "Germanized" despite the existing close economic interrelations and actually in particular since joining the EU in 1995, Austria became more and more "independent" from Germany. It is not unlikely that the same would happen to Canada when joining NAMU with the U.S.A. and Mexico because there are various policy tools for each member within an economic and further on within a monetary union to state one's opinion and ideology to certain issues such as the various diplomatic tools, not signing common agreements, heavy political debates or veto-policy being the ultimate tool to disagree with common policy.

As the fixed exchange rates during the 1960s showed, Canada was able to go into a different direction regarding social policy than the U.S.A. *Courchene* (2001, 24) even argued that buying into U.S. monetary policy in the 1960s did not mean that Canada bought into U.S. social policy but that instead the opposite was the case.

Another aspect that has to be kept in mind is that unlike dollarization, which would mean the disappearance of the Bank of Canada and the likely integration of Canada's financial infrastructure into the American institutional environment, NAMU would on the one side preserve Canada's financial environment and due to my suggestions of establishing seven new Canadian Reserve Banks even improve the Canadian financial infrastructure. Furthermore, under a single currency, the national banks will still be responsible – among various other things – for monitoring and research functions, meaning that their influence on monetary and economic policy in general should not be underestimated at all.

However, even though Canada might in the future opt for monetary integration, the big question arises if the Americans would ever embrace NAMU. Among Canadians the widespread view is that the U.S.A. would never agree to NAMU which may well be true under the current U.S. administration. Nevertheless, the answer can not be a simple "no", because especially since the Euro rebounded from its mid-80 cent range to e.g. 1.1933 US-$ in May 2003, the European single currency has become a serious competitor to the US-$ in global portfolios and business transactions. The Euro will face an additional impact when it will be the effective circulating currency in twenty-five European countries in the future and maybe become the *de facto* currency in several more through currency boards and fixed exchange rates. Anyhow, these recent developments will cause the Americans to be in favour of having a larger formal US-$ (or single currency area they are participating in) area as well, especially given the (traditional) U.S. proclivity to run enormous current account deficits. In addition to this, the relatively recent currency implosions in Latin America are definitely not in the economic and geopolitical interest of the U.S.A. Someone could now argue that this line of reasoning could just encourage the U.S.A. to enforce dollarization. This may well be true and therefore it seems to be more realistic that the U.S.A. would not make the first step into this direction. However, Canada has to watch the U.S. and Mexican developments closely because a dollarization in Mexico would have dramatic implications for the country, especially since there are serious concerns about Canada's shrinking North American share of inward FDI. It should always be kept in mind that if Mexico is able to combine its existing wage advantage with a stable currency regime, its attractiveness as a North American business location would be much enhanced to the detriment of Canada. Therefore, it would be in the Canadian interest to pursue monetary integration in North America, in order not to be the "odd man out"!

Conclusions

The discussion above showed that monetary integration in North America is definitely possible if certain criteria are met and especially if Canadians and their political leaders realize the economic advantages of NAMU. Canada will sooner or later have no other choice than pursuing monetary integration in North America because there is already fear that Mexico could become the much more attractive North American business location than Canada. Nevertheless, the proposals by the former Mexican president *Vicente Fox* in terms of an eventual broadening and deepening of NAFTA, including the adoption of a common North American currency, should already be a necessary incentive for Canada to start leading this process and to seek for Mexican co-operation to convince the United States of the advantages and necessity of NAMU. Now the question arises if NAMI could be an optimum at all?

By using the proposed *multi-dimensional approach*, a currency or monetary union, being the final stage of NAMI, can only constitute an OCA if it meets the following criteria:
- geographical proximity of the (potential) members
- similar economic developments, disturbances and structure as well as intensive trade links (economic integration), in particular a high integration of the product markets as well as factor markets
- the political will of the citizens and political leaders to deepen economic integration with the neighbour countries (regions) until achieving the final stage of a complete monetary union
- a common monetary policy, preferably based on fixed exchange rates
- a central bank (e.g. NACB) being responsible not only for price stabilization but also for a wide range of common monetary policy and being controlled by political bodies (necessarily on the supranational level)
- states and state control on a national and supranational level, in order to have control over the integration process as well as to guide the integration into the right direction

After evaluating all these criteria, it has to be concluded that even the EMU does not constitute an OCA *yet* but nevertheless it should be emphasized that Europe is on a good way to become an OCA. North America now has the big advantage to observe the European developments and to be convinced that such a project of monetary integration on a larger scale can turn out successfully. Contrary to Europe,

North America has much better economic pre-conditions in terms of intra-regional trade, labour mobility and so on. Therefore it should be in the interest of Canada, the United States and Mexico as well to use this potential to successfully compete with Europe and the rest of the world in the future. However, there exists an enormous lack of political will in Canada and probably in the USA as well and therefore the process of monetary integration in North America has not yet started. As the new model of the *multi-dimensional approach* of OCA theory clearly points out, monetary integration and further on constituting an OCA always needs a political dimension which has mostly been excluded in standard OCA theory. In this light, the developed model shall be considered as a further evolution of OCA theory, representing the necessary addition of a political dimension to its famous and necessary economic dimension primarily invented by *Mundell*, *McKinnon* and *Kenen*.

However, if North America and in particular Canada can find a common political will for further economic integration in terms of NAMI and finally NAMU, the excellent – already existing – economic pre-conditions would certainly have the necessary impact that North American monetary integration would be the optimum for this continent and its countries. Besides that we should never forget that *national, ethic and liturgical languages are here to stay, but a common world language, understood as a second language everywhere would obviously facilitate international understanding ...*

References

Bayoumi, Tamim, 1994, "A Formal Model of Optimum Currency Areas", *IMF Staff Papers*, 41, 537-53.
Bayoumi, Tamim, 1997, *Financial Integration and Real Activity*, The University of Michigan Press.
Cohen, Benjamin J., 1997, *International Trade and Finance: New Frontiers for Research*, New York, Cambridge University Press.
Commission of the European Communities, 1990, "One Market, One Money", in: *European Economy*, No 44, October.
Courchene, Thomas J., 2001, "A Canadian Perspective on North American Monetary Union", in: Joint NAEFA/ASSA Session, *Currency Consolidation in the Western Hemisphere*, New Orleans, Louisiana, Conference Version.
Courchene, Thomas J. (ed.), 2002, *Money, Markets, and Mobility* – Celebrating the ideas of Robert A. Mundell, Nobel Laureate in Economic Sciences, John Deutsch Institute for the Study of Economic Policy, IRPP.
Courchene, Thomas J. / Richard Harris, 1999, "Canada and a North American Monetary Union", www.cabe.ca/cbe/vol7_4/courchene.pdf
De Grauwe, Paul, 2000, *Economics of Monetary Union*, 4th Edition, Oxford University Press.
Demopoulos, George D. / Nicholas A. Yannacopoulos, 2000, "Structural Convergence and Divergence in Monetary Unions", in: Cristos C. Paraskevopoulos / Andreas A. Kintis / T. Georgakopoulos (eds.), *Global Financial Markets and Economic Development*, Studies in Economic Transformation and Public Policy, The Athenian Policy Forum Inc., APF Press, Toronto.

Eichengreen, Barry, 1992, *Should the Maastricht Treaty Be Saved?*, Princeton Studies in International Finance No 74, International Finance Section, Princeton University, December.

Friedman, Milton, 1953, "The Case for Flexible Exchange Rates", *Essays in Economics*, University of Chicago Press, Chicago, 157-203.

Frankel / Rose, 1998, "The Endogeneity of the Optimum Currency Area Criteria", *The Economic Journal*, 108, 1009-1025.

Gandolfo, Giancarlo, 2001, *International Finance and Open – Economy Macroeconomics*, Springer Verlag.

Goodhart, Charles A.E., 1998, "The two concepts of money: implications for the analysis of optimal currency areas", *European Journal of Political Economy*, Vol. 14, 407-432.

Grubel, Herbert G., 1999, *The Case for the Amero: The Merit of Creating a North American Monetary Union*, Fraser Institute, Vancouver.

Hallwood, C. Paul / Ronald MacDonald, 2000, *International Money and Finance*, 3rd Edition, Blackwell Publishers, Malden Oxford.

Harris, Richard, 2001, "North American Economic Integration: Issues and Research Agenda", in: Industry Canada, ed., *Research Publications Program*, Discussion Paper Number 10.

Kammel, Armin J., 2003, "Optimum Currency Areas & Monetary Integration", Bachelor Thesis in Economics, University of Graz.

Kenen, Peter B., 1969, "The Theory of Optimum Currency Areas: An Eclectic View", in: Robert A. Mundell / Alexander K. Swoboda (eds.), *Monetary Problems of the International Economy*, Chicago, University of Chicago Press, 41-60.

Kenen, Peter B., 2002, "Currency Unions and Policy Domains", in: David M. Andrews / C. Randall Henning / Louis W. Parly (eds.), *Governing the World's Money*, Cornell University Press, Ithaca, London.

Krugman, Paul, 1991, *Geography and Trade*, MIT Press, Cambridge, Mass.

Krugman, Paul / Maurice Obstfeld, 2000, *International Economics*, 5th Edition, Addison-Wesley Publishing Company.

McKinnon, Ronald, 1963, "Optimum Currency Areas", *American Economic Review* 53, 717-725.

Melitz, Jacques, 1995, "A Suggested Reformulation of the Theory of Optimum Currency Areas", *Open Economies Review* 6, 281-98.

Mundell, Robert A., 1961, "A Theory of Optimum Currency Areas", *American Economic Review* 51, November, 509-517.

Pilbeam, Keith, 1998, *International Finance*, 2nd Edition, palgrave.

Sarno, Lucio / Mark P. Taylor, 2002, *The Economics of Exchange Rates*, Cambridge University Press.

Sebastiàn, Saturnino Aguado, 2003, "La Opción de la Dolarizaciòn", in: Gonzalo Rodrìguez Prada (ed.), *Tipos de Cambio y Crisis Financieras*, Servicio De Publicaciones, Universidad de Alcalá.

Tavlas, George S., 1993, "The 'New' Theory of Optimum Currency Areas", *World Economy* 16, 663-85.

Tavlas, George S., 1994, "The Theory of Monetary Integration", *Open Economies Review* 5, 211-30.

Trivisvavet, Thanawat, 2001, "Do East Asian Countries Constitute An Optimum Currency Area?", www.econ.duke.edu/Journals/DJE/dje2001/trivisvavet.pdf

Zhang, Zhaoyong / Sato, Kiyotaka / McAleer, Michael, 2002, "Is East Asia An Optimum Currency Area?", www.iemss.org/iemss2002/proceedings/pdf/volume%20due/438_zhang.pdf

FALKO BREDE

Politikberatung im Vergleich: *Royal Commissions* und deutsche Expertenkommissionen

―――――――――――

Abstract

The use of expert knowledge and expert commissions to prepare policy initiatives is strongly influenced by the political culture and the political framework of the country, where the advisory work takes place. Detailed case studies of advisory commissions are an essential precondition for studies on this interrelatedness of the political culture, the political system and the work of advisory bodies. Several recent studies on the work of Royal Commissions in Canada and expert commissions in Germany have made it possible to conduct an in-depth analysis of the functioning of advisory bodies in these two countries. This article compares the legal framework for advisory commissions, their staff members, the role of the chairperson, the instruments of knowledge generation and the role of the public. This comparative analysis shows that expert commissions in Canada and Germany not only have different modes of operation but that they also fulfill different functions that are closely related to the incentive structure of the political system and the political culture.

Résumé

La culture et le cadre politiques d'un pays jouent un rôle essentiel en ce qui concerne l'usage que fait ce pays du savoir des experts et des commissions spécialisées quand vient le temps de préparer des initiatives politiques. Les études détaillées concernant le travail de ces commissions constituent une condition cruciale pour savoir comment sont liés la culture politique, le système politique et le travail des comités conseil. De nombreuses études effectuées au sujet du travail des commissions royales au Canada et des commissions d'experts en Allemagne permettront désormais une analyse complexe en ce qui concerne le fonctionnement des conseils dans les deux pays. Cet article comparera les conditions juridiques générales pour les comités conseil, leurs membres, le rôle du président, les instruments d'enquête et le rôle du public. Cette analyse comparative montre que les comités conseil au Canada et en Allemagne ne se distinguent pas seulement par leur mode de travail mais aussi par leur fonctions qui sont étroitement liées à la structure des incitations présentes dans le système politique et la culture politique.

―――――――――――

1. Einleitung

Nach der Bundestagswahl von 1998 entwickelte sich die Analyse politikberatender Prozesse in Deutschland zu einem der großen politikwissenschaftlichen Trendthemen. Hierbei wurden vor dem Hintergrund der Nutzung von sachverständiger Expertise durch die erste Regierung Schröder insbesondere die möglichen negativen Auswirkungen der Hinzuziehung von externem Sachverstand thematisiert. Warnungen vor einer „Kommissionitis" (Leersch 2001), einer „Räterepublik" (Heinze 2002, Sebaldt 2004) sowie vor einer „Deparlamentarisierung" (Kropp 2003) blieben längerfristig im wissenschaftlichen und im öffentlichen Bewusstsein. Neuere wissenschaftliche Analysen der Aufgaben und Rollen politikberatender Expertenkommissionen nach dem Regierungswechsel 1998 kamen jedoch zu dem Ergebnis, dass zumindest quantitativ keine signifikante Zunahme der Verwendung beratender Gremien in Deutschland nach 1998 nachweisbar ist (vgl. Siefken 2003 und 2007).

Spätestens seit der Bundestagswahl von 2005 hat das öffentliche Interesse an Politikberatung deutlich nachgelassen. Dies hat positiv dazu geführt, dass heute kaum noch alarmistische Stellungnahmen in Presse und Wissenschaft zur Politikberatung veröffentlicht werden. Negativ ist jedoch anzumerken, dass die Untersuchung des Zeitraums 1998-2005 zwar zu Fortschritten in der Analyse politikberatender Prozesse geführt hat; diese Fortschritte sind jedoch bis heute kaum systematisiert. Insbesondere fehlt es bisher an vergleichenden Ansätzen für die Untersuchung von Politikberatungsinstitutionen und -prozessen in verschiedenartigen politischen Systemumfeldern und Kulturen.

Dabei bietet sich aufgrund einer Reihe von neuen Studien zur Arbeit von *Royal Commissions* das Länderbeispiel Kanada mehr denn je für eine Untersuchung der Frage an, welche Funktionen Beratungsgremien in unterschiedlichen politischen Systemen übernehmen und anhand welcher Kriterien vergleichende Untersuchungen von Politikberatungsprozessen durchgeführt werden können. Bereits 1999 stellten Rainer-Olaf Schultze und Tanja Zinterer in einem Aufsatz die Frage, ob das kanadische Beratungsinstrument der *Royal Commission* ein Modell für den Abbau des bundesdeutschen Reformstaus sein könnte (Schultze/Zinterer 1999).

Aufbauend auf neueren Fallstudien zur Arbeit kanadischer *Royal Commissions* (insbesondere Lindner 2000, Zinterer 2004 und Brede 2006) sowie zur Arbeit von Expertenkommissionen der Bundesregierung (Weimar 2004, Siefken 2003 und 2007) lässt sich untersuchen, inwieweit sich vor dem Hintergrund verschiedenartiger politischer Systeme und Kulturen insbesondere auf funktionaler Ebene Anhaltspunkte für eine *policy convergence* bei der Hinzuziehung von externem Sachverstand im Rahmen politikberatender Kommissionen in Kanada und Deutschland nachweisen lassen.

Bevor man sich den Fallanalysen zuwendet, sind einige einleitende Anmerkungen zum Forschungsfeld Politikberatung notwendig. Im *Handbuch Politikberatung* wird festgestellt: „Politikberatung ist ein Untersuchungsgegenstand mit beträchtlicher

Variationsbreite und -tiefe." (Falk / Rehfeld / Römmele / Thunert (Hrsg.) 2006a, 13) Dies gilt in besonderer Weise für den internationalen Vergleich der Inanspruchnahme von Politikberatungsangeboten. Angesichts des großen politikwissenschaftlichen Interesses am Phänomen Politikberatung muss die begrenzte Reichweite der bisherigen Analysen von Politikberatungsprozessen und -institutionen sowie der theoretischen Fundierung dieser Studien jedoch überraschen.

Im Regelfall wurden bisher im Zuge von Forschungsvorhaben zu Politikberatungsprozessen Einzelfälle – zumeist einzelne Beratungskommissionen – untersucht (vgl. etwa Weimar 2004). Nur selten werden mehr als zwei Expertenkommissionen vergleichend untersucht (so etwa bei Brede 2006 und Siefken 2007). Noch seltener wurden international vergleichende Studien durchgeführt. So finden sich etwa im *Handbuch Politikberatung* (Falk / Rehfeld / Römmele / Thunert 2006b) im Abschnitt „Politikberatung international" zwar vier Länderstudien, jedoch keinerlei vergleichende Ausführungen zu unterschiedlichen Beratungsinstitutionen sowie den Funktionen von Expertise in verschiedenartigen politischen Systemen und Kulturen. Ein Vergleich der Erfahrungen aus Kanada und Deutschland dürfte vor diesem Hintergrund für die weitere wissenschaftliche Analyse von Politikberatungsprozessen besonders anregend sein.

Im Folgenden wird ausgehend von diesen Überlegungen anhand mehrerer Faktoren die Arbeit politikberatender Expertenkommissionen in Kanada – unter Bezugnahme auf die Situation in Deutschland – analysiert. Hierbei wird vor allem auf die Arbeitsweise der Politikberatungsgremien abgestellt. Eine alle Rahmenbedingungen und Faktoren umfassende, also etwa eine auch den output der Beratungsarbeit beinhaltende, Analyse kann und soll hingegen mit diesem Beitrag nicht geleistet werden. Diese Vergleichsstudie soll verdeutlichen, dass die Nutzung von Sachverstand im Rahmen von Expertenkommissionen in unterschiedlichen Ländern zum Teil erhebliche Unterschiede im Hinblick auf die Funktion der Beratung aufweist. Gleichzeitig soll die folgende Gegenüberstellung neue Anregungen für den internationalen Vergleich von Politikberatungsprozessen liefern. Hierzu wurden bewusst Kontextfaktoren ausgewählt, die in Kanada und Deutschland besonders unterschiedliche Wirkungen entfalten.

2. *Royal Commissions* im politischen System Kanadas

Kanada ist ein multikultureller und bilingualer Bundesstaat sowie eine Einwanderernation. Die Institutionen des politischen Systems und auch die politische Kultur sind bis heute in erheblicher Art und Weise geprägt durch die Strukturen des „Mutterlandes" Großbritannien. Da die Hinzuziehung von externer Expertise immer im Kontext der Rahmenbedingungen des jeweiligen politischen Systems sowie unter dem Einfluss politisch-kultureller Faktoren stattfindet, lohnt zunächst ein Blick auf das Wechselspiel zwischen diesen Faktoren und der politischen Beratungsarbeit. Besonders bedeutsam für die Ausgestaltung von politikberatenden Prozessen ist der Aspekt der starken Elitenzentrierung, der in Kanada generell bei der Entwicklung von Politikprogrammen nachweisbar ist (vgl. auch Brede / Schultze 2008, 319 und 323f). In Kanada als hochgradig dezentralisiertem Bundesstaat besteht außerdem eine signifikante regionale Konfliktdimension, die in nahezu jedem Politikfeld Wirkungen entfaltet. Zu vermuten ist, dass der Faktor Regionalismus in Politikberatungsprozessen daher eine weitaus größere Rolle spielt als in Deutschland. Unter Bezugnahme auf die Untersuchungen von Lipset (1990) ist außerdem noch folgende Charakterisierung der politischen Kultur Kanadas (in Abgrenzung zu den USA) anzuführen: klassenbewusster, statischer sowie stärker kollektiv orientiert und auf den Kompromiss als beste Lösung politischer Konflikte hin ausgerichtet. Zusammenfassend kann man festhalten: „Die kanadische Gesellschaft war [...] von Beginn an: gemeinschaftsorientiert – askriptiv – partikularistisch und elitär; sie ist bis heute konservativ – traditional und statisch." (Schultze 1989, 22). Dass dieser spezifische Charakter der kanadischen Gesellschaft und des politischen Systems Rückwirkungen auf das Verhältnis von externem Sachverstand bzw. Wissen und Politik hat, liegt nahe.

Das Beratungsinstrument der *Royal Commission* wurde in Kanada nach der *Confederation* von 1867 in enger Anlehnung an die aus Großbritannien übernommenen Strukturen ausgestaltet. Von Schultze und Zinterer werden *Royal Commissions* beschrieben als die „[...] großen, einflussreichen politikberatenden Kommissionen, die in angelsächsischen Ländern zur Formulierung von grundlegenden Politik-Programmen eingesetzt werden und oft signifikanten Politik-Wandel eingeleitet haben." (Schultze / Zinterer 1999, 881)

Grundsätzlich lassen sich zwei Formen von kanadischen *Royal Commissions* unterscheiden:

1.) Skandal-Enqueten, die eng umgrenzte Sachverhalte (meist Skandale oder begrenzte Problemfelder) bearbeiten und Lösungen entwickeln,

2.) *policy-Royal Commissions*, die mit einem breit gefassten Mandat eingesetzt werden und grundsätzliche politische Fragestellungen (etwa Zukunftsfähigkeit des Gesundheitssystems, Stand und Perspektiven der Wirtschaftspolitik, Umgang mit Verfahren der assistierten Reproduktion) bearbeiten.

Auf letzteren Kommissionstyp beziehen sich sowohl Schultze / Zinterer als auch die folgenden Ausführungen, da jene Beratungsgremien am ehesten das funktionale Äquivalent zu Expertenkommissionen der deutschen Bundesregierung darstellen. Wiederholt konnten diese *Royal Commissions* einen tief greifenden Paradigmenwechsel oder zumindest einen Pfadwandel in dem von ihnen bearbeiteten Politikfeld einleiten. Zahlreiche dieser Kommissionen prägten die folgenden politischen Debatten sowie die wissenschaftliche Analyse des bearbeiteten Politikfeldes nachhaltig. Auch ihre Wirkung in die kanadische Öffentlichkeit hinein ist im Vergleich zur Tätigkeit von Expertenkommissionen in Deutschland überdurchschnittlich hoch. Die Vielfalt der bisher bearbeiteten Themen macht bereits die überblicksartige Darstellung ausgewählter *Royal Commissions* deutlich, wobei festzuhalten ist, dass die *Rowell-Sirois Commission* als erste „Royal Commission on Everything" gilt (Bradford 1999, siehe auch Schultze / Zinterer 1999, 888ff):

Ausgewählte kanadische *policy-Royal Commissions*		
Royal Commission on Railways		1886-1887
Royal Commission on the Relations of Labour and Capital		1886-1889
Royal Commission on Banking and Currency	Macmillan Commission	1928-1933
Royal Commission on Radio Broadcasting	Aird Commission	1929
Royal Commission on Dominion-Provincial Relations	Rowell-Sirois Commission	1937–1940
Royal Commission on National Development of the Arts, Letters and Sciences	Massey Commission	1949-1951
Royal Commission on Broadcasting	Fowler Commission	1955-1957
Royal Commission on Canada's Economic Prospects	Gordon Commission	1955–1958
Royal Commission on Transportation	MacPherson Commission	1959-1961
Royal Commission on Health Services	Hall Commission	1961-1964
Royal Commission on Bilingualism and Biculturalism	Laurendeau-Dunton Commission	1963-1967
Royal Commission on the Status of Women	Bird Commission	1967-1970
Royal Commission on the Economic Union and Development Prospect for Canada	Macdonald Commission	1982-1985
Royal Commission on Electoral Reform and Party Financing	Lortie Commission	1989-1991
Royal Commission on New Reproductive Technologies	Baird Commission	1989-1993
Royal Commission on Aboriginal Peoples		1991-1996
Commission on the Future of Health Care in Canada	Romanow Commission	2000-2002

Die Mitgliederzahl dieser Kommissionen lag zwischen einem (Romanow Commission) und dreizehn Mitgliedern (Macdonald Commission). Die im Vergleich zur deutschen Situation kleine Mitgliederzahl verdeutlicht, dass hier nicht versucht wird, bereits durch die Besetzung der Gremien eine Ausgewogenheit der Arbeit oder einen Interessenausgleich herbeizuführen (vgl. auch Schultze/Zinterer 1999, 887f).

Die Kosten für die Arbeit einer *policy-Royal Commission* sind sehr unterschiedlich und unter anderem von der Größe der Kommission (Mitglieder- und Mitarbeiterzahl) sowie von der Aufgabenstellung bzw. dem Thema der Untersuchung abhängig. So kostete die bisher letzte *Royal Commission* (die *Romanow Commission*) rund 15 Mio. Can$ (Brede 2006, 120), die *Macdonald Commission* kostete als bisher mitgliederstärkste Kommission 20,6 Mio. Can$ und die *Royal Commission on Aboriginal Peoples* mit ihren sieben Mitgliedern war mit über 50 Mio. Can$ die bisher teuerste Kommission (Lindner 2000, 110 sowie Zinterer 2004, 373).

Untersuchungskommissionen, die zwar ebenfalls unter den *Inquiries Act* fallen, jedoch im Gegensatz zu *policy-Royal Commissions* nur eng begrenzte Fragestellungen untersuchen, werden hingegen zumeist als *Commissions of Inquiry* betitelt und entsprechen eher den deutschen Untersuchungsausschüssen. Besetzt werden diese Kommissionen jedoch nicht mit Parlamentariern, sondern mit externen Sachverständigen, wobei in der Vergangenheit durchaus auch ehemalige Politikerinnen oder Politiker den Vorsitz einer solchen Kommission übernommen haben.

Ausgewählte kanadische *Commissions of Inquiry*		
Commission of Inquiry into the Non-Medical Use of Drugs	Le Dain Commission	1969–1973
Commission of Inquiry into Certain Activities of the RCMP	McDonald Commission	1977–1981
Commission of Inquiry into the Deployment of Canadian Forces in Somalia		1994-1997
Commission of Inquiry on the Blood System in Canada	Krever Commission	1995-1997
Commission of Inquiry into the Sponsorship Program and Advertising Activities		2004-2006
Commission of Inquiry into the Actions of Canadian Officials in Relation to Maher Arar		2004-2006

3. *Royal Commissions* in Kanada – Rahmenbedingungen und Funktionen im Vergleich zu deutschen Expertenkommissionen

Politikberatung findet immer in einem Spannungsfeld von Ideen, Institutionen und Interessen statt (Falk / Rehfeld / Römmele / Thunert 2006a, 17). Die Verwendung und die Ausgestaltung politikberatender Expertenkommissionen hängen daher eng mit der Struktur und den Anreizen des jeweiligen politischen Systems zusammen. Ausgehend von dieser Überlegung soll im Folgenden anhand ausgewählter Rahmenbedingungen und Kontextfaktoren die Tätigkeit und die Funktion(en) von kanadischen *Royal Commissions* analysiert werden.

3.1. Verhältnis von *Royal Commissions* zur Ministerialverwaltung und zu den Parteien

Von herausragender Bedeutung für die politisch-gestalterische Arbeit einer Regierung sind das Potential und die Struktur der Ministerialverwaltung(en). In Kanada verfügt die Ministerialbürokratie jedoch nur über ein begrenztes Potential, um längerfristige, kohärente Politikprogramme zu entwickeln. Sie wirkt aus diesem Grunde nur selten als zentrale Kraft bei politischen Reformprojekten (vgl. Bradford 1999, 546).

Royal Commissions der Bundesregierung werden daher oft genutzt, um Defizite in der Fähigkeit zur Programmgestaltung auf Seiten der Ministerien zu kompensieren (vgl. auch Jenson 1994, 51). Bereits mehrfach wurden durch *Royal Commissions* neue bzw. alternative *policy*-Paradigmen (vgl. Zinterer 2004, 313ff und Brede 2006, 75ff) entwickelt, was sich nachhaltig auf die weitere Entwicklung des jeweils bearbeiteten Politikfeldes ausgewirkt hat. Im Gegensatz zur Situation in Deutschland prägen starke Ressortgrenzen zwischen den Ministerien die Hinzuziehung von externem Sachverstand hierbei kaum. Neben der Kompensation von Defiziten in der Programmgestaltung auf Seiten der kanadischen Bundesministerien dient die Beratung auch dazu, *windows of opportunity* für größere Reformvorhaben zu öffnen, oder aber die Voraussetzungen für die Durchführung einer bereits geplanten Reform zu schaffen (Legitimationsfunktion).

Eine Untersuchung des Wechselspiels von Parteien und *Royal Commissions* führt zu ähnlichen Ergebnissen. Die beiden großen kanadischen Parteien (Konservative Partei und Liberale Partei) lassen sich als *catch-all parties* oder *brokerage parties* umschreiben. Sie sind ideologisch kaum gefestigt und zeichnen sich durch einen pragmatischen Umgang mit politischen Programmen aus. Bradford stellt hierzu fest: „[…] brokerage politics supplies few incentives for governing parties to produce their own ideas, much less to use such novel concepts in seeking mandates from voters for policy innovation." (Bradford 2000, 140) Das Potential der kanadischen Parteien zur Entwicklung langfristiger Politikprogramme ist entsprechend begrenzt (vgl. auch Aucoin 1990, 203).

Vergleicht man dies mit der Situation in Deutschland, so fällt auf, dass die Parteien nur über wenige Ressourcen verfügen, um längerfristige Politikprogramme zu entwickeln. In Deutschland hingegen erfüllen unter anderem die Stiftungen der Parteien diese Aufgabe (vgl. auch Thunert 2003). Durch die Beteiligung an Regierungen in den Bundesländern verfügen die deutschen Parteien außerdem über einen – mehr oder weniger – direkten Kanal zu spezialisierten Ministerialbürokratien. Auch wenn sich etwa eine der beiden Volksparteien im Bundestag in der Opposition befindet, so kann sie meist dennoch beispielsweise über ein Landes-Finanzministerium einen Plan für eine Steuerreform fachkundig bewerten oder gegebenenfalls detailliert ausarbeiten lassen. Da die Parteien zwischen Bund und Provinzen nur schwach integriert sind, steht diese Option in Kanada kaum zur Verfügung.

Die programmatischen Defizite sowie die begrenzte Innovationsfähigkeit der Bundesparteien werden in Kanada durch die Arbeit von *Royal Commissions* teilweise kompensiert. Dies ist ein wichtiger Grund, warum *Royal Commissions* wiederholt einen starken Einfluss im jeweiligen Politikfeld ausüben konnten, in Deutschland die Aufgabenstellung für Politikberatungsgremien hingegen meist weniger umfassend ist und die Nutzung von externem Sachverstand zumeist auf der Basis pragmatischer Überlegungen und nicht selten in Reaktion auf unvermittelt auftretende Herausforderungen erfolgt (vgl. auch Siefken 2007, 315).

Neben dem Blick auf die Funktionen von *Royal Commissions* im Wechselverhältnis zu Ministerialbürokratie und Parteien müssen auch die konkreten Rahmenbedingungen der Arbeit von Expertenkommissionen in Kanada analysiert werden, um ein umfassendes Bild der Funktionen und Arbeitsweise von *Royal Commissions* – im Vergleich zu deutschen Expertenkommissionen – zu erhalten.

3.2. Rechtlicher Handlungsrahmen

Royal Commissions arbeiten in Kanada auf Grundlage eines Bundesgesetzes, des *Inquiries Act* und werden formal durch den *Governor General* eingesetzt bzw. berufen. Faktisch entscheidet jedoch der jeweilige Regierungschef im System des *prime-ministerial government*, ob eine *Royal Commission* eingerichtet wird und welchen Arbeitsauftrag sie erhalten soll (vgl. Schultze / Zinterer 1999, 887f). In der gesetzlichen Grundlage sind hierzu einige eher allgemein gehaltene Regelungen – etwa die Rechte des Vorsitzenden einer *Royal Commission* betreffend – festgeschrieben. Im Gegensatz hierzu verfügen Expertenkommissionen der Bundesregierung nicht über eine einheitliche Rechtsgrundlage. Vielmehr werden für jede Kommission in Deutschland – zumeist in der jeweiligen Ressortkompetenz – Verfahrensregelungen wie etwa Geschäftsordnungen oder Maßgaben für die Arbeit der Geschäftsstelle neu entwickelt, wobei durchaus Erfahrungen aus früheren Kommissionen aufgenommen werden (vgl. Brede 2006, 262ff).

Durch die einheitliche Rechtsgrundlage in Kanada sind die Erwartungen der Öffentlichkeit an die Tätigkeit und den Bericht einer *Royal Commission* vergleichsweise klar, da das Instrument bekannt ist und bestimmte Erwartungen etwa im Hinblick auf den Einfluss einer solchen Kommission bestehen. Auch die Möglichkeiten eines institutionellen *polity-/policy*-Lernprozesses sind hierdurch größer als in Deutschland. Dies wirkt sich positiv auf den Einfluss der *Royal Commissions* aus. Gleichzeitig werden allerdings auch die Chancen für eine pragmatische Nutzung von Politikberatungsgremien verringert, da die Abwesenheit eines verbindlichen Rechtsrahmens (wie in Deutschland) die Optionen für Politik und Verwaltung erweitert, je nach aktueller Gesamtsituation die Form der politischen Beratungsarbeit auszugestalten und spezifischen Anforderungen der Politik an die externe Expertise Rechnung zu tragen.

3.3. Kommissionsmitarbeiter

Royal Commissions verfügen im Gegensatz zu deutschen Expertenkommissionen meist über einen großen Mitarbeiterstab von 50 oder mehr Personen (vgl. Brede 2006, 126, Zinterer 2004, 124; siehe auch Lindner 2000, 59f). Dieser wird nur selten mit Mitarbeitern aus der Ministerialbürokratie besetzt. Stattdessen arbeiten oftmals Sozialwissenschaftler mit universitärem Hintergrund in den Geschäftsstellen. Nach Abschluss der Kommissionsarbeit entwickeln einige dieser Personen die Ideen und Konzepte der *Royal Commission* nicht nur an den Universitäten zu neuen wissenschaftlichen Ansätzen oder Paradigmen, sondern auch in Verwaltungen des Bundes oder der Provinzen zu konkreten politischen Programmen weiter.[1] Dieses Vorgehen unterscheidet sich erheblich von demjenigen in Deutschland, da hier oftmals Verwaltungsmitarbeiter die Arbeit in den Geschäftsstellen von Expertenkommissionen der Bundesregierung prägen (für das Fallbeispiel der Hartz-Kommission siehe Siefken 2007, 195). Die Einbeziehung von Personal aus dem universitären Umfeld oder aus anderen wissenschaftlichen Einrichtungen ist vergleichsweise selten nachweisbar. *Royal Commissions* nutzen somit auch die Möglichkeit, durch einen Transfer von Personen neue Ideen in den politischen Prozess und in die wissenschaftliche Debatte einfließen zu lassen.

3.4. Wissensgenerierung und -verarbeitung

Im Gegensatz zu deutschen Expertenkommissionen nutzen *Royal Commissions* nicht nur bereits bestehende Wissensbestände im Rahmen ihres Deliberationsprozesses, sondern sie generieren auch neues Wissen durch eigene Forschungsprogramme. Seit der *Royal Commission on Dominion-Provincial Relations* sind wissenschaftliche Forschungsprogramme ein fester Bestandteil der Arbeit von *policy-Royal Commissions* (Lindner 2000, 60ff, vgl. auch Zinterer 2004, 129ff). So gab beispielsweise die *Commission on the Future of Health Care in Canada* im Rahmen der wissenschaftlichen Begleitforschung 40 Diskussionspapiere bei Wissenschaftlerinnen und Wissenschaftlern in Auftrag. Diese durchliefen ein eigenes *peer review* Verfahren, was den wissenschaftlichen Anspruch des Vorgehens der *Royal Commission* verdeutlicht. Des Weiteren gab diese Kommission drei umfangreiche Gutachten in Auftrag, da sich einige der zu bearbeitenden Themenfelder nach Auffassung der Kommission nicht hinreichend durch die Aufarbeitung bereits verfügbarer wissenschaftlicher Abhandlungen und Studien im Rahmen kleinerer Gutachten aufarbei-

---

[1] So wurde etwa der Mitarbeiter der *Commission on the Future of Health Care in Canada*, Pierre-Gerlier Forest, zeitweise Mitarbeiter des kanadischen Gesundheitsministeriums (im Rahmen des *G.D.W. Cameron Visiting Chair*). Heute ist Forest unter anderem Professor an der Universität Laval, Quebec. Greg Marchildon – ein weiterer ehemaliger, leitender Mitarbeiter dieser *Royal Commission* – ist heute Professor an der Universität von Regina, Saskatchewan.

ten ließen.[2] Anhand dieses Fallbeispiels wird deutlich, dass *Royal Commissions* im Gegensatz zu deutschen Expertenkommissionen neben der politischen Beratungsfunktion auch zur Fundierung und Fortführung der wissenschaftlichen Diskussionen beitragen (für weitere Beispiele siehe Schultze / Zinterer 1999, 894ff).

Viele der wissenschaftlichen Auftragsarbeiten werden im Anschluss an die Kommissionsarbeit publiziert. So wurde etwa eine Auswahl der wissenschaftlichen Auftragsarbeiten für die *Commission on the Future of Health Care in Canada* in drei Buchbänden durch leitende Mitarbeiter der Kommission herausgegeben (Forest / Marchildon / McIntosh 2004, Marchildon / McIntosh / Forest 2004 sowie McIntosh / Forest / Marchildon 2004). Die Generierung von neuem Wissen und das Wirken in die *scientific community* hinein sind somit wesentliche Bestandteile der Arbeit kanadischer *Royal Commissions*.

Deutsche Expertenkommissionen nutzen stattdessen in erster Linie die in Verwaltung und Parlament üblichen Verfahren (Stellungnahmen, Anhörungen, usw.) zur Generierung von neuen Erkenntnissen. Dieses Vorgehen eignet sich besser zur Beteiligung möglichst vieler Interessengruppen und Verbände und entspricht dem deutschen, neokorporatistisch geprägten Politikstil. Gleichzeitig wird durch den Vergleich mit dem kanadischen Beratungsansatz offenkundig, dass deutsche Expertenkommissionen keine wissenschaftlich arbeitenden Beratungseinrichtungen sind, die neues Wissen generieren sollen. Ihr Vorgehen und auch ihre Funktion unterscheiden sich in diesem Punkt signifikant von denjenigen kanadischer *Royal Commissions*.

3.5. Besetzung des Postens des Vorsitzenden

Bereits anhand der Umschreibung diverser *Royal Commissions* sowie deutscher Expertenkommissionen mit dem Namen der oder des Vorsitzenden wird die herausgehobene Stellung dieser Personen im Beratungsprozess offenkundig. In Kanada wird der Posten des Vorsitzenden vergleichsweise oft mit (ehemaligen) Richtern besetzt,[3] aber auch Journalisten, Unternehmer und ehemalige Politiker wurden in der Vergangenheit zu Vorsitzenden einer *Royal Commission* berufen. Der Grund für die vergleichsweise häufige Berufung von Richtern oder anderen, eher politikfernen Persönlichkeiten dürfte sein, dass die Nützlichkeit einer *Royal Commission* im kanadischen Kontext nicht zuletzt davon abhängt, dass es ihr gelingt, sich personell und strukturell vom elitenzentrierten Politikstil, der im politischen System Kanadas vorherrscht (und seit Jahren unter einem erheblichen Legitimationsdefizit leidet), ab-

---

2 Die drei Themen waren *Globalization and Health*, *Fiscal Federalism and Health* sowie *Health Human Ressources* (Brede 2006, 130).
3 Als Beispiel für dieses Vorgehen lässt sich etwa die *Royal Commission on Health Services (Hall Commission)* anführen (vgl. Brede 2006, 64ff.). Ein weiteres Fallbeispiel wäre die *Macmillan Commission*. Für weitere Beispiele zur Arbeit von Richtern in *Royal Commissions* siehe Zinterer 2004, 111ff. Für weitere Ausführungen siehe Cole 2007, 137f.

zugrenzen.[4] Denkbar ist, dass sich hierin auch die größere Konsensorientierung der kanadischen Gesellschaft widerspiegelt, da etwa einem Richter eher als einem Politiker ein erfolgreiches Zusammenführen unterschiedlicher Positionen und Wertungen zugetraut wird.

An diesem Punkt wird ein weiterer signifikanter Unterschied zum deutschen Umgang mit Expertenkommissionen offensichtlich. Zu Zeiten der ersten Regierung Schröder 1998-2002 wurden mehrfach ehemalige Politikerinnen und Politiker in Expertenkommissionen berufen und zu Vorsitzenden ernannt (Süßmuth-Kommission, Weizsäcker-Kommission).[5] Man kann dies mit der Überlegung begründen, dass auf diesem Wege eine parteiübergreifende Konsensbildung befördert werden sollte. In den beiden genannten Fällen scheinen jedoch vor allem Anreize des Parteienwettbewerbs eine Rolle gespielt zu haben. Die Regierung Schröder beschritt etwa mit der Berufung von Rita Süßmuth zur Vorsitzenden der „Unabhängigen Kommission Zuwanderung" den Weg der parteipolitischen Konfrontation mit der CDU/CSU, welche noch vor der Bekanntgabe der weiteren Mitglieder und somit auch deutlich vor Beginn der eigentlichen Sacharbeit einsetzte (vgl. Zinterer 2004, 262ff und Siefken 2007, 146f) und den langfristigen Einfluss der Beratungsergebnisse dieser Kommission nachteilig beeinflusst hat. Eine Berufung von parteipolitisch weniger stark eingebundenen Persönlichkeiten hätte dazu beigetragen, diese negativen Reaktionen zu vermeiden. Angesichts der späteren Berufung von Peter Hartz und Bert Rürup zu Vorsitzenden von Expertenkommissionen der Bundesregierung ist zu vermuten, dass hier auf Seiten der Bundesregierung ein Lernprozess stattgefunden hatte.

3.6. Bezug zur Öffentlichkeit

Die politischen Entscheidungsträger stehen seit der der Gründung des *Dominion of Canada* vor der dauerhaften Herausforderung, einen bilingualen und multikulturellen Bundesstaat Kanada zu einen. *Royal Commissions* haben mit ihren umfassenden Aufgabenstellungen zu Themen wie Freihandel, ökonomische Integration, Zuwanderung, Bilingualismus, usw. wiederholt einen bedeutsamen Beitrag zur nationalen Integration geleistet (vgl. auch Bradford 2000). Hieraus ergeben sich konkrete Folgen für die Arbeitsweise dieser Expertenkommissionen. So bereisen *Royal Commissions* üblicherweise im Rahmen ihrer Arbeit alle Landesteile. Dieses Vorgehen ist auf die in vielen Politikfeldern bestehende regionale Konfliktdimension zurückzuführen. Auch nutzen die Gremien Anhörungen und in jüngerer Vergangenheit verstärkt das Internet, um einen nationalen Diskurs über ihr Untersuchungsthema zu initiieren (für eine Analyse dieses Phänomens siehe Brede 2006, 132ff.). Sie sind daher nicht nur rein regierungsberatende Gremien, sondern sie

---

4   Zur Legitimationsproblematik des elitenzentrierten Politikstils vgl. auch Cameron/Simeon 2001, 71.
5   Die Hartz-Kommission wurde erst im Wahljahr 2002 eingesetzt, die Rürup-Kommission erst nach der Bundestagswahl von 2002.

bilden auch eine Keimzelle und ein Forum für einen nationalen *policy*-Diskurs (vgl. Jenson 1994: 39). Insofern findet in Kanada bereits statt, was in Deutschland unter der Trendbeschreibung „Von der Politik- zur Gesellschaftsberatung" (Leggewie 2007) seit kurzem verstärkt diskutiert wird.

Expertenkommissionen der Bundesregierung versuchen bisher nur selten, die Öffentlichkeit (zumeist die entsprechenden Teilöffentlichkeiten) in ihren Beratungsablauf einzubinden. Hierin spiegelt sich auch ein grundlegend anderes Verständnis in Bezug auf die Nutzung von Sachverstand und Experten, welches in Deutschland einen stark instrumentellen Charakter aufweist. Die Herbeiführung eines nationalen Diskurses über das Beratungsthema einer Expertenkommission ist kaum Teil der Aufgabenstellung deutscher Politikberatungsgremien und ausgehend von Fallbeispielen lässt sich die These formulieren, dass eine starke öffentlichkeitsbezogene Komponente in der Kommissionsarbeit sogar negativ bewertet wird. Zu verweisen ist diesbezüglich etwa auf die Arbeit der Kommission „Nachhaltigkeit in der Finanzierung der Sozialen Sicherungssysteme" (Rürup-Kommission), deren starke Medienpräsenz von Seiten der politischen Entscheidungsträger eher negativ bewertet wurde (vgl. Brede 2006, 271). Zu bedenken ist, dass durch öffentliche Stellungnahmen zu politischen Fragen die Berater ein Stück weit in das Tätigkeitsfeld der Politiker hineinwirken, was diese wiederum als Beschränkung ihrer eigenen Handlungsspielräume interpretieren können.

4. Fazit

Die Untersuchung der Arbeitsweise und Funktionen von *Royal Commissions* im Vergleich zu deutschen Expertenkommissionen verdeutlicht erhebliche Unterschiede in der Ausgestaltung politikberatender Kommissionen und der Nutzung von externem Sachverstand in Kanada und Deutschland. Eine *policy convergence*, wie sie etwa im Kontext von Debatten über Wissensgesellschaft und Globalisierung immer wieder diskutiert wird, ist im Bereich der Politikberatung in den beiden untersuchten Länderbeispielen nicht erkennbar. Eine Annäherung beider Beratungstraditionen lässt sich lediglich in Ansätzen bezüglich der Einbeziehung der Öffentlichkeit in den Diskussionsprozess konstatieren.

Ein Ergebnis der vorliegenden Vergleichsstudie ist die Beobachtung, dass sich die institutionelle Ausgestaltung politikberatender Gremien in den beiden Länderbeispielen nicht nur strukturell unterscheidet, sondern dass sich auch die den Sachverständigen zugedachten Funktionen und Rollen sowie das Selbstverständnis im Umgang mit externem Wissen erheblich unterscheiden. Dennoch lohnt es sich, aufbauend auf den dargelegten Forschungserkenntnissen die Frage nach dem Modellcharakter kanadischer *Royal Commissions* für die bundesdeutsche Politik zu stellen. Einige der Erfahrungen aus Kanada bieten durchaus Anknüpfungspunkte für die Debatte über die Funktionen und die Ausgestaltung der Arbeit von Expertenkommissionen in Deutschland. So ist zu vermuten, dass eine einheitliche Rechtsgrundlage die Arbeit von Expertenkommissionen verstetigen würde und

Chancen für neue *policy-/polity*-Lernprozesse bieten könnte. Allerdings würde dies auch zu einer Einschränkung der bisher noch recht freien Ausgestaltung der institutionellen Rahmenbedingungen für Expertenkommissionen in Deutschland führen. Die starke Ministerialbürokratie präformiert hier die Nutzung von Expertenkommissionen bis heute in erheblichem Umfang, und entsprechend dürften Restriktionen wie etwa ein deutscher *Inquiries Act* nur geringe Umsetzungschancen haben. Ohne den Nachweis von Defiziten aufgrund des Fehlens einer entsprechenden Rechtsgrundlage muss die Begründung der Erforderlichkeit einer solchen, die Handlungsfreiheit der Exekutive einschränkenden, Regelung schwer fallen.

Deutsche Expertenkommissionen agieren in einem stark von Neokorporatismus, Parteienwettbewerb und Politikverflechtung geprägten Systemumfeld. Sie sind, wie es Schultze / Zinterer ausdrücken, „[…] nur Teil eines vielstimmigen Chores von Interessen, die Einfluß auf die Politikformulierung zu nehmen versuchen und sich dabei vielfach neutralisieren und blockieren." (Schultze / Zinterer 1999, 902). Dies trägt dazu bei, dass hier externe Beratung zumeist unter instrumentellen Gesichtspunkten und entlang parteipolitisch-pragmatischer Erwägungen ausgestaltet und genutzt wird. Dies begrenzt insbesondere im Vergleich zur Situation in Kanada die Möglichkeiten, mittels externer Expertise einen grundlegenden Politikwandel herbeizuführen. Im vorliegenden Ländervergleich wird des Weiteren deutlich, dass in Deutschland dem Parteienwettbewerb als Faktor in der politischen Beratungsarbeit eine größere Bedeutung zukommt als in Kanada.

Die vielfältigen Unterschiede in der Ausgestaltung und Nutzung der Arbeit von Expertenkommissionen in Kanada und Deutschland machen deutlich, dass Modelle für einen *policy-* und/oder Institutionen-Transfer in der Politikberatung mit großer Vorsicht entwickelt werden müssen. Gerade aus diesem Grunde hat der Ansatz von Schultze / Zinterer aus dem Jahr 1999 bis heute nichts an Aktualität verloren, da hier nach *best practices* im internationalen Vergleich der Nutzung von Politikberatungseinrichtungen gefragt wurde, ohne einfache Transferempfehlungen zu formulieren.

Es bleibt zu hoffen, dass sich die Politikwissenschaft mehr als bisher dem internationalen Vergleich von Politikberatungsprozessen und -gremien zuwenden wird. Denkbar wären hier unter anderem Studien zu den Rollen und Funktionen, die Sachverständigen zugedacht werden sowie zum Umgang mit externem Wissen oder zum Verständnis von Expertenwissen und – wissenschaftlicher – Expertise in Anknüpfung an die Untersuchungen von Peter Weingart (2005a und 2005b). Diese Analysen ließen sich – etwa um ideengeschichtlich untermauerte – Fragen nach dem Wechselspiel von Staatsverständnis und Politikberatung erweitern und könnten eine neue Grundlage für den internationalen Vergleich von Politikberatungsprozessen bilden.

Literatur

Abelson, Donald E., 1999, "Public Visibility and Policy Relevance. Assessing the Impact and Influence of Canadian Policy Institutes", *Canadian Public Administration*, Jg. 42, Nr. 2, S. 240-270.

Aucoin, Peter, 1990, "Contributions of Commissions of Inquiry to Policy Analysis: An Evaluation", in: A. Paul Pross / Innis Christie / John A. Yogis (Hrsg.), *Commissions of Inquiry. Dalhousie Law Journal*, Jg. 12, Nr. 3, S. 197-208.

Bakvis, Herman, 1997, "Advising the Executive. Think Tanks, Consultants, Political Staff and Kitchen Cabinets", in: Patrick Weller / Herman Bakvis / R.A.W. Rhodes (Hrsg.), *The Hollow Crown. Countervailing Trends in Core Executives*, London u.a., S. 84-125.

Berg-Schlosser, Dirk 2003, „Politische Kultur", in: Dieter Nohlen (Hrsg.), *Lexikon der Politik*, 3. Auflage, S. 397-398.

Bleek, Wilhelm, 2002, „Politikwissenschaftliche Politikberatung in Geschichte und Gegenwart", in: Jens Uwe / Hajo Romahn (Hrsg.), *Der Einfluss der Wissenschaft auf die Politik*, Marburg, S. 75-94.

Berger, Thomas, 2003, "Canadian Commissions of Inquiry: An Insider's Perspective", in: Allan Manson / David Mullan (Hrsg.), *Commissions of Inquiry. Praise or Reappraise*, Toronto, S. 13-28.

Bogner, Alexander / Wolfgang Menz, 2002, „Wissenschaftliche Politikberatung? Der Dissens der Experten und die Autorität der Politik", *Leviathan*, Jg. 30, Nr. 3, S. 384-399.

Bradford, Neil, 1998, *Commissioning Ideas: Canadian National Policy Innovation in Comparative Perspective*, Toronto u.a.

Bradford, Neil, 1999, "Innovation By Commission. Policy Paradigms and the Canadian Political System", in: Alain G. Gagnon / James Bickerton (Hrsg.), *Canadian Politics*, 3. Auflage, Peterborough, S. 541-564.

Bradford, Neil 2000, "Writing Public Philosophy. Canada's Royal Commissions on Everything", *Journal of Canadian Studies*, Jg. 34, Nr. 4, S. 136-167.

Brede, Falko / Rainer-Olaf Schultze, 2008, „Das politische System Kanadas", in: Klaus Stüwe / Stefan Rinke (Hrsg.), *Die politischen Systeme in Nord- und Lateinamerika. Eine Einführung*, Wiesbaden, S. 314-340.

Brede, Falko 2005a, „Ethikrat, Enquete, oder ...? Perspektiven der bioethischen Politikberatung", *Zeitschrift für Biopolitik*, Jg. 4, Nr. 1, S. 29-36.

Brede, Falko, 2005b, "Medicare at the Crossroads? Gesundheitsreformvorschläge im kanadischen Bundeswahlkampf 2004", *Zeitschrift für Kanada-Studien*, Jg. 25, Nr. 1 S. 23-38.

Brede, Falko, 2006, *Gesundheitspolitik und Politikberatung. Eine vergleichende Analyse deutscher und kanadischer Erfahrungen*, Wiesbaden.

Cairns, Alan C., 1990, "Reflections on Commission Research", in: A. Paul Pross / Innis Christie / John A. Yogis (Hrsg.), *Commissions of Inquiry. Dalhousie Law Journal*, Jg. 12, Nr. 3, S. 87-110.

Cameron, David R. / Richard Simeon, 2001, "Intergovernmental Relations and Democratic Citizenship", in: B. Guy Peters / Donald J. Savoie (Hrsg.), *Governance in the Twenty-First Century, Revitalizing the Public Service*, Montreal u. a., S. 58-118.

Clarkson, Stephen / Timothy Lewis, 1999, "The Contested State. Canada in the Post-Cold War, Post-Keynesian, Post-Fordist, Post-National Era", in: Leslie A. Pal (Hrsg.), *How Ottawa Spends 1999-2000. Shape Shifting. Canadian Governance Toward the 21st Century*, Toronto u.a., S. 293-340.

Cole, Stephen J., 2007, "Commissioning Consent: An Investigation of the Royal Commission on the Relations of Labour and Capital, 1886-1889", QSpace at Queen's University, http://hdl.handle.net/1974/963 (Zugriff: 28. November 2008).

d'Ombrain, Nicholas, 1997, "Public Inquiries in Canada", *Canadian Public Administration*, Jg. 40, Nr. 1, S. 86-107.

Falk, Svenja / Dieter Rehfeld / Andrea Römmele / Martin Thunert, 2006a, „Einführung: Politikberatung – Themen, Fragestellungen, Begriffsdimensionen, Konzepte, Akteure, Institutionen und

Politikfelder", in: Svenja Falk / Dieter Rehfeld / Andrea Römmele / Martin Thunert (Hrsg.), Handbuch Politikberatung, Wiesbaden, S. 11-19.
Falk, Svenja / Dieter Rehfeld / Andrea Römmele / Martin Thunert (Hrsg.), 2006b, *Handbuch Politikberatung*, Wiesbaden.
Forest, Pierre-Gerlier / Gregory P. Marchildon / Tom McIntosh, 2004, *Changing Health Care in Canada: Romanow Papers*, Band 2, Toronto.
Heinze, Rolf G., 2002, *Die Berliner Räterepublik. Viel Rat – wenig Tat?*, Wiesbaden.
Heinze, Rolf G., 2004, „Verwissenschaftlichung der Politik? Zur neuen Rolle von Expertenkommissionen", *Zeitschrift für Sozialreform*, Jg. 50, Nr. 1/2, S. 51-55.
Hodgetts, J.E., 1964, "Should Canada Be De-Commissioned?", *Queen's Quarterly*, Jg. 70, Nr. 4, S. 475-490.
Iacobucci, Frank, 1990, "Commissions of Inquiry and Public Policy in Canada", in: A. Paul Pross / Innis Christie / John A. Yogis (Hrsg.), *Commissions of Inquiry. Dalhousie Law Journal*, Jg. 12, Nr. 3, S. 21-28.
Jasanoff, Sheila, 1990, *The Fifth Branch: Science Advisers as Policymakers*, Cambridge u.a.
Jasanoff, Sheila, 2000, "The 'Science Wars' and American Politics", in: Meinolf Dierkes / Claudia von Grote (Hrsg.), *Between Understanding and Trust – The Public, Science and Technology*, Amsterdam, S. 39-60.
Jenson, Jane, 1994, "Commissioning Ideas: Representation and Royal Commissions", in: Susan D. Philips (Hrsg.), *How Ottawa Spends 1994-1995: Making Change*, Ottawa, S. 39-70.
Kropp, Sabine, „'Deparlamentarisierung' als Regierungsstil?", in: Antonia Gohr / Martin Seeleib-Kaiser (Hrsg.), *Wirtschafts- und Sozialpolitik unter Rot-Grün*, Wiesbaden, S. 329-344.
Leersch, Hans-Jürgen, 2001, „Diagnose: Kommissionitis", *Die Welt* vom 8. August 2001.
Leggewie, Claus (Hrsg.), 2007, *Von der Politik- zur Gesellschaftsberatung. Neue Wege öffentlicher Konsultation*, Frankfurt/Main.
Lindner, Ralf, 2000, „Politikberatung und Politikwandel. Der Beitrag der Macdonald Commission am wirtschafts- und sozialpolitischen Paradigmenwechsel in Kanada", Augsburg (unveröffentlichte Diplomarbeit).
Lipset, Seymour Martin, 1990, *Continental Divide: The Values and Institutions of the United States and Canada*, New York.
Mackay, A. Wayne, 1990, "Mandates, Legal Foundations, Powers and Conduct of Commission of Inquiry", in: A. Paul Pross / Innis Christie / John A. Yogis (Hrsg.), *Commissions of Inquiry. Dalhousie Law Journal*, Jg. 12, Nr. 3, S. 29-50.
Marchildon, Gregory P., 2001, "Royal Commissions and the Policy Cycle in Canada: The Case of Health Care", The Scholar Series, Saskatchewan Institute of Public Policy, University of Regina, http://www.uregina.ca/sipp/documents/pdf/ssgm.pdf (Zugriff: 28 November 2008).
Marchildon, Gregory P. / Tom McIntosh / Pierre-Gerlier Forest, 2004, *The Fiscal Sustainability of Health Care in Canada: Romanow Papers*, Band 1, Toronto: University of Toronto Press
Mayntz, Renate, 1994, „Politikberatung und politische Entscheidungsstrukturen. Zu den Voraussetzungen des Politikberatungsmodells", in: Axel Murswieck (Hrsg.), *Regieren und Politikberatung*, Opladen, S. 17-30.
McCamus, John D., 2003, "The Policy Inquiry: An Endangered Species?", in: Allan Manson / David Mullan (Hrsg.), *Commissions of Inquiry. Praise or Reappraise*, Toronto, S. 211-228.
McIntosh, Tom / Pierre-Gerlier Forest / Gregory P. Marchildon, 2004, *The Governance of Health Care in Canada: Romanow Papers*, Band 3, Toronto: University of Toronto Press
Murswieck, Axel, 2003, „Des Kanzlers Macht: Zum Regierungsstil Gerhard Schröders", in: Christoph Egle / Tobias Ostheim / Reimut Zohlnhöfer (Hrsg.), *Das rot-grüne Projekt. Eine Bilanz der Regierung Schröder 1998–2002*, Wiesbaden, S. 117-136.
Murswieck, Axel, 1994, „Wissenschaftliche Beratung im Regierungsprozeß", in: Axel Murswieck (Hrsg.), *Regieren und Politikberatung*, Opladen, S. 103-120.

Nevitte, Neil (Hrsg.), 2002, *Value Change and Governance in Canada*, Toronto.
Salter, Liora, 2003, "The Complex Relationship Between Inquiries and Public Controversy", in: Allan Manson / David Mullan (Hrsg.), *Commissions of Inquiry. Praise or Reappraise*, Toronto, S. 185-210.
Salter, Liora, 1990, "The Two Contradictions in Public Inquiries", in: A. Paul Pross / Innis Christie / John A. Yogis (Hrsg.), *Commissions of Inquiry. Dalhousie Law Journal*, Jg. 12, Nr. 3, S. 173-196.
Schmidt, Manfred G., 2002, „Politiksteuerung in der Bundesrepublik Deutschland", in: Frank Nullmeier / Thomas Saretzki (Hrsg.), *Jenseits des Regierungsalltags. Strategiefähigkeit politischer Parteien*, Frankfurt/Main u.a., S. 23-38.
Schultze, Rainer-Olaf, 1985, *Das politische System Kanadas im Strukturvergleich*. Studien zur politischen Repräsentation, Föderalismus und Gewerkschaftsbewegung, Bochum.
Schultze, Rainer-Olaf, 1989, *Kanada und die Vereinigten Staaten. Ungleiche Nachbarn in Nordamerika*, Augsburg.
Schultze, Rainer-Olaf, 2004, „Bundesstaaten unter Reformdruck: Kann Deutschland von Kanada lernen?", *Zeitschrift für Staats- und Europawissenschaften*, Jg. 2, Nr. 2, S. 191-211.
Schultze, Rainer-Olaf / Tanja Zinterer, 1999, „Kanadische Royal Commissions: Ein Vorbild für den Abbau von Reformstaus?", *Zeitschrift für Parlamentsfragen*, Jg. 31, Nr. 4, S. 881-903.
Schwartz, Bryan 2003, "Public Inquiries", in: Allan Manson / David Mullan (Hrsg.), *Commissions of Inquiry. Praise or Reappraise*, Toronto, S. 443-460.
Sebaldt, Martin, 2004, „Auf dem Weg zur ‚Räterepublik'? – Expertengremien und ihr Einfluss auf die deutsche Bundesgesetzgebung", *Zeitschrift für Gesetzgebung*, Jg. 19, Nr. 2, S. 187-200.
Siefken, Sven T., 2003, „Expertengremien der Bundesregierung – Fakten, Fiktionen, Forschungsbedarf", *Zeitschrift für Parlamentsfragen*, Jg. 34, Nr. 3, S. 483-504.
Siefken, Sven T., 2007, *Expertenkommissionen im politischen Prozess. Eine Bilanz der rot-grünen Bundesregierung 1998-2005*. Wiesbaden.
Steinmeier, Frank Walter, 2001, „Konsens und Führung", in: Franz Müntefering / Matthias Machnig (Hrsg.), *Sicherheit im Wandel*, Berlin, S. 263-272.
Thorburn, Hugh G. / Alan Whitehorn (Hrsg.), [8]2001: *Party Politics in Canada*, Kingston.
Thunert, Martin, 2004, „Politikberatung in der Bundesrepublik Deutschland: Entwicklungslinien, Leistungsfähigkeit und Legitimation", in: André Kaiser / Thomas Zittel (Hrsg.), *Demokratietheorie und Demokratieentwicklung. Festschrift für Peter Graf Kielmansegg*, Wiesbaden, S. 391-422.
Thunert, Martin, 2003, „Think Tanks in Deutschland – Berater der Politik?", *Aus Politik und Zeitgeschichte*, Heft B51/03, S. 30-38.
Weimar, Anne-Marie, 2004, *Die Arbeit und die Entscheidungsprozesse der Hartz-Kommission*, Wiesbaden.
Weingart, Peter, 2005a, *Die Stunde der Wahrheit? Zum Verhältnis der Wissenschaft zu Politik, Wirtschaft und Medien in der Wissensgesellschaft*, Weilerswist.
Weingart, Peter, 2005b, *Die Wissenschaft der Öffentlichkeit. Essays zum Verhältnis von Wissenschaft, Medien und Öffentlichkeit*, Weilerswist.
Zinterer, Tanja, 2004, *Politikwandel durch Politikberatung? Die kanadische Royal Commission on Aboriginal Peoples und die Unabhängige Kommission „Zuwanderung" im Vergleich*, Wiesbaden.

MIRIAM RICHTER

Constitutional 'Equality of Status' – From Political Program to Fictional Reality

The Relationship between Anglo- and Franco-Canadians in Anglo-Canadian Children's Literature

___

Zusammenfassung
Vor dem Hintergrund, dass das Verhältnis der beiden Gründungskulturen Kanadas nach wie vor einen zentralen Stellenwert für den heutigen Nationalcharakter besitzt, soll in diesem Aufsatz untersucht werden, wie anglo-kanadische Jugendbuchautoren des 20. und 21. Jahrhunderts den Kontakt zwischen Engländern und Franzosen im Akadien des 18. Jahrhunderts, d.h. zur Zeit der Deportation der Akadier, darstellen. Hauptziel wird sein, eine Entwicklung in der literarischen Beschreibung dieser beiden Bevölkerungsgruppen in Romanen aufzuzeigen, die vor und nach der Verabschiedung der Canadian Charter of Rights and Freedoms verfasst wurden, um daraus Rückschlüsse darauf zu ziehen, wie die Texte politisch-ideologische Veränderungen widerspiegeln und welche Rolle den historischen Jugendromanen bei der Herausbildung der nationalen Identität Kanadas zukommt.

Résumé
Les liens entre les deux cultures fondatrices du Canada revêtant, aujourd'hui comme hier, une importance fondamentale dans la constitution de l'identité nationale contemporaine de ce pays, cet exposé a pour ambition de montrer comment des auteurs anglo-canadiens de livres pour la jeunesse des XXe et XXIe siècles décrivent les relations existant entre les Français et les Anglais dans l'Acadie du XVIIIe siècle, au moment où les Acadiens furent déportés. Il s'agit avant tout de mettre en lumière l'évolution que nous avons pu constater dans la représentation littéraire de ces deux fractions du peuple à travers des romans ayant été écrits avant et après l'adoption de la Charte canadienne des droits et libertés afin d'étudier de quelle manière ces textes reflètent des mutations d'ordre à la fois politique et économique et quel rôle revient aux romans historiques pour la jeunesse dans la formation de l'identité nationale du Canada.

___

Sections 16 to 22 of the 1982 *Canadian Charter of Rights and Freedoms* confirm the equality of status of Canada's two official languages. The fact that seven sections alone of the charter's 34 sections are devoted to the country's bilingualism clearly emphasizes its importance to Canada's national character. It reflects the facet that the two initial European founding cultures still form the two largest groups in today's Canadian society, their relationship thus constituting a crucial issue of the country's national identity. What is often called "the great debate in the 1960s" (Canadian Consultative Council on Multiculturalism 1975, iii) is still topical today.

Historical youth fiction represents a genre that is especially appropriate to enhance the development of a nation, above all because literary renderings of a country's history possess the capability to construct identity by establishing a collective memory in Maurice Halbwachs's sense. In this context, the impact of fiction is particularly strong for, as Sheila Egoff claims, "only invention can bring the reader to an identification with the past" (Egoff 1966, 44). As, naturally, young readers are considerably more susceptible to this, their literature enables educational intervention in the country's next generation. Therefore, the analysis of this genre offers insights into the role literature plays in the process of constructing a national identity against an internal 'Other' and in conjunction with this same internal 'Other'.

It is not only identification with a country's history but also identification with its geography which possesses major significance for a feeling of national belonging. With regard to the Canadian situation, this topographical component is of special importance as – due to the relatively young character of a large corpus of homegrown Canadian (children's) literature – the availability of Canadian settings does not constitute an asset to be taken for granted. Not least since Northrop Frye's influential "Where is here?" a particular occupation with a Canadian literary space can be stated; Margaret Atwood also emphasized this when she stated that Canadian literature can function as a map to Canadians

> if we can learn to read it as *our* literature, as the product of who and where we have been. [...] we need to know about here, because here is where we live. For the members of a country or a culture, shared knowledge of their place, their here, is not a luxury but a necessity. (Atwood 2004, 27)

The "idea of place" (Hunt 1992, 86), which Peter Hunt defines as one of the most crucial aspects children's literature can convey to its readers, constitutes an element which was missed by many of today's Canadian authors of children's literature when they were children and had to resort to youth fiction from Great Britain or the United States, territories unfamiliar to them. The awareness of this necessity – intertwined with nationalist motives – has been a trigger to many of them to compose youth fiction set in Canada. The recent boom of Canadian historical youth fiction underlines the ongoing perception of this relevance, while the combination of history and geography presents itself as an ideal tool for the creation of the country's national narrative.

Hence, this article will examine how Canadian authors for young readers characterize the relationship between Anglo- and Franco-Canadians in their novels dealing with the deportation of the Acadian population in 1755. Against the background of the change in the makeup of the Canadian population and of political moves such as the charter, a development can be expected with regard to the portrayal of these two cultural groups in novels written before and after the repatriation of the constitution. The overall aim will be to detect this development, and the three novels under analysis have, therefore, been chosen to represent different times of publication – before and after 1982. In order to provide the reader with a deeper understanding of the character of this development in the ideological rhetoric longer quotations from all three novels will be included. Peter Hollindale's distinction between the "surface ideology" – i.e. the message voluntarily conveyed by the author – and the "passive ideology" – i.e. the subconsciously transmitted values of society – of a text (cf. Hollindale 1988, 11–13) will be applied in the course of the analysis to pinpoint the change of policies. Acadia constitutes a model region for a close look at Canada's national identity: It is not only the place of the first permanent European settlements on Canadian soil and, thus, Canada's nucleus but it is also a region that has been inhabited and contested by both, Anglo- and Franco-Canadian populations. Although the Acadians consider themselves a cultural group different from all others in the country, they still share language, ethnic origin, and religion with the other French-Canadian groups and can therefore be classified as a variety of French-Canadians as Alan B. Anderson and James S. Frideres suggest (cf. Anderson/Frideres 1981, 93). Consequently, it is legitimate to treat the relationship between Acadians and the English depicted in the novels as reflective of the relationship between Anglo- and Franco-Canadians in general. The question of the individual ethnic identities of the two groups will be largely disregarded in the following; the purpose of this examination is to shed some light on the literary representation of the relationship between Canada's two European founding nations and the interrelatedness of these literary renderings with the country's national identity.

I.

The first novel examined is John Francis Hayes's *A Land Divided*. It was originally published in 1951 and received a Governor General's Literary Award in the year following its publication, which indicates political approval of the author's stance. Hayes's adventure stories for young readers predominated the historical fiction market in Canada for close to twenty years (cf. Egoff/Saltman 1990, 108). While their tone is typical of traditional adventure stories, the setting of all his historical novels in Canada underlines a specificity of Canadian adventure literature: Contrary to adventure story conventions of other national literatures "gemäß derer exotisierend die ferne Fremde imaginiert wird" (Seifert 2006, 960), Canadian novels of this genre are mostly set in the home country. This reflects the thirst for literature set in Canadian home ground; as readers are, thus, offered a strong idea of place, this specificity may be interpreted as representing the Canadian preoccupation with the constant search for a national identity, which has come to be regarded as an element of the country's national identity in itself.

In *A Land Divided*, the English protagonist Michael and his Acadian cousin Pierre go on a quest to search for Michael's father, an English army officer, who has been kidnapped by a French villain. Because of this constellation of characters one would expect a well-balanced description that takes into account both points of view of the deportation, the English as well as the French, all the more as Michael is half-Acadian, half-English. However, although it is mentioned that the expulsion causes the Acadians difficulties and grief, the author presents a purely one-sided English version, which leaves no doubt that the deportation was the only possible decision on the part of the English, with the Acadians being portrayed as a threat to the latter:

> All efforts to get the Acadians to abide by English law had been fruitless, and the rising strength of French garrisons in the disputed land of Acadia was giving the settlers new hope that the British would soon be driven from the country. [...] Brash boasts of an early defeat of the English were openly expressed. (Hayes 1951, 34)

The dramatic style of the quotation illustrates that the English are depicted as only reacting to the situation and defending themselves. In situations where doubts concerning their actions could arise in the readers, the English characters' behaviour is excused by their soldierly obedience to orders. Service to the cause is, thus, ranked above loyalty towards one's own family.

> Again and again Captain Harvey repeated that he was under orders, but there seemed to be no escape from the cold fact that he was taking part in sending his wife's family into exile. He was helpless to do otherwise, but he felt his duty keenly [...]. He peered across the table at his wife: 'I'm sorry, Marcelle. I wish there was some other way out.' (Hayes 1951, 233)

This English value operates at both of Hollindale's levels of ideology: The principle itself is introduced to the readers at the level of surface ideology; at the level of passive ideology, the preservation of a British value by a Canadian author reveals the Canadian society's deep-rootedness in the British heritage and Canada's continuing strong ties to her former mother country in the middle of the 20th century. This is equally reflected in the military dominance of the English, which constitutes only one example of the English colonial attitude that is displayed in every part of the novel without the author's questioning it. The region is under British rule, and it is presented as a sign of British generosity that the French population, i.e. the Acadians, is allowed to live there, as becomes evident in Captain Harvey's address to the Acadians:

> Gentlemen, you are called together today to hear His Majesty's final resolution concerning the French inhabitants of this His province of Nova Scotia, who for almost half a century have had more indulgence granted them than any of his subjects in any part of his dominions … (Hayes 1951, 237)

From their possession of the land the English derive the right to dictate the conditions, including the right to expel anyone. The colonial mentality becomes visible again at the time of the deportation: The superior English have to take care of the helpless Acadians, who would be at a complete loss without the soldiers' organisational skills.

> [The Acadians were] making no effort to stow their belongings which lay in scattered heaps over the decks. Sailors were trying to sort out their passengers, but only a few of the settlers did anything to help themselves. (Hayes 1951, 251)

Hayes reports that the English even help the Acadians get settled and build a new life after deportation – the Acadians' best interests are, thus, presented as important to the English, i.e. the latter are beyond all criticism. Therefore, Hayes's account of the deportation and the English role in it can only be called euphemistic from today's point of view. What Konrad Gross states for early English-Canadian adult fiction dealing with French-Canada holds true for *A Land Divided* as well: The authors make it seem that "a happier calamity never befell a people than the conquest of Canada by British arms" (Gross 1981, 69).

On condition that the English maintain their ruling power, the relationship between Acadians and the English is portrayed as a good one, which is underlined by a great number of mixed marriages, the classical device; not only Michael's father but "scores of British soldiers" stationed at Fort Annapolis and "most of the officers" (Hayes 1951, 47) are married to Acadian women of the region. Furthermore, Pierre is not only Michael's cousin but has also been his best friend since earliest childhood, which exemplifies that Anglo- and Franco-Canadians are compatible. With family members and Acadian neighbours positive experiences are described; it is only outsiders who pose a threat – or as Patricia E. Johnston puts it: there is "an obvious cast of good guys and bad guys. The bad guys are the extremist, militant Acadians led by Lucien Vaudreuil and the good guys are everyone else" (Johnston 1981, 52).

The friendship between Michael and Pierre could therefore be seen as pointing the way ahead for the country's two principal cultural groups – were it not for the imbalance of power in their relationship: the English boy Michael is the strong one who decides what to do, colonial mentality yet again. Reviews from the 1950s greeted *A Land Divided* enthusiastically and praised it as "an excellent background novel for any young Canadian: history is made to come to life. For boys 12-15, especially" (Review of *A Land Divided* 1951). This underscores that the book was in accordance with the zeitgeist, and that the political attitudes and the values expressed in *A Land Divided* were by no means Hayes's alone but representative of the period.

Unlike most adolescents whose parents are of different cultural origin, Michael's identity is neither torn nor shattered but he feels completely English although he would have been predestined to incorporate the union of the two cultures in Canada. When they try to put this down simply to the author's not exploiting the conflicts inherent in his characters, Egoff and Saltman do not cover all relevant explanations (cf. Egoff/Saltman 1990, 108). Societal aspects should also be considered to account for this surprising characterization: First, Michael's unwavering English identity, again, reflects the notion of English superiority, thus reinforcing the existing imbalance of power. Second, it continues what the title, *A Land Divided*, announces already; it proves to be highly reminiscent of Hugh MacLennan's *Two Solitudes*. This landmark in Canadian nationalist fiction, published only six years prior to *A Land Divided*, paved the ground for the theme of Canadian unity and disunity respectively. By placing his historical novel in this tradition, Hayes signals his intention to contribute to the formation of a Canadian national identity in its own right, in times of a nationalist atmosphere around the introduction of Canadian citizenship.

II.

Like John F. Hayes, Anne Carter also anchors her time-slip novel *The Girl on Evangeline Beach* (published in 2000) in the literary tradition already by the title. By choosing the site of Evangeline Beach in modern Nova Scotia as central to the setting, the author conjures up Henry Wadsworth Longfellow's 1874 poem *Evangeline: A Tale of Acadie*, which has since become an Acadian identity myth, although it was written by an American poet. Here, parallels between the literary namesakes are even greater. Both are told against the historical background of the Acadian expulsion and Carter's principal Acadian character Marie has to watch her newly "betrothed" die in her arms as does Evangeline. The tragic character of the expulsion is, hence, transferred very clearly. Carter's using an existing identity myth suggests her intention to contribute to the renegotiation of a Canadian identity which includes the open acceptance of past wrongs.

The actual protagonist of *The Girl on Evangeline Beach,* Michael Denshaw, is a 20th century Torontonian boy who is attacked by two "thugs" (Carter 2000, 46) at his school, and falls – badly injured – into a coma. He finds himself travelling back to Grand Pré, Acadia, in 1755 with the task to save the Acadian girl Marie from the same two "thugs". As Martina Seifert has shown, time-slip fantasies possess even more than conventional historical novels the power to help young Canadian readers understand the importance of their history, their country and the people with whom they belong because the search for identity is inherent in this genre (cf. Seifert 2001, 119). This genre enables young readers still more than traditional historical fiction to draw the connection between history and present and understand the relevance. That way, they can develop an even deeper idea of place and consequently a sense of national belonging and identity. Carter's choice of genre, hence, constitutes another case in point of her intentions in this respect.

The depiction of the Acadians' deportation in this novel is the complete opposite of that presented by Hayes almost half a century earlier: Although the protagonist Michael is Anglo-Canadian like Hayes's Michael, Carter's Michael sides with the Acadians as he explicitly states – "I'm on your side" (Carter 2000, 112). Contrary to Hayes, Carter does not offer a justification for the English acts but rather an accusation of the English throughout her whole novel; the "injustice of the Acadian fate" (Carter 2000, 47) is declared more than once and it is underlined by the choice of words: "the English *deported* their families and *stole* all these lands" (Carter 2000, 4; my emphasis). The English argument that the Acadians form a threat is included in the book, but the fact that this accusation is a pretext becomes obvious by the author's constant emphasis on the Acadians' neutrality, which is historical reality as well as a central part of the Acadian auto-image at least at the time of deportation.

> It's urgent that we convince Lawrence of our neutrality. […] He calls us a security threat. He says all the Acadians will fight alongside Father LeLoutre against the English. Or failing that, we will supply aid to the French soldiers in Fort Beauséjour. We must persuade him that we don't take sides, that we're peaceful farmers like the generations before us. (Carter 2000, 98)

The author's using the Acadian neutrality as a keyword of her novel, almost a leitmotif, constantly reinforces the injustice of the deportation and the guilt of the English. The above quotation exemplifies that the content is underlined by the choice of words: While the urgency of the matter is clearly discernible here, the tone is considerably less dramatic than in Hayes's description of the Acadian threat, suggesting that in Carter's characterisation the Acadians are indeed peaceful whereas the English are the aggressors. In opposition to Hayes, Carter leaves no doubt about the fact that it is the land where the Acadians have been living for centuries and where they therefore belong. She underlines this by a motif often to be found in Canadian adult literature as well as in Canadian youth fiction on Loyalist refugees to Canada (cf. Richter 2004): By presenting the indigenous population, i.e. the

Mi'kmaq, as allies and friends of the Acadians, the author naturalizes the French population. For instance Marie's mother has got an aboriginal cousin with the French name of Louis, who is in close contact with the family. Furthermore, cases of exogamy, i.e. mixed marriages between Acadian and Mi'kmaq partners, lay further emphasis on their firm bonds. The English soldiers in Acadia are portrayed as enemies of the First Nations – "the English have been killing Mi'kmaq on sight; there's a bounty on their scalps" (Carter 2000, 127) – and are, thus, clearly characterized as intruders. The Mi'kmaq's hatred for the English constitutes another case in point (cf. Carter 2000, 223). Like in *A Land Divided*, the English also display a strong colonial attitude; however, in *The Girl on Evangeline Beach*, this attitude is not regarded as natural but on the contrary it is strongly criticized. This becomes particularly evident in an explanation Marie's father provides:

> They [the English] are driven to own land, put up fences, slop on taxes. […] *This is mine*. The Mi'kmaq have been here, maybe forever, and never tried to own the land. But those English – they don't listen to anybody. (Carter 2000, 88)

Carter's presentation indicates a shift in power at least in Canadian literature: As the past acts of injustice are condemned, English supremacy in Canada has come to an end in children's fiction. This change clearly reflects the development in Canada's official policy over the past half century towards a policy of equality, starting with a policy of equality between Anglo- and Franco-Canadians in the 1960s, which was later extended to the multiple ethnic groups living in Canada.

Although the principle of equality was finally anchored in the *Canadian Charter of Rights and Freedoms*, the process of negotiating the relationship of Anglo- and Franco-Canadians is not completed yet, as the literary evidence suggests. Not only is the issue dealt with at the level of surface ideology but also, different from Michael Harvey in *A Land Divided,* Michael Denshaw's identity is torn and he questions his belonging, which can be seen as a symbol of the discussion of Canadian national identity. Michael Denshaw is Anglo-Canadian with a grandmother of Acadian descent, attends a French immersion school, and possesses an "uncanny facility for French" (Carter 2000, 29). Nevertheless, he feels English in the scenes set in the present. In the past, however, he identifies completely with the Acadians: He is afraid of the English soldiers and speaks and thinks of "the English" (Carter 2000, 188) as if he were Acadian. Therefore, when he introduces himself to Marie and her family as a half-Acadian, half-English boy from Boston (cf. Carter 2000, 53), this does not only help him get along but it also describes his feeling of identity best. His flexible first name underlines his being able to understand both cultures and also to belong to both: In an English environment his name is *Michael*, while his French-Canadian grandmother and the Acadians during his time travel call him *Michel*. After initial mistrust and fear on the side of the Acadians, they accept him as one of their own and come to the conclusion that they were "so wrong about you. You were a blessing, not a curse" (Carter 2000, 249). These aspects make him a model for modern Canadian society: Both, English and French parts of the population can get along well and bear each other respect and understanding. And, what is more, they can even form one nation incorporating both cultures of equal status, which once more mirrors the political goal of equality. The English soldiers, clearly marked as the 'bad guys' to remain in Johnston's terminology, serve as a deterrent example.

The fact that modern Anglo-Canadians acknowledge the deportation of the Acadians as a reprehensible act in their history is an important step in the process of national identity formation because it constitutes a sign of respect. In the book such a self-critical awareness of historical legacies of guilt is aroused in Michael. The readers are taught a similar awareness by means of the book as becomes particularly evident in one commentary made by Michael's grandfather: "Nowadays they'd call it ethnic cleansing, without the mass graves. Protestant English getting rid of Catholic French" (Carter 2000, 6). This reproach of atrocity also evokes a sense of equality of the two groups in the readers. The sense is underlined by the scenes set in the present where equal rights of Anglo- and Franco-Canadians are uncontested fictional reality. In spite of the described barbarities, the novel's ending is, hence, reconciliatory with regard to Anglo-/Franco-Canadian relations, which both suggests an achievement in that changes have occurred already and holds further promises for the future.

III.

With regard to the general stance taken, the most recent of the three youth novels analyzed here, Sharon Stewart's *Banished from Our Home. The Acadian Diary of Angélique Richard* (published in 2004), does not differ greatly from Carter's novel. This does not seem surprising since only four years had elapsed between the publication of the two books. The changes which can be stated are mostly changes in degree. *Banished from Our Home* also presents the point of view of the Acadians. Like Carter before her, Stewart expresses the wrongness of the deportation and the guilt of the English but she renders their cruelty as well as the Acadians' sufferings still more drastically. Again the English are presented as the aggressors – "*Les Anglais* are like a nest of wasps [who] keep stinging us" (Stewart 2004, 39) – and contrary to *A Land Divided*, they are depicted as responsible for their actions and not as merely reacting out of necessity. "*Les Anglais* have done us a great wrong" (Stewart 2004, 134) – "What a muddle [they] have made of things!" (Stewart 2004, 132) Powerful examples illustrate the underhandedness of the English; for instance Colonel Winslow issues a proclamation summoning all Acadian men and boys over 10 to the church to "hear a message" (Stewart 2004, 79), yet as soon as they are inside the church, "the guards closed the doors and set a great bar across them [...]. Why would they lock up our menfolk when all had come freely?" (Stewart 2004, 81) The even greater brutality of the descriptions can in part be put down to the type of the novel; as the title suggests, the work is written in the form of a diary. However, it can also be accounted for by further political actions: In 2003 a Royal Proclamation from Britain, supported by the Government of Canada, was issued, which acknowledges the sufferings of the Acadians during the expulsion. Stewart's changes in degree can, hence, also be seen as a reaction to this proclamation, indicating that the recognition of guilt on the part of the Anglo-Canadian population has gained further ground.

The English feeling of colonial superiority is topicalized here as in the two previous novels – for instance the English make their announcements to the Acadians in English, not caring if they understand (cf. Stewart 2004, 34, 73). In opposition to *A Land Divided,* in *Banished from our Home* the colonial, supremacist attitude is clearly condemned by the Anglo-Canadian author. The change in ideology since the middle of the 20th century is, thus, evidenced once more. Like in *The Girl on Evangeline Beach*, this critical stance, or rather confession, suggests present equality of the two cultural groups – at least as fictional reality.

Throughout the entire time, the Acadians endure the aggravating situation, they remain peaceful and even so trustful as not to suspect any evil of the English: Angélique's father reassures his family that "though the British may bluster, they never do anything" (Stewart 2004, 22). The Acadians do not give up sending delegations to Halifax with new petitions and – like in *The Girl on Evangeline Beach* – they keep emphasizing their neutrality.

> The governor greeted Papa and the others in a rage. He demanded that they at once swear an oath promising to take up arms against the French if they are asked to do so. Papa has always said that Acadians are neutrals. That means we do not fight either the French or the English. [...] The French are our kinfolk. How could we ever fight against them? When our elders said that to Governor Lawrence he clapped them in jail. (Stewart 2004, 57)

Here, the Acadians are clearly assigned the role of innocent victims – still more strongly than in Carter's novel – and they can only be fatalistic: "Maman says we can only wait and pray. Well, I am going to pray to *le bon Dieu* to send a plague upon that wicked governor!" (Stewart 2004, 57) The victim motif constitutes another element which firmly roots the two more recent novels in the Canadian literary tradition. According to Atwood, it is one of the principal motifs of Canadian literature in general with one variety of the motif regarding French-Canadians in French-Canadian literature – "'[...] French Canadians are to the English as the natives are to the whites,' that is, exploited victims threatened with extinction" (Atwood 2004, 120-121). It seems to be a new variation here that Anglo-Canadian authors adopt this motif for their work; again, this development points to the societal impact of the Royal Proclamation.

The loss of home which the Acadians experience is a major issue in *Banished From Our Home* not least due to the diary form; completely disregarded in Hayes's novel, this topic is mentioned but neglected in Carter's. The Acadians refuse to believe that they will be deported; they are "sick with sorrow" (Stewart 2004, 101) and the extent of their devastation becomes evident:

> Our dear familiar world is dead. It was killed by the British two days ago. Perhaps it would be kinder if they killed all of us, too. (Stewart 2004, 98)

This quotation powerfully illustrates the extraordinary significance of home, not least through its dramatic wording. The deportation deprives the Acadians of the point of reference which constitutes a central pillar of their sense of life. Consequently, their loss of home shatters them so deeply that they would even prefer the loss of their lives over this experience. By underlining this attitude, the author arouses in her readers an awareness of the significance of home at an abstract level. She, thus, goes one step further than merely providing young Canadians with a strong idea of place in Hunt's sense through the setting of her novel. This awareness possesses special weight in Canada with its large immigrant influx: Canadian-born children can gain an understanding of a central issue their New Canadian classmates have to struggle with. What is more, this knowledge fosters their sense of national belonging.

The Acadians' feeling of being entirely uprooted and their planning to return to Acadia after the deportation constitute further instances which demonstrate the utmost importance of home for a person's identity. From this results the importance of a strong regional and, based on this, national identity, all the more as the strong regional diversity constitutes one of the elements Canadians define their country by. As Mavis Reimer and Anne Rusnak point out, "to study the representation of home in fiction is to study an aspect of the narrative by which a nation produces and reproduces itself" (Reimer/Rusnak 2000/2001, 10).

The issue of national identity can be found in yet another context in *Banished from Our Home*: The Acadians distinguish rigorously between the terms *the French* and *the Acadians*, while to the British all are alike, namely all are (French) enemies. When Acadians speak of *the French* they designate the French of European origin, i.e. in the first place French soldiers stationed in Acadian forts. The Acadians define themselves as not-English, so there is an assertion against the internal 'Other'; they are very proud of their French heritage, and call their ancestors' home country "*la douce* France" (Stewart 2004, 18). Hence, one of the principal elements of Canadian national identity, the country's being an immigration country, is included in the novel. Acadians in this book like in Carter's do not consider themselves continental French but have developed their own identity as Acadians, as descendants of the first settlers in Canada; this symbolizes a colony's having become independent of her mother country. In this regard as well, the two authors writing after the repatriation of the constitution display respect towards French-Acadians. Hayes does not clearly distinguish between Acadians and French in *A Land Divided* but uses both terms interchangeably throughout the entire book when he refers to the Acadian population. Hence, the change in policy towards the equality of Anglo- and Franco-Canadians becomes visible once more; in the historical youth novels published at the beginning of the 21st century, the Acadians have come to be recognized as an integral part of the Canadian population and no longer as a foreign threat. The fact that the evidence lies at the level of passive ideology indicates that this is fully shared by today's Canadian society; hence, it not only constitutes fictional reality but presents itself as part of everyday reality.

IV.

In conclusion, it can be stated that an obvious development has indeed taken place in Canadian historical fiction for young readers: The justification of the Acadians' deportation and a natural, uncontested English predominance before the repatriation of the constitution have given way to the condemnation of the same disrespectful actions and of the same predominance of the English in recent works. All three authors are Anglo-Canadian, their characterization of the English-French relationship therefore offers insights into the Anglo-Canadian political ideology during the respective periods. The development detected involves not only a greater respect for one another but also a shift in power between Canada's two European founding cultures; this change in the literary portrayal can be explained by a change in the political and societal climate. Therefore, the novels analyzed provide an understanding of the auto-image of Canadian society while simultaneously helping construct this same image and by promoting it among the country's next generation. The stated shift in Canada's collective memory constitutes a significant step in the negotiation of the country's national identity: By means of the two recent novels examined, Anglo-Canadians acknowledge and take responsibility for their ancestors' unjust actions, and the writings can therefore be seen as apologies. This reading suggests itself all the more because of the temporal closeness of the literary apology with the 2003 proclamation, which recognized the sufferings of the Acadians – one more case in point for the close interrelatedness of a country's literature and its politics. The fact that Hayes's novel is out of print underlines the development of positions in the past decades; his presentation of the historical events is no longer in conformity with today's official political opinion. A general renegotiation of Canada's collective memory seems to be in progress, as is also indicated by Harper's 2008 apology to Native Canadians concerning residential schools.

Although it would be an overinterpretation to credit the *Canadian Charter of Rights and Freedoms* alone to have brought about this significant change in attitude, it doubtlessly played a major role – first, in its function as the country's constitution, i.e. the foundation of national life, which still serves as the "ultimate point of reference" (Kamboureli 1993, 208) in the national narrative; second, as the final step to leave colonial dependency on Britain behind. Furthermore, his bicultural vision was a principal motive of Trudeau's for advancing the repatriation – and as Richard Clippingdale points out "the constitution had meant for some time the Quebec issue in the consciousness of most Canadians" (Clippingdale 1983, 92). A case in this point is the above mentioned emphasis on Canada's bilingualism – for "the written constitution [...] is a powerful symbolic statement of inclusion or exclusion" (Cairns 1993, 205). In addition, since the repatriation the federal government has employed the constitution "to strengthen allegiance to Canada and to promote Canadian identity" (Laforest 1995, 45). But further circumstances have also contributed to the development. The *Canadian Multiculturalism Act*, which is generally seen as a consequence of the constitution (cf. Kamboureli 1993, 207), on the one hand reinforces the status of the two official languages. At the same time, it encourages the preservation of the varieties of cultural heritage existing in Canada – thus elaborating on section 27 of the *Charter*. Furthermore, the consciousness and preservation of Acadian heritage in present-day Nova Scotia are very vivid, as testified not least by the dedicated maintenance of national sites like Grand Pré. A recently created *lieu de mémoire* in Pierre Nora's sense offers further enhancement: July 28, 2004, was designated as a commemorative day to honour Canada's Acadian people nationwide, concurrent with the 400th anniversary of French settlement in North America. A special urge to politically and literarily acknowledge past injustices and emphasize present improvement was certainly also fostered by the repeated upsurges of separatist movements, most recently, the 1997 Referendum on Quebec's independence; its narrow result has doubtlessly aroused what Gross has called in a different context "the need for stroking French-Canadian sensibilities" (Gross 1981, 73) in the English-Canadian part of the population. Stephen Harper's latest move in this matter, i.e. granting Quebec the status of a nation within the nation in the fall of 2006, equally has to be interpreted in this way.

The friendships which are emphasized between individual English people and Acadians in all three novels pave the ground for a positive common future. The novels published after the repatriation of the constitution incorporate a promotion of the country's bicultural character on the premise of equality, which proves that the two cultures have moved closer together on the whole over the past half-century. This greater rapprochement is also evidenced by the fact that some of the aspects dealing with their relationship – especially those that demonstrate acceptance – are not presented at the level of surface ideology but have moved on to the level of passive ideology in the later novels. These observations reflect the results of Stéphane Dion's study concerning the realm of Anglo- and Franco-Canadian values.

En fait, de plus en plus d'études montrent qu'il n'y a plus de différences significatives entre l'échelle des valeurs des francophones et celle des anglophones. La similarité des attitudes est frappante sur des sujets aussi divers que l'échelle de prestige de professions, les questions morales, le rôle du gouvernement, le droit de grève, les droits des autochtones, le rapport à l'autorité, la notion d'égalité, les valeurs à transmettre aux enfants, etc. (Dion 1991, 301)

The negotiation of the two groups' relationship, however, is not complete yet as becomes visible in the fact that the authors present many aspects concerning the Anglo-/Franco-Canadian relationship at the level of surface ideology; this not only highlights the topicality of the issue but also its particular relevance to the Canadian psyche. In the novels under examination, the Acadians' will to return and continue life in Acadia under the English rule in spite of their horrible experiences further emphasizes that the two cultural groups are not incompatible bodies of population. The authors' turning towards the history of Acadia in the novels reinforces the existence of a shared Anglo-/ Franco-Canadian identity because the historical events common to both cultural groups offer elements for identification and, thus, enhance national unity. My findings hence substantiate Claude Romney's claim that "la littérature canadienne d'enfance et de jeunesse constitue, selon moi, un excellent moyen de rapprocher jeunes anglophones et francophones au pays" (Nodelman 1997, 27). The novels analyzed here clearly serve this purpose. The constitutional equality of status has evolved from a political program into – at least – fictional reality.

References

Primary Literature

Carter, Anne, 2000, *The Girl on Evangeline Beach*. Toronto/New York: Stoddart Kids.
Hayes, John Francis, 1951, *A Land Divided*. Toronto: Copp Clark.
Longfellow, Henry Wadsworth, 2003, *Evangeline: A Tale of Acadie*. Halifax: Nimbus Publishing. (first published in 1874)
MacLennan, Hugh, 1945, *Two Solitudes*. Toronto: William Collins, Sons & Company.
Stewart, Sharon, 2004, *Banished from Our Home: The Acadian Diary of Angélique Richard: Grand Pré, Acadia, 1755*. Markham: Scholastic (Dear Canada series).

Secondary Literature

Anderson, Alan B./James S. Frideres, 1981, *Ethnicity in Canada: Theoretical Perspectives*. Toronto: Butterworths.
Atwood, Margaret, 2004, *Survival: A Thematic Guide to Canadian Literature*. Toronto: McClelland & Stewart. (first published in 1972)

Cairns, Alan C., 1993, "The Fragmentation of Canadian Citizenship", in: William Kaplan (ed.), *Belonging – The Meaning and Future of Canadian Citizenship*, Montreal/Kingston: McGill/Queens University Press, 181-220.
Canadian Consultative Council on Multiculturalism, 1975, *First Annual report of the Canadian Consultative Council on Multiculturalism*, Ottawa.
Clippingdale, Richard T., 1983, "Canada's Unfinished Constitutional Crisis 1980-1981", *Zeitschrift der Gesellschaft für Kanada-Studien*, 3.1, 91-103.
Dion, Stéphane, 1991, "Le nationalisme dans la convergence culturelle – Le Québec contemporain et le paradoxe de Tocqueville", in: Raymond Hudon/Réjean Pelletier (eds.), *L'engagement intellectuel – Mélanges en l'honneur de Léon Dion*, Sainte-Foy, Québec: Presses de l'Université Laval, 219-312.
Egoff, Sheila, 1966, "Canadian Historical Fiction for Children", *Canadian Literature*, 27, 44-52.
Egoff, Sheila/Judith Saltman, 1990, *The New Republic of Childhood: A Critical Guide to Canadian Children's Literature in English*. Toronto: Oxford University Press.
Gross, Konrad, 1981, "The Image of French-Canada in Early English-Canadian Fiction", in: Konrad Gross/Wolfgang Klooss (eds.), *English Literature of the Dominions: Writings on Australia, Canada and New Zealand*, Würzburg: Könighausen & Neumann, 69-79.
Hollindale, Peter, 1988, "Ideology and the Children's Book", *Signal: Approaches to Children's Books*, 55, 3-22.
Hunt, Peter, 1992, *Approaching Arthur Ransome*. London: Cape.
Johnston, Patricia E., 1981, "Atlantic Canadian Historical Fiction: Where Is the Drama?", *Canadian Children's Literature*, 23/24, 51-58.
Kamboureli, Smaro, 1993, "The Technology of Ethnicity", *Open Letter*, 8.5-6, 202-217.
Laforest, Guy, 1985, *Trudeau and the End of a Canadian Dream*. Montreal/Kingston: McGill/Queen's University Press.
Nodelman, Perry, 1997, "What's Canadian about Canadian Children's Literature? A Compendium of Answers to the Question", *Canadian Children's Literature*, 87, 15-35.
Reimer, Mavis/Anne Rusnak, 2000/2001, "The Representation of Home in Canadian Children's Literature/La Représentation du chez-soi dans la littérature de jeunesse canadienne", *Canadian Children's Literature*, 100/101, 9-46.
Review of *A Land Divided* by John F. Hayes, no author indicated, in: *SN* [?], Dec. 8, 1951, page "For Younger Readers" (available in: Lyn Cook Fonds, Box 8.8: *Reviews The Little Magic Fiddler*; The Osborne Collection of Early Children's Books, Toronto/Canada).
Richter, Miriam, 2004, "*Underground to Canada* and *On Loyalist Trails* – Canada as a Safe Haven to American Refugees"; paper presented at the conference "Cultural Approaches to the Study of Canadian Nationalism", Nipissing University, North Bay/Ontario, August 12–14, 2004.
Seifert, Martina, 2001, "'Unmagical Canada'? – Phantastische (Zeit-)Reisen in der englischsprachigen kanadischen Kinder- und Jugendliteratur", *Inklings-Jahrbuch*, 19, 109-135.
-----, 2006, "Kulturtransfer: Studien zur Repräsentanz einzelner Herkunftsliteraturen", in: *Entfernungen. Fremdwahrnehmung und Kulturtransfer in der deutschsprachigen Kinder- und Jugendliteratur seit 1945*. Band 2: Martina Seifert/Gina Weinkauff, *Kulturtransfer: Studien zur Repräsentanz einzelner Herkunftsliteraturen: Literaturverzeichnis: Personenregister: CD-ROM*, München: Iudicium Verlag, 791-1005.

CHRISTIAN J. KRAMPE

Inserting Trauma into the Canadian Collective Memory: Lawrence Hill's *The Book of Negroes* and Selected African-Canadian Poetry

___

Zusammenfassung

Die afro-kanadische Literatur ist ein aufstrebendes Segment der kanadischen literarischen Szene. Dies drückt sich in steigenden Auflagen, wachsendem Angebot, aber auch in einer sich ausweitenden populären und akademischen Rezeption aus. In diesem Artikel wird anhand des aktuellen Romans Lawrence Hills (The Book of Negroes, 2007; Gewinner des Commonwealth Writers' Prize 2008) und einer Auswahl afro-kanadischer Lyrik nachgezeichnet, inwiefern die behandelten Autor(inn)en individuelle und kollektive Trauma-Erfahrungen in ihre Werke einfließen lassen. Die afro-kanadische Literatur insgesamt zeigt die Tendenz, ein kollektives Gegengedächtnis zu etablieren, welches diese Erfahrungen in den Vordergrund stellt. Ziel ist es, das von den schwarzen kanadischen Autor(inn)en als einseitig und 'weißgewaschen' perzipierte Majoritäts-Selbstbild Kanadas zu korrigieren. Die stereotypisierte Darstellung Kanadas als ein 'Kanaan' sowohl in der Vergangenheit (im Sinne eines sicheren Hafens angesichts der U.S.-amerikanischen Sklaverei) als auch in der Gegenwart (im Sinne eines multikulturellen Paradieses) wird somit kritisch hinterfragt.

Résumé

La littérature afro-canadienne est une branche en essor dans le milieu littéraire au Canada. Phénomène visible non seulement dans le nombre croissant de tirages et de nouvelles parutions, mais aussi dans l'intérêt grandissant que portent la population et le milieu académique à ce genre littéraire. Par l'intermédiaire du nouveau roman de Lawrence Hill (The Book of Negroes, 2007; prix Commonwealth Writers en 2008) et grâce à un choix de poésies afro-canadiennes, cet article permettra de constater dans quelle mesure les expériences traumatisantes individuelles ou collectives se retrouvent dans les œuvres des auteurs traités. L'ensemble de la littérature afro-canadienne a tendance à établir une « contre-mémoire » collective qui met ces expériences au premier plan. Le but étant de corriger l'image générale, perçue par les auteurs afro-canadiens comme unilatérale, d'un Canada qui tend à « se blanchir ». Il s'agit donc d'une remise en question d'une vision stéréotypée du Canada en tant que « pays de Canaan » – dans le passé (fuite devant l'esclavage aux États-Unis) et paradis multiculturel de nos jours.

> The construction of a national memory in particular is concerned with those points of reference that strengthen a positive self-perception and which are consistent with certain objectives of action. Victories are more easily memorized than defeats. […] It is far more difficult to incorporate into [a group's] memory moments of shame and guilt, as these cannot be integrated into a positive collective self-perception. This applies to the persecution and eradication of Native peoples on different continents, to the deportation of African slaves, to the victims of a genocide in the shades of World War One and Two. (A. Assmann 2001, 309; translation CJK)

In this paper, I will argue that African-Canadian[1] authors aim at an insertion of trauma into the Canadian collective memory. They embark on the difficult endeavour of integrating "moments of shame and guilt" – particularly "the deportation of African slaves" (cf. introductory quote) and the ensuing discrimination and maltreatment of enslaved, indentured or free Blacks – into a Canadian collective memory that has been constructed to reflect a (distorted) self-perception of Canada as a 'Canaan' for Blacks in both the past and the present. African-Canadian literature thus constitutes a counter-memory whose goal is a restructuring of the prevalent, 'whitewashed' national memory of Canada. It undermines common stereotypes and notions of Canadian moral superiority and acknowledges memories that have been virtually purged from mainstream discourse for centuries.

There are three levels of dealing with trauma in the subsequent literary analysis: One level is the individuals' immediate experience of trauma. On this personal scale, Lawrence Hill's *The Book of Negroes* will be discussed and individual characters' exposure to different traumata, particularly the experience of dehumanization and objectification as well as the experience of utter disillusionment will be illustrated. On a social or collective scale, the characters of *The Book of Negroes* – particularly its female protagonist – are archetypes and stand *pars pro toto* for the experiences of Black Loyalists coming to Canada in the 1780s. Hill unambiguously collectivises the experience of his characters so that we arrive at a description of a collective trauma

---

1   Due to spatial limitations, I will not justify at length my choice of terminology. "Black Canadian" and "African-Canadian" will be used interchangeably in this paper, agreeing with Clarke (2002, xi-ii), who expresses confidence in using both terms synonymously (as well as his favorite coinage "Africadian" for Maritime African-Canadians). For a thorough discussion of terminology cf. Tettey/Puplampu 2005.

caused by slavery and continuing racism. On a third, and more theoretical level, this paper reasons that the continued and prevalent preoccupation of Black Canadian authors with issues of slavery and racial discrimination (both historical and current) aims at keeping these memories alive and seeks to bring them to the fore – where 'standard' Canadian self-perception has never allowed them to be. This point will be further substantiated by a brief outlook beyond *The Book of Negroes*, i.e. with a survey of several African-Canadian poems.

Trauma and the theory of collective memory

Current approaches to theories of collective memory are largely based on the ground-breaking works of French philosopher/sociologist Maurice Halbwachs.[2] In the 1920s, Halbwachs, a student of Bergson and Durkheim, developed a theory of collective memory based on three main assumptions:

First, memory is seen as the basis of identity (cf. e.g. Assmann 1988, Weber 2001). Without distinct memories, individuals would not be able to establish coherent identities, i.e. diachronically and synchronically stable versions of self-perception (cf. Halbwachs 1967, 74). Individuals (as well as groups) strive to ascertain coherent versions of who they are, hence two features of memory are of eminent importance: Memory is selective and it is constructed (cf. Halbwachs 1966, 22). Unlike modern computer hard drives, human memory does not faithfully retrieve information it has stored; instead, it selects and (re-)constructs, modifying memories according to current needs of identity construction (cf. Halbwachs 1966, 126).

Second, individual memory is framed and thus shaped by social memory, which Halbwachs calls *cadres sociaux*. These *cadres sociaux* – provided by social milieus such as friends, colleagues, families, religious groups etc. – influence the contents and processes of saving and retrieving memories (cf. e.g. Halbwachs 1967, 35-38). Halbwachs uses the now famous 'walk through London' as an illustration: On an imaginary walking tour through London, Halbwachs' perspective, his way of noticing and perceiving certain features of the city, is influenced by his friends and colleagues, even though he is taking the walk in absolute solitude. Still, he takes notice of architectural designs as if in conversation with an architect friend, notices certain monuments as if in conversation with an art historian etc.[3] Our perception, and thus the contents and modes of what and how we remember, are hence pre-structured by our social framework (even *in absentia*).

---

2   Cf. Halbwachs' chief works (Halbwachs 1966 and 1967). A biographical sketch is provided in Halbwachs 1966, 11-23. For a good summary of Halbwachs' theories as well as current developments, cf. Erll 2003. Brief introductory articles on collective and cultural memory: Assmann 2001 and Bering 2001. Neumann 2005 provides a good overview with some detailed criticism before presenting her own analyses.

3   Cf. the opening of Halbwachs' seminal *Das kollektive Gedächtnis* (The Collective Memory) (Halbwachs 1967).

The third main assumption is the concept of a *collective* memory as opposed, or rather in addition, to individual memory. Not only are individual memories shaped by the individual's social surroundings; there is a memory that is genuinely social: the memory of a group. This memory, due to a lack of a unified neuronal basis in which to store information, by necessity relies on the individual members' cerebral networks.[4] It is, however, externalised in that it is an abstract agglomeration of the individual group members' memory. As such, it is as selective and constructed as individual memory. A group structures its collective memory hierarchically as well, attributing different levels of importance to certain memories. Accordingly, the processes of 'forgetting' are considered not as an arbitrary loss of information, but as a deliberate (though not always consciously planned and executed) way of selection. Those memories deemed important for a group are kept 'alive', while memories either unimportant or harmful to a group's identity are deleted. A group – in analogy to individuals – strives to arrive at a coherent memory version and thus at an identity that is positive and devoid of major contradictions (cf. Halbwachs 1966, 382).

Collective memory is thus a volatile entity: Processes of selection, interpretation and (re-)construction render and re-render information into modifications of the 'original' information (which, as such, is a detested concept in itself). Modern theories of collective memory have focused on a number of aspects, often dealing critically with Halbwachs' assumptions, though largely adopting the three main tenets of collective memory as identity-informing (and as such selective and constructed), socially framed and externalised as a 'meta'-memory. A number of scholars have warned against easy analogies between individual and collective memory processes. One strand of scholarship is devoted to the research of the media of collective memory, dealing with issues such as literate vs. oral communities, the impact of the advent of electronic storage devices and the internet etc. (cf. e.g. Erll/Nünning 2004). Other strands have attempted to render the theory of collective memory compatible with different scholarly disciplines, such as psychology, sociology, history, communication sciences or cultural studies. Cultural studies in particular have adopted collective memory as a powerful tool for analysis. The prolific works of Aleida and Jan Assmann[5] above all have provided the theoretical foundations for the use of collective memory as an analytical approach in the humanities. Their thoughts on memory as *ars* and *vis* (cf. A. Assmann 1999, 29), the differences between cultural and communicative memory (cf. J. Assmann 1992, 56) as well as the concept of functional and storage memory (cf. A. Assmann 1999, 134) are elements of the theoretical underpinnings of this paper. Aleida and Jan Assmann's elaborate

---

4   Cf. Halbwachs 1967, 35. Halbwachs himself, however, did not subscribe to theories of neuronal activity within cerebral networks as storage processes, cf. 1966, 21-22.
5   Both Aleida and Jan Assmann have edited numerous collections and published a wide range of monograph and articles. For introductory purposes, cf. their key works (A. Assmann 1999, J. Assmann 1992).

distinctions and modifications to Halbwachs' concepts have been exceedingly important for the terminology and conceptual clarity needed in e.g. literary analyses lest the term 'collective memory' become a universalised shell and mere catchphrase.[6]

It has become a commonplace that the same danger looms large over the term 'trauma'. Originally designating violent physical injury, psychoanalytical approaches in particular have employed the term for instances of intense psychological injury, its causes, processes and effects. The connection of physical trauma to psychological trauma as a causal relationship is still a dominant aspect, as cases of intense violence, sexual abuse, the experience of major bodily harm or the witnessing thereof are key sources of psychological trauma (cf. Eggers 2001). Yet the concept of trauma has been widened to include experiences of psychological or structural violence (particularly in child- or early adulthood) as well as the threat or imminent danger of violence. In connection to the theory of collective memory, the most salient aspect of trauma is its problematic integration into coherent and positive memory versions and thus self-identifications: The "moments of guilt and shame" identified in the introductory quote by Aleida Assmann are obstacles to such a coherent and positive, *ergo* successful and stable, construction of identity. Assmann argues that only recently have societies begun to integrate into their national self-perceptions the darker moments of their histories, thus embarking on what she calls a "therapeutic surmounting of the paralysing repercussions" of these traumatic instances (Assmann 2001, 310). My argument here is that African-Canadian authors are paving the way for this therapeutic surmounting of the omission/denial of slavery and discrimination in hegemonic constructions of a Canadian collective memory. The dominant Canadian collective memory is still constructed along the presumption of a benevolent Canada in both the past and the present. In order to maintain a fissure- and blotch-free Canadian identity, the existence of slavery and the ensuing experience of Canadian Blacks (namely disillusionment, segregation and continuing discrimination) have been blanked out for centuries (cf. Cooper 2007, 68-70; Foster 1996, 31-32; Walker 1982, 6). African-Canadian authors challenge this 'whitewashed' conception of Canada as a 'Promised Land', thus attempting to insert their traumatic experiences into a Canadian collective memory of which they should rightfully be a part.

Lawrence Hill: *The Book of Negroes*

The Book of Negroes (2007; abbreviated as 'BN') is the third novel by Lawrence Hill, son of social activists and US émigrés to Canada. In his works, which include non-fictional writings as well, Hill places particular importance on the passing on of memories, on keeping forgotten or suppressed aspects of (Black North American)

---

6 Others have furthered the task of providing enhancements to the adaptability of collective memory theory to the study of literature; cf. for instance Erll / Gymnich / Nünning 2003.

history alive.[7] He often focuses on the traumatic elements of the Black presence in North America, such as segregation, discrimination, racism, limited upward social mobility for Blacks, stereotyping, violence and racial hatred. In *The Book of Negroes*, Hill explores, through the eyes of his protagonist Aminata Diallo, the trials and tribulations – yet also the small triumphs – of an 11-year-old girl captured by slave-traders in Mali in 1756 who is sold to a plantation-owner in the United States. Hill does not shy away from gory detail when relaying the atrocities of the Middle Passage ensuing Aminata's abduction. The reader is also painfully confronted with notions of total ownership and de-humanization that were so blatantly central to the institution of slavery and the Atlantic slave trade. Barely surviving the slave coffle from her native village to the coast and the subsequent Middle Passage, Aminata is put to work on an indigo plantation in South Carolina. In 1775, she manages to run away from her new master in New York City. Fluent in three languages and literate, Aminata is then hired by the British Army to work on the name-sake Book of Negroes, a ledger that contains the names of those Blacks who, by serving the British, have qualified for shipment to Nova Scotia as Black Loyalists. In 1783, Aminata joins the exodus of Blacks – partly runaway slaves, partly indentured or free persons – to Canada. Settling in Birchtown, Nova Scotia, Aminata helps to organize a second exodus: The Sierra Leone Company, in 1792, ships 1,200 African-Canadians from Nova Scotia to Sierra Leone, the first independent Black colony. Aminata joins the ones willing to cross the ocean once more. After an abortive quest to go back inland to her native village of Bayo in 1800, Aminata agrees to sail the Atlantic a final time in order to accompany a British abolitionist to London, fostering the abolitionist cause by giving testimony of her life.

The story of Aminata's life, presented by Hill in a fictionalized autobiography recorded by Aminata in the early 1800s, explores traumata in a variety of constellations and levels of intensity. The text furthermore includes discussions of coping with trauma and the inability to do so, thus confronting the reader with an intricate treatment of issues revolving around remembering and forgetting, suffering and surviving.[8]

---

7   Hill's first two novels, *Some Great Thing* (1992) and *Any Known Blood* (1997) both feature protagonists who explore their family history, uncover a larger (Black Canadian) history beyond their immediate families' stories and set out to write down what they have learned about their literal and metaphorical ancestors in order to pass their newly found knowledge on. For insightful reviews of *Any Known Blood*, cf. Clarke 2002, 310-312 and Bailey Nurse 2003, 173-174.

8   *The Book of Negroes* deals with trauma both in detail and in broad scope. Instances of trauma include – but are not limited to – racial and sexual violence, dehumanization, impotence vis-à-vis cruelty and humiliation, loss of family and friends, loss of identity, disillusionment and broken promises, subhuman living conditions and preventable sickness, total heteronomy and dispossession of self, and structural violence in general. Given the fact that the 486-page novel spans, among others, the histories of the abduction of Africans by slave-traders, the Middle Passage, plantation slavery, indentured labor, broken promises in Nova Scotia, and the impossibility to return 'home', it should be obvious that no single paper can adequately deal with all of

Textual level: diverging reactions to trauma

The novel opens with a scene set in London in 1802, headlined "And now I am old" (BN 1). Despite her old age, Aminata is haunted by memories of her abduction and enslavement as an 11-year-old. Her traumatic recollections are still present and vivid through sensory perceptions: "I still can smell trouble riding on any wind [...]. And my ears still work as good as a hound dog's." (BN 1)[9] The trauma that most haunts and aggrieves Aminata at her old age is having lost her family. Having neither parents nor children to comfort her is the one regret that stands out among the others. Interestingly, the loss of her own children – both of them torn away from her by whites – is rivalled by a longing for her parents.[10] Aminata has her own way of dealing with the loss of her parents, who have been killed by slave traders in the raid that sent her into slavery: she imagines their presence. When young, it had been impossible for Aminata to be without the counsel of her parents, so she holds imaginary conversations with both her father and her mother (cf. e.g. BN 28, 82, 132-133). Accordingly, in absence of the living parents, her memory of them guides and advises her. The imaginary conversations serve, in Halbwachs' terminology, as *cadres sociaux*, the social framings exemplified in the London walk with physically absent friends. This psychological mechanism is preserved in Aminata up to her old age. In 1802, when writing her memoir, she says:

> Most of my time has come and gone, but I still think of them as my parents, older and wiser than I, and still hear their voices, sometimes deep-chested, at other moments floating like musical notes. I imagine their hands steering me from trouble, guiding me around cooking fires and leading me to the mat in the cool shade of our home. I can still picture my father with a sharp stick over hard earth, scratching out Arabic in flowing lines and speaking of the distant Timbuktu. (BN 3)

It is Aminata's literacy, initiated by her father in Bayo, that sets her apart from other slaves and qualifies her for services such as book-keeping and the recording

---

these aspects – let alone all of the individual instances, circumstances, responses and results of the traumata being inflicted on the novel's characters. Consequently, the reading offered here will by necessity remain cursory and eclectic.

9   Sensory perceptions play an important role in mnemonic contexts; cf. van der Kolk and van der Hart 1995, particularly 173. Also cf. e.g. Kölbl 2001 on olfactory memory and Hartmann 2001 on taste.

10 "[...] I wish my parents were still here to care for me." (BN 3) Aminata has lost her parents and both of her children to the *buckra*, the whites. Her parents were killed in the slave-traders' raid on her village; her first child was sold by her master and died in his infancy; her second child was abducted by a white couple for whom Aminata worked. Deprived of her family, Aminata, at 57, feels like an amputee: "I have escaped violent endings even as they have surrounded me. But I never had the privilege of holding my own children [...]. I long to hold my own children, and their children if they exist, and I miss them the way I'd miss limbs from my own body." (BN 2)

of names for the exoduses to Nova Scotia as well as to Sierra Leone. It is important not to underestimate the social aspect of Aminata's literacy, as it designates Aminata as both a survivor and a teacher. Part of Aminata's strength – next to the almost miraculous fact of her sheer physical survival – indeed lies in encouraging, teaching and inspiring her fellow people, in not letting her and her fellow Blacks' memories slip away.[11] Notions of transmitting memories are repeated throughout *The Book of Negroes*, strongly emphasized by Aminata's ability to indeed externalize her memories into written form (the ledger called the Book of Negroes as well as her autobiography). Yet remembering and reifying trauma is not only a life-saver for Aminata; it is also a painful process.[12] Aminata admits: "It was less painful to forget, but I would look and I would remember." (BN 190) Which, of course, Aminata does in writing her life's account, in producing (not simply retelling, but restructuring, reconstructing) the narrative that gives meaning to her life: "I have my life to tell, my own private ghost story, and what purpose would there be to this life I have lived, if I could not take this opportunity to relate it?" (BN 7)

It is through the task of record-keeping and the passing on of memories that Aminata is able to sustain herself psychologically throughout the atrocities of the Middle Passage. Most of her fellow slaves are less fortunate. Fanta, fifth wife of Bayo's chief and captured alongside Aminata, is a case in point. The very thought that her status as a slave will be entailed to her child, that the trauma of her objectification will be passed on, makes her kill her own child as well as the child of a fellow slave.[13] Aminata recalls the foreshadowing of the infanticide and the gruesome murder itself:

---

11 Lawrence Hill, in an as of yet unpublished interview I conducted with him in April 2007, asserts that Aminata's key strength, however, is constituted by the fact that she retains a capacity to love in spite of all the suffering she has lived through and all the pain she has witnessed. This view certainly matches the notion that trauma of a scope such as the one presented bears the almost insurmountable danger of rendering positive emotions impossible. For instances of Aminata's sustained capacity for love, cf. e.g. the birth of her second child May (BN 330) or the reunion with May at the very end of the novel.

12 Which of course is a well-explored concept; cf. in the Canadian minority context for instance the masterful treatment of this conflict in Joy Kogawa's *Obasan* (1994, particularly 218, 232-235, 237-238). Lawrence Hill cites Joy Kogawa as an example of how to insert history into fiction in order to pass on forgotten memories: "Dramatizing critical moments of our past can produce excellent fiction. Joy Kogawa comes to mind. Many Canadians might not have known about the experience of Japanese-Canadians during the Second World War if she hadn't written about it in *Obasan*." (Thomas 2006, 135)

13 The notion of trauma breeding trauma, of entailing the status of slave, and thus of property, through (racial) ancestry is maintained throughout the novel. As Georgia, Aminata's surrogate mother on the South Carolina indigo plantation, tells Aminata: "Got a slave mama, then you is slave. Got a slave daddy, then you is slave. Any nigger in you at all, then you is slave as clear as day." (BN 134) For a discussion of the term "slave" as a possible "misnomer" for African-Canadians' ancestors, cf. Prince 2001, 39-49.

> I put my hand on [Fanta's] shoulder and told her to think about the baby. She grunted. 'I stopped caring about that a long time ago. No toubab will do to this baby what they have done to us.' A shiver ran through my body. (BN 82-83)
> Fanta brought out the knife from the medicine man's room, placed a hand over the baby's face and jerked up his chin. She dug the tip of the knife into the baby's neck and ripped his throat open. Then she pulled the blue cloth over him, stood and heaved him overboard. (BN 90)

While Aminata's reaction to the trauma of the Middle Passage is to survive in order to testify, thus reconstructing subjects through narration, Fanta can see no other way of escape than to disrupt the chain of objectified selves by murder. Fomba, the *woloso* (intra-African slave) of Bayo's chief, reacts differently to the humiliation and pain of the Middle Passage. In contrast to Aminata, who witnesses to testify, and to Fanta, who kills to break the chain of entailing subhuman status, Fomba completely retreats and falls silent. At the slave auction in South Carolina, Fomba is among the 'leftover' slaves – the old, sickly and useless – just as Aminata:

> I caught a glimpse of Fomba, sitting on the ground, elbows around his knees, palms over his ears, eyes shut, rocking back and forth. [...] Dead weight, but not dead. [...] Fomba opened his mouth, but nothing – not one sound – came from his lips. (BN 115)

Aminata claims that Fomba's mind is "gone" (BN 114); he refuses to interact with the world of cruelty that surrounds him. The scene described above is an almost stereotypical depiction of a deeply traumatized person. Later on, Fomba is able to work again, but he never recovers his ability to communicate. Tragically, his social death[14] also precipitates physical death: Fomba is shot by a guard when he fails to identify himself (BN 214).

Aminata, in contrast, in a limbo of wanting to witness and having to suffer terribly throughout the process of witnessing, cannot and will not shut herself off from the pain: "I shut my eyes and plugged my ears, but could not block out all the shrieking." (BN 93) There are two factors that secure Aminata's psychological survival (though a mere 'survival' it is indeed): her young age and the notion of being a *djeli*.[15] At the

---

14 Cf. the widely discussed work of Orlando Patterson (1982).
15 Though the conception of being a *djeli*, a storyteller, is the more interesting one from a literary perspective (as it ties into narrative modes and roles), Aminata's young age provides her mind with a certain flexibility that she claims is lost in adults. Aminata recalls her time aboard the slave vessel and how she was able to endure the horrors aboard the ship: "But also, the child's mind has elasticity. Adults are different – push them too far and they snap. Many times during that long journey, I was terrified beyond description, yet somehow my mind remained intact." (BN 56) Also cf. Aminata's surrogate mother Georgia, who, in the plantation English usually re-

very beginning of the Middle Passage, Aminata decides to act as if she were a *djeli*. A *djeli*, occasionally written *jeli* or *jali*, is a West African storyteller; *griot* is the term predominantly used in Anglophone contexts.[16] His obligation is to relate and pass on oral history (cf. Schulz 2001, 240-241). As such, he is the quintessential specialist in the field of preserving and transmitting identity-informing collective memories (cf. distinctions between cultural and communicative memory, e.g. J. Assmann 1992, 50-52). Aminata, after her passage to London almost 45 years after her abduction, bears witness before the King and Queen as well as before Parliament. By subsequently writing her memoir, thus rendering her story into a durable medium, Aminata – as a *djeli*-cum-writer – externalizes and spreads those memories.

> Some of us still scream out in the middle of the night. But there are men, women and children walking about the streets without the faintest idea of our nightmares. They cannot know what we endured if we never find anyone to listen. In telling my story, I remember all those who never made it through the musket balls and the sharks and the nightmares, all those who never found a group of listeners, and those who never touched a quill to an inkpot. (BN 56-57)

Aminata wants to share her pain (or rather: *their* pain, as she explicitly speaks for a collective, including those who have died), she must pass on her/their memories lest the nightmares of the abducted Africans die with the slaves themselves and be forgotten.[17] Two levels of dealing with trauma are reflected in this quotation: The immediate reaction to trauma (nightmares) and the need to keep alive the traumatic memory (either orally: "listeners", or through writing: "quill to an inkpot"). In effect, thus, the insertion of the traumatic memory of slavery into a mainstream collective memory unperturbed by these recollections ("without the faintest idea of our nightmares") is at the core of Aminata's testimony.

---

served for communication with whites, contrasts Aminata with Fomba: "You done cross the river [the Atlantic], and your head is on fire. But grown man done cross the river and shut his mouth forever." (BN 130) The elasticity of her mind is thus presented as a major factor in Aminata's ability to cope with trauma. For Fomba, however, the ocean has proved to be "one nasty shut-mouth river." (BN 130)

16 Cf. for instance the collection *T-Dot Griots: An Anthology of Toronto's Black Storytellers* (Richardson / Green 2004).

17 This notion is repeated a number of times in *The Book of Negroes*; the collective voice embodied by Aminata is an important aspect of stressing collective rather than personal memory, even though on the surface we are dealing with a fictionalized individual autobiography. Cf. for instance: "They [the people of Canvas Town, NYC] took me into their dancing, and did not ask where I came from, for all they had to do was look at me and hear my own sobs in my maternal tongue and they knew I was one of them. The dead infant was the child I had once been; it was my own lost [son] Mamadu; it was every person who had been tossed into the unforgiving sea on the endless journeys across the big river [the Atlantic]." (BN 256)

Consequently, Aminata – in contrast to Fanta or Fomba – has both the predisposition (her young age) and a reason to survive physically as well as mentally. She brings herself to channel her traumatic experiences and renders the process of witnessing usable against caving in: "*No*, I told myself. *Be a djeli. See, and remember.*" (BN 64)

The Canadian perspective: Canaan denied

In 1783, Aminata is asked to work for the British Army – by then preparing to retreat from New York City, their last stronghold south of the 49th parallel separating the two North American countries – by helping to compile the Book of Negroes. This list of Black Loyalists signifies, so Aminata and her fellow Canvas Town residents are promised, their ticket to a life in freedom and equality under the lion's paw of British rule in the North. "Nova Scotia, Miss Diallo, will be your promised land," Aminata is told by a British officer (BN 286). All Blacks registered in the Book of Negroes (an actual historical document that has survived and is available to scholars today) were guaranteed to be "as free as any [white] Loyalist" (BN 286) in the British colony of Nova Scotia.

The history of Black Canadians, however, has been a history of broken promises. Hill describes Aminata's first day of recording the names of those willing to leave New York City for Nova Scotia:

> A group of ten Negroes was called up to the deck [where Aminata logs the names of those Blacks wishing to sail for Nova Scotia]. I had never seen them before. 'Who are they?' I asked [Captain] Waters. 'Slaves and indentured servants,' he said. 'But I thought...' 'We will get around to evacuating the refugees in Canvas Town,' Waters said. 'But first, we register the property of white Loyalists.' [...]
> A girl appeared before me. [...] I could see that nothing about this trip suggested freedom. *Hana Palmer*, I wrote, again taking down the colonel's words. *15, stout wench. Ben Palmer of Frog's Neck, Claimant.* 'Claimant?' I asked the colonel when the white man had taken away the girl. 'It means that he owns her,' the colonel said. (BN 293; italics in the original)

In a twist of sardonic irony, Hill has Aminata record the name of a slave once belonging to Lord Dunmore, the British governor who issued the very declaration promising Blacks freedom if they joined the British ranks. "Virginia governor got to have his slaves," Dunmore's blind ex-slave squarely comments (BN 299). Through Aminata's entries in the Book of Negroes, Hill thus discerns the fact that slavery – contrary to popular opinion – indeed existed in Canada. The text also cites advertisements for runaway slaves (slave-owners promised rewards for captured and re-enslaved fugitives) and describes raids for these fugitives. Aminata summarizes the British policy which so blatantly violates the promises made to Blacks:

> I came to understand that if you had come to Nova Scotia free, you stayed free – although that didn't prevent American slave owners from sailing into town and attempting to snatch back their property. However, if you came to Nova Scotia as a slave, you were bound as fast as our brothers and sisters in the United States. (BN 321)

The first crucial element of the traumatic treatment of Blacks as presented in *The Book of Negroes* is thus: Slavery existed in Canada as well as in the United States, though certainly on a smaller scale in terms of numbers and economic and social enmeshment (particularly due, of course, to the absence of an extensive plantation economy in Canada). As Aminata observes in the summary that was just quoted, there are also those Blacks for whom the promised land indeed meant freedom. But even for those who had come as free people and managed to evade (re-)capture, Nova Scotia turned out to be anything but the Canaan they had hoped for. First of all, due to the economic dependence of Blacks on the white population, the institution of indentured labour constituted a prolongation of slavery under only slightly better terms. Aminata, discussing the difference between slavery and indenture, resolves: "After such a long journey to freedom, I couldn't imagine agreeing to" indenture (BN 295), yet many of her fellow exiles hardly had a choice. And for those Blacks who, like Aminata, avoided both (re-)enslavement and indenture, Nova Scotia did not materialize as the land of milk and honey they had been led to anticipate either.

Aminata's first encounter with white Canadians is marked by her apparent invisibility ("as if I didn't exist," "without stopping to look at me," BN 313), which of course alludes both to well-known African-American literary notions (cf. Ralph Ellison's *Invisible Man*, 1952, and its perception) and the impression that 'white Canada' largely has and continues to ignore the Black presence. Aminata is refused service in a coffee house and British soldiers pelt her with nuts; segregation and racial hatred are the bottom line of the Black Loyalists' experience. In terms of trauma, the disillusionment that a vast majority of Black Loyalists experienced has left obvious scars that still reverberate in contemporary African-Canadian literature. In general, this aspect of the Black experience is the most distinctly *Canadian* one: Slavery, indenture, racism, and segregation all existed in the United States (most of the time more harshly so than in Canada). But Canadian Blacks *expected otherwise*. They had been promised a refuge but got only a continuation of their suffering and hardships under slightly improved conditions.[18]

---

18 Disillusionment is one of the most pervasive themes in African-Canadian literature in general. It has been explored from the onset of the Black Canadian literary landscape in the 1960s (by Austin Clarke, cf. Bailey Nurse 2006, XIV-XV) and is applied to historical as well as to contemporary issues (cf. ibid.). For a survey of the African-Canadian literary field, cf. Lutz 2005, 313-319.

In Birchtown, a segregated Black community halfway between Yarmouth and Annapolis Royal, Nova Scotia, Aminata lives among the disappointed and disgruntled Black Loyalists waiting for the promised land allocations.

> Nova Scotia had more land than God could sneeze at, [the blind pastor] Daddy Moses said, but hardly any of it was being parcelled out at black folk. 'But the British said we could have land,' I said. 'Get good and comfortable at the back of the line,' he said. 'There are a thousand coloured folks waiting before you. And, ahead of them, a few thousand white people. They call this place Nova Scotia, but folks in Birchtown have another name for it.' 'What's that?' I asked. 'Nova Scarcity.' (BN 317)[19]

As the ironic usage of the name "Moses" suggests, the Black exodus to Nova Scotia has thus turned out to be a continuation of the structural racism experienced by Blacks in the United States. The scale of traumatic experiences has been reduced, yet their underlying factors, such as assumptions of racial superiority, persist. Those African-Canadians who have been granted freedom – and thus humanity and the status of subject, not object – still remain second-class citizens and humans.[20]

Clearly, *The Book of Negroes* presents a picture of the exodus of Blacks to Canada in terms of a Canaan *not* secured, thus contradicting the common notion of Canadian moral superiority vis-à-vis the slave-ridden United States. Hill seems to discern a need to correct the lopsided perception of Canadian history and national identity – in unison with a large number of African-Canadian writers. This endeavour to insert trauma into the Canadian collective memory will be further illustrated by a closer look at a number of poems by Black Canadian writers in the following section.

Beyond *The Book of Negroes*: selected African-Canadian poetry

As I have exemplified in the discussion of *The Book of Negroes* above, one of the goals of African-Canadian literature is to present little-known memories regarding the Black presence in Canada. The impetus behind much of African-Canadian literature is the fact that life for Black Canadians has incorrectly, yet consistently been portrayed as a bed of roses by Canadian mainstream (historical) discourse. The cur-

---

19 If land plots were allotted to Blacks at all, they were indeed second-rate or worse. Boyko summarizes: "Freed slaves fared little better than those still in bondage. […] Whites were afforded land grants of fifteen to 150 acres and given their choice of location. Freed Blacks were given an average of less than twenty acres and were assigned land that was nearly all rocky, swampy or far from fresh water." (Boyko 1998, 159) Walter Borden describes the land allocation to Black Loyalists in his poem "The Hebrew Children": "Ham's descendants [Blacks] / shouted HALLELUYAH, / Caught a train [the Underground Railroad] / And travelled / To the Warden of the North [Halifax] / Who counted heads, / Heaved a sigh, / And told them: / Go, and make potatoes / Out of rocks!" (Borden 1992, ll. 18-27)

20 This treatment of the newly-arrived Black Loyalists is well-documented; cf. e.g. the seminal works of Winks (1997) and Walker (1982) and particularly Walker's *The Black Loyalists* (1992).

rent Canadian self-perception, based on a continuation of the assumed historical absence of "moments of guilt and shame" (cf. the introductory quote by Assmann), consequently ascribes a Canaanite status to the life of Blacks in Canada:

> In Canada, the prevailing view suggests, nobody has doors slammed in their faces because of the colour of their skin, for Canada has the potential to be one big, comfortable home for all people fortunate to live within its boundaries. [...] No, the prevailing view argues, minority groups have no reason to whine or complain. Not in Canada, not in the place that had been the terminus of the Underground Railroad for American Blacks fleeing slavery. (Foster 1996, 31-32)[21]

A similar analysis regarding the lack of acknowledgement of the Canadian history of slavery and suppression has long been presented by a number of Black scholars, yet the charge that mainstream Canada still refuses to recognize this particular, traumatic aspect of its collective memory is still being upheld by African-Canadian authors. Compare, for instance, the following remarkably similar statements, made in a 1982 and a 2007 publication respectively:

> [From the end of the 17th century] until the early nineteenth century, throughout the founding of Nova Scotia, New Brunswick and Ontario, there was never a time when blacks were not held as slaves in Canada. Slavery is thus a very real part of our history, yet the fact that slavery ever existed here has been one of our best-kept historical secrets. (Walker 1982, 19)
> Slavery is Canada's best-kept secret, locked within the national closet. And because it is a secret it is written out of official history. But slavery was an institutionalized practice for over two hundred years. (Cooper 2007, 68)

Throughout African-Canadian fictional as well as non-fictional writing, this concept of a 'dual denial' is strongly emphasized: the historical denial of actual freedom and equality is closely followed by the denial of the existence of slavery and racism in the first place. Accordingly, African-Canadian authors claim that two promises

---

21 An excellent example of lopsided assumptions about African-Canadian history and social reality is provided by Africville, an all-Black community just outside Halifax, torn down in the early 1970s because of its alleged 'backwardness'. Africville's symbolic nature and its salience as an almost quintessential contested memory have been well-documented in fictional as well as non-fictional literature. For an overview cf. the study by Clairmont and Magill (1999), a children's version of the story of Africville by Perkyns (2003), a number of poems (e.g. Nolan 1992, Tynes 1990c, Ward 1997, Clarke 1994) and the scholarly articles by Bast (2003), Gerlach (1997), Moynagh (1998), and Nelson (2002).

have been broken. The first promise is an historical one, illustrated in *The Book of Negroes* – full equality under the lion's paw.²² The second one is the contemporary promise of multiculturalism, viz. the pledge of full participation in the life and identity of the country. African-Canadian literature dissects the mechanisms of what I have called a 'dual denial', laying bare the actual racism of both the past and the present as well as the tendency to erase the acknowledgement of these shortcomings from the Canadian collective memory – and consequently, from the construction of a national identity. While *The Book of Negroes,* necessitated by its autobiographical narrative structure, cannot comment on the contemporary suppression of memories directly (but does so indirectly by presenting the ignorance of Canadians concerning the country's history of slavery²³), many African-Canadian poets, for instance, very consciously link the wrongs of the past to the shortcomings of the present: The same mechanisms of dual denial (first the social policy of denying full equality, then the refusal to remember the policy) are attributed to both the past and the present. The Underground Railroad as a marker of freedom in the North, the exodus of Black Loyalists to Canada and the multiculturalism doctrine of today are thus linked and exposed as pretences that allow Canadian society to perpetuate discriminatory actions while simultaneously denying them in order to arrive at a self-perception that describes Canada as a historical and current paradise – in particular as opposed to the immoral United States of both the past and the present.

George Borden's poem "Empathy" (1988) is a case in point. Its unostentatious style and structure as well as its straightforwardness in terms of content underline the primal and essential nature of the connection between the past and the present in African-Canadian literature. This link is not poetically encrypted or delicately alluded at; instead, the text's lyrical I quite literally remembers the suffering of his ancestors, bridging the gap between slavery ("this dastardly deed", l. 3²⁴) and his current situa-

---

22 "As the freed slaves of Nova Scotia had discovered, however, slavery's death did not mark the birth of true freedom." (Boyko 1998, 160) The racist practices of e.g. indenture or unfair land allocations presented in *The Book of Negroes* are of course only a small aspect of the discrimination Blacks have faced in Canada. Boyko for instance also deals with issues such as discriminatory admittance into the military, limited upward social mobility, segregation, and racist immigration practices, tracing racial discrimination against Blacks from the time of slavery up to the 1970s.

23 "But there are men, women and children walking about the streets without the faintest idea of our nightmares. They cannot know what we endured if we never find anyone to listen." (BN 56, also quoted in the analysis of *The Book of Negroes* above)

24 It is worthwhile mentioning the ironic usage of the Biblical quote employed here by Borden, as it bears resemblance to Hill's ironic usage of "Daddy Moses": The first lines of "Empathy" read: "'In as much / as you have done / this dastardly deed / to those of my heritage - / you have done it unto me.'" (Borden 1988, ll. 1-5) The original Biblical passage ("And the King shall answer and say unto them, Verily I say unto you, Inasmuch as ye have done it unto one of the least of these my brethren, ye have done it unto me." Mt 25, 40) would primarily suggest a reward for a positive deed done, while the poem can only be read in terms of retribution for the "dastardly deed"

tion ("With them - / I have suffered", l. 9). Borden creates a collective of African-Canadians through diachronic unity, a feat that might be deemed lofty as even synchronic unity is disputed due to the multiplicity of backgrounds, immigration histories, countries of origin etc. of people(s) subsumed under the umbrella term 'African-Canadian'.[25] Still, it is the poem's imperative impetus that the shared memory, as Aminata's shared pain in *The Book of Negroes,* is upheld and passed on: a trauma remembered and brought to the fore time and time again.

One of the literary mechanisms through which the bridging of past and present is achieved in Black Canadian poems is the use of sound/music or other sensory perceptions. Slavery and field work, for example, are often alluded to through music (*The Book of Negroes* makes use of field songs as well; cf. BN 136-137; also cf. notions of sensory perceptions triggering memories in Aminata as discussed above). Olive Senior, for instance, writes: "Now against the rhythms / of subway trains my / heartbeats still drum / worksongs. Some wheels / sing freedom, the others: / home." (Senior 1980, ll. 40-45) Worksongs – songs based on field hollers, spirituals and African call-and-response patterns – have come to represent both the unendurable slave work and the hope of freedom. Senior combines these memories with the current "rhythms / of subway trains", keeping the memory of slavery and indentured labour closely connected to the present situation of the lyrical I.

Similarly, a sensory perception triggers memories of past injustices in the lyrical persona of Maxine Tynes' "Black Heritage Photos: Nova Scotia Archives" (1987b). In another poem, Tynes (1990a) strongly asserts the Black presence in Nova Scotia:

> *Black Song Nova Scotia*
> We are Africville and Preston,
> North and East
> We are Portia White singing to a long-ago king
> We are Edith Clayton weaving the basketsong of life
> Black and old with history
> and strong with the new imperative.
> We are Graham Jarvis bleeding on the road in Weymouth Falls.
> We are the Black and the invisible
> We are here and not here

---

of slavery – again a reversal of expectations, as in the hope of being led to the promised land by (blind Daddy) Moses.

25 Other poets go beyond the creation of a collective memory shared by African-Canadians as a locally defined group, speaking of 'race memory' ("The ritual [of planting] was ingrained / in the blood, embedded / in the centuries of dirt / beneath his fingernails / encased in the memories / of his race," Senior 1980, ll. 17-22). Also cf. Afua Cooper, who quotes Jan Carew in her poem "Roots and Branches": "Names are like magic markers in the long and labyrinthine stream of racial memory, for racial memories are rivers leading to the sea where the memory of mankind [sic] is stored." Cooper 1992, 23 ([sic] in the original).

> We are gone but never leave
> We have voice and heart and wisdom
> We are here
> We are here
> We are here.

The lyrical I (really, a collective 'lyrical we') in "Black Song Nova Scotia" identifies so completely with both the heroines (White, Clayton) and the victims (Jarvis) of Black Maritime Canadian history that again, an absolute diachronic unity – identity in the original sense of the word – is created: 'we *are* these people.' It thus transcends even the collectivization of Aminata's suffering in *The Book of Negroes*. Like Aminata, the persona(e) also experience(s) the apparent invisibility of Blacks (l. 8). The transmission of memories is a central element once more: The memory of the Black experience in Canada will be upheld, though the actual witnesses may long be departed (ll. 9-10). The concluding lines again emphasize vigorously the need to assert the Black presence against a collective memory that has erased the traumata (ll. 7-8) and the achievements (ll. 3-4) of African-Canadians from dominant national self-definitions.

Another writer who has extensively dealt with the literary revival of the Black presence, particularly in Nova Scotia, is George Elliott Clarke. He has emerged as the foremost scholar and one of the most highly acclaimed authors of African-Canadian literature. His *Execution Poems* (2001) antedate his 2005 novel *George and Rue* in tone and in content. Both the novel and the collection of poems tell the story of two Africadians, based on the true story of two of Clarke's cousins who killed a white taxi driver with a hammer to rob him. The unorthodox question Clarke confronts the reader with is: Could this crime be even remotely justified (or at least triggered) by the traumata and the vicious circle created by centuries of slavery, indenture, discrimination and disillusionment? In "The Killing", Clarke uses these suggestive lines for Rue's defence statement in court:

> Here's how I justify my error:
> The blow that slew Silver [the taxi driver] came from two centuries back.
> It took that much time and agony to turn a white man's whip
> into a black man's hammer.
> (Clarke 2001, ll. 36-39)

Whether or not the moral burden of the murder might be eased by the history of African-Canadians may be up to each reader to decide; in any case, the effect of this moral judgment is that Clarke virtually *forces* his audience to confront and deal with the issues of Canadian slavery and racism in the first place (using, as many contemporary Black Canadian authors do, the easily recognizable image of the whip to conjure up the institution of slavery). Other authors employ the richly metaphorical tropes of the Middle Passage to recall the traumata suffered by slaves; the persona in Claire Harris' "A Dream of Valor and Rebirth" (1989), for instance, in a dream- or trance-like state "sees slow swelling moon tastes the flow / of blood and tides knows centuries / knows nothing ever changes in fact" (ll. 50-52). Later on in the poem, Harris describes in gruesome lines the memory of the slave ships, including several aspects – such as the olfactory onslaught of the slave ship – also employed in *The Book of Negroes*: "she swallows the wail stench / of men shackled spoon shaped" (ll. 106-107).[26] Harris concludes this scene by connecting the pain and suffering of the slaves to the lyrical I of today as the contemporary persona's "cramped legs burn at the ankles" (l. 115) in empathy with the slaves. Consequently, for the poem's persona, the traumatic experience (here also in the original meaning of the word as being physically hurt) is vividly present. Likewise, Harris' "Sister (y)our Manchild at the Close of the Century" (1996) deals with the atrocities of and the particular Canadian involvement with the slave trade from a contemporary perspective, emphasizing the link between past and present.

On the larger scale of African-Canadian literature, then, the constant conjuring up of these traumatic issues points to the importance contemporary Black Canadian writers place on the historical and current Black experience as well as to the perceived need to assert and re-assert, to tell and re-tell these memories (whether in full length as novels or in metaphorical density in poems) lest they remain blanked out. The very titles of African-Canadian poems suggest a strong preoccupation with issues of slavery and bondage: "Chains and Shackles", "VIII – Exodus", "Forgotten Holocaust", "Breaking Chains", "Patterns of Escape", "Fashions of Slavery", "Plantation North", "A Century after Slavery" are only a small sample. These poems frequently add specifically Canadian elements to make sure that their direction of impact is not misunderstood as an attack against the United States (and thus, again, as an excuse for Canadian mainstream discourse to exclude their own traumatic historical moments by pointing south).

G. A. Borden, in his poem "I Never Heard Their Cry", summarizes this re-calling to attention, this need to establish and to assert the memories of African-Canadians as part of the larger collective memory, in the following way:

> Today, centuries later, in
> the quiet of the evening,
> as I gaze about this
> wretched plantation-like
> Black Nova Scotia community,

---

26 In *The Book of Negroes*, the stench of the slave ship haunts and tortures Aminata (the smell of the slave ship is the first thing she notices about the vessel she is forced to board after her abduction, cf. BN 50), yet she is also spellbound by it years later – a remnant of her urge to witness and not turn away: "The stink grew as the [slave] ship drew closer. Some of the Nova Scotians went […], but I was transfixed." (BN 378-379)

> I can hear their cry ... and
> feel their pain.
> (Borden 1988, ll. 46-52)

The reference to a "plantation-like / Black Nova Scotia community" is of course historically counter-factual in its allusion: Nova Scotia has never been a place of plantation slavery. Yet the combination of a marker of forced labor and a specifically Canadian locale illustrates the underlying similarities between the plantation economy and the Canadian treatment of Blacks (e.g. notions of racial superiority). Though lacking actual plantations, these lines seem to suggest, Nova Scotia has been "plantation-*like*" (l. 49, emphasis added) in its dealings with African-Canadians.

As a final example, the following excerpt from Maxine Tynes' "Black Teacher: To this World, To my Students" underlines the salience of witnessing (cf. the similarity to Aminata's wish to be a *djeli*, i.e. her urge to witness in Hill's *The Book of Negroes*), the connection of past and present through strong ties to the ancestors (l. 45) as well as the aspiration to be part of the (historical) discourse by asserting, through literature, the Black aspects of a rewritten Canadian collective memory (Tynes 1987c, ll. 44-48):

> take me as a true Black statement
> take me as a legacy of the fathers
> take me as a witness
> for I demand to read every word
> and to write some of my own.

Conclusion

This paper has explored questions of trauma and slavery in African-Canadian literature. A closer look at the way in which trauma is dealt with in Lawrence Hill's 2007 novel *The Book of Negroes* has yielded results on three different levels. On a personal or individual level, Hill presents a range of possible reactions to the trauma of objectification and dehumanization through slavery. The novel's protagonist, Aminata Diallo, is able to sustain herself psychologically to a degree that allows her to continue living. While even her sheer physical survival is against all odds, her ability to lead a purposeful life with a distinct possibility of retaining her capacity for love is simply astonishing. This achievement largely rests on her self-proclaimed mission to be a *djeli*, to record and pass on the memories of both her own enslavement as well as that of her fellow slaves. Her survival is contrasted with other characters' caving in or "snap[ping]" (BN 56) – remembering and telling are thus presented as the alternative to destructive reactions such as infanticide or complete retreat. On a second level, Hill portrays a part of Canadian history that has largely been forgotten ('forgetting' here implies the ranking of certain memories on a scale of alleged importance for a group, with those memories of lesser salience being relegated to the background of the collective memory).²⁷ As such, the experiences made by the novel's characters are representative of the fate of many Black Loyalists migrating from the United States to Canada in the 1780s. On a third level, *The Book of Negroes*, by the very fact of reviving these 'inactive' memories (Assmann calls them 'uninhabited', cf. Assmann 1999, 133), works towards a more encompassing ambition of African-Canadian literature: to assert the (historical) Black presence in Canada, which, for reasons of cleansing the national self-perception of the cracks and blotches of inflicting traumata on one of Canada's – officially cherished – minorities, has remained widely unacknowledged. Hill's novel is only one example of this tendency. Several more examples have been given in the section on Black Canadian poetry. The list of authors striving to revive the Black Canadian experience and to incorporate these traumatic memories into the Canadian self-perception could easily be expanded; though African-Canadians account for only about three per cent of the total population, and although there is still a lack of scholarly interest in Black Canadian literature, it is a literary strand both prolific and increasingly appreciated by a wider public. As such, Black Canadian literature stands a good chance to cause a positive rupture in the fabric(ation) of a coherent Canadian collective memory and identity that is based on superficial notions of a benevolent, Canaanesque nation, and to bring to the fore traumatic memories of slavery and racial discrimination in order to arrive at a more detailed and more faithful representation of a national 'self'.

References

Assmann, Aleida, 1995, "Funktionsgedächtnis und Speichergedächtnis – Zwei Modi der Erinnerung", in: Kristin Platt / Mihran Dabag (eds.), *Generation und Gedächtnis. Erinnerungen und kollektive Identitäten*, Opladen: Leske + Budrich, 169-185.
----, 1999, *Erinnerungsräume. Formen und Wandlungen des kulturellen Gedächtnisses.* München: C.H. Beck.
----, 2001, "Kollektives Gedächtnis", in: Pethes / Ruchatz, 308-310.
Assmann, Jan, 1988, "Kollektives Gedächtnis und kulturelle Identität", in: Jan Assmann / Tonio Hölscher (eds.), *Kultur und Gedächtnis*, Frankfurt a. M.: Suhrkamp, 1-19.
----, 1992, *Das kulturelle Gedächtnis. Schrift, Erinnerung und politische Identität in frühen Hochkulturen.* München: C.H. Beck.
Bailey Nurse, Donna, 2003, *What's a Black Critic to Do? Interviews, Profiles and Reviews of Black Writers.* Toronto: Insomniac Press.
----, 2006, "Introduction", in: *Revival. An Anthology of Black Canadian Writing*, Toronto: McClelland & Stewart, XI-XXII.
Bast, Heike, 2003, "The Ghosts of Africville, Acadia and the African Continuum. (Re)claiming Ethnic Identity in Africadian Literature", *Zeitschrift für Kanada-Studien*, 23.2, 129-142.
Bering, Dietz, 2001, "Kulturelles Gedächtnis", in: Pethes / Ruchatz, 329-332.

---

27 A process aptly described by Aleida Assmann's conception of functional vs. storage memory, cf. Assmann 1995.

Borden, George A, 1988a, "Empathy", in: *Canaan Odyssey. A Poetic Account of the Black Experience in North America,* Dartmouth, NS: Black Cultural Centre for Nova Scotia, 5.
----, 1988b, "I Never Heard Their Cry", in: *Canaan Odyssey. A Poetic Account of the Black Experience in North America,* Dartmouth, NS: Black Cultural Centre for Nova Scotia, 12-13.
Borden, Walter, 1992, "The Hebrew Children", in: Clarke, 40-42.
Boyko, John, 1998, *Last Steps to Freedom. The Evolution of Canadian Racism.* 2nd rev. ed., N/A: J. Gordon Shillingford.
Clairmont, Donald H. / Dennis William Magill, 1999, *Africville. The Life and Death of a Canadian Black Community,* 3rd ed. Toronto: Canadian Scholars' Press.
Clarke, George Elliott, 1992, *Fire on the Water. An Anthology of Black Nova Scotian Writing, Volume 2.* Lawrencetown Beach, NS: Pottersfield Press.
----, 1994, "Campbell Road Church", in: *Lush Dreams, Blue Exile: Fugitive Poems, 1978-1993,* Lawrencetown Beach, NS: Pottersfield Press, 73.
----, 2001, "The Killing", in: *Execution Poems,* Wolfville, NS: Gaspereau Press, 35.
----, 2002, *Odysseys Home. Mapping African-Canadian Literature.* Toronto: University of Toronto Press.
----, 2005, *George & Rue.* Toronto: HarperCollins.
Cooper, Afua, 1992, "Roots and Branches", in: *Memories Have Tongue,* Toronto: Sister Vision, 23.
----, 2007, *The Hanging of Angélique: The Untold Story of Canadian Slavery and the Burning of Old Montréal.* Athens: The University of Georgia Press.
Eggers, Michael, 2001, "Trauma", in: Pethes / Ruchatz, 602-604.
Ellison, Ralph, 1952, *Invisible Man.* New York: Random House.
Erll, Astrid / Marion Gymnich / Ansgar Nünning (eds.), 2003, *Literatur – Erinnerung – Identität, Theoriekonzeptionen und Fallstudien (Studies in English Literary and Cultural History Series).* Trier: WVT.
Erll, Astrid, 2003, "Kollektives Gedächtnis und Erinnerungskulturen", in: Ansgar Nünning / Vera Nünning (eds.), *Konzepte der Kulturwissenschaften, Theoretische Grundlagen - Ansätze - Perspektiven,* Stuttgart: J. B. Metzler Verlag, 156-186.
Erll, Astrid / Ansgar Nünning (eds.), 2004, *Medien des kollektiven Gedächtnisses, Konstruktivität – Historizität – Kulturspezifität.* Berlin / New York: Walter de Gruyter.
Foster, Cecil, 1996, *A Place Called Heaven: The Meaning of Being Black in Canada.* Toronto: HarperCollins.
Gerlach, Andrea, 1997, "Africville. Die Zerstörung des Bewusstseins einer 'Ethnic Community'", *Zeitschrift für Kanada-Studien,* 17.2, 153-165.
Halbwachs, Maurice, 1966, *Das Gedächtnis und seine sozialen Bedingungen.* Berlin: Luchterhand.
----, 1967, *Das kollektive Gedächtnis.* Stuttgart: Enke.
Harris, Claire, 1989, "A Dream of Valor and Rebirth", in: *The Conception of Winter,* Stratford, ON: Williams-Wallace, 28-31.
----, 1996, "Sister (y)our Manchild at the Close of the Century", in: *Dripped in Shadow,* Fredericton: Goose Lane Editions, 51-62.
Hartmann, Andreas, 2001, "Geschmack", in: Pethes / Ruchatz, 230-232.
Hill, Lawrence, 1992, *Some Great Thing.* Winnipeg: Turnstone Press.
----, 1997, *Any Known Blood.* Toronto: HarperCollins.
----, 2007, *The Book of Negroes.* Toronto: HarperCollins.
Kogawa, Joy, 1994, *Obasan.* New York: Anchor Books.
Kölbl, Carlos, 2001, "Olfaktorisches Gedächtnis," in: Pethes / Ruchatz, 425.
Lutz, Hartmut, 2005, "Multikulturalität als Stärke der zeitgenössischen kanadischen Literatur", in: Konrad Groß / Wolfgang Klooß / Reingard Nischik (eds.), *Kanadische Literaturgeschichte,* Stuttgart / Weimar: J. B. Metzler, 310-335.
Moynagh, Maureen, 1998, "Africville, an Imagined Community", *Canadian Literature,* 157 (Summer), 14-34.

Nelson, Jennifer J., 2002, "The Space of Africville. Creating, Regulating, and Remembering the Urban 'Slum'", in: Sherene Razack (ed.), *Race, Space, and the Law: Unmapping a White Settler Society,* Toronto: Between the Lines, 211-232.

Neumann, Birgit, 2005, *Erinnerung – Identität – Narration, Gattungstypologie und Funktionen kanadischer "Fictions of Memory".* Berlin / New York: Walter de Gruyter.

Nolan, Faith, 1992, "Africville", in: Clarke, 118.

Patterson, Orlando, 1982, *Slavery and Social Death: A Comparative Study.* Cambridge, MA: Harvard University Press.

Perkyns, Dorothy, 2003, *Last Days in Africville.* Toronto: Dundurn Press.

Pethes, Nicolas / Jens Ruchatz (eds.), 2001, *Gedächtnis und Erinnerung, Ein interdisziplinäres Lexikon.* Reinbek: Rowohlt.

Prince, Althea, 2001, *Being Black: Essays by Althea Prince.* Toronto: Insomniac Press.

Richardson, Karen / Steven Green (eds.), 2004, *T-Dot Griots: An Anthology of Toronto's Black Storytellers.* Victoria, BC: Trafford Publishing.

Schulz, Dorothea E, "Griot", in: Pethes / Ruchatz, 240-242.

Senior, Olive, 1980, "Ancestral Poem", in: Pamela Mordecai / Morris Mervyn (eds.), *Jamaica Woman: An Anthology of Fifteen Jamaican Women Poets,* Kingston, Jamaica: Heinemann Educational Books, 77-78.

Tettey, Wisdom J. / Korbla P. Puplampu, 2005, "Continental Africans in Canada: Exploring a Neglected Dimension of the African-Canadian Experience", in: *The African Diaspora in Canada, Negotiating Identity and Belonging,* Calgary: University of Calgary Press.

Thomas, Nigel H. (ed.), 2006, *Why We Write. Conversations With African Canadian Poets and Novelists.* Toronto: TSAR Publications.

Tynes, Maxine, 1987a, *Borrowed Beauty.* Porters Lake, NS: Pottersfield.

----, 1987b, "Black Heritage Photos: Nova Scotia Archives", in: Tynes, 41.

----, 1987c, "Black Teacher: To this World, To my Students", in: Tynes, 43-44.

----, 1990a, *Woman Talking Woman.* Porters Lake, NS: Pottersfield.

----, 1990b, "Black Song Nova Scotia", in: Tynes, 63.

----, 1990c, "Africville", in: Tynes, 62.

Van der Kolk, Bessel A. / Onno van der Hart, 1995, "The Intrusive Past: The Flexibility of Memory and the Engraving of Trauma", in: Cathy Caruth (ed.), *Trauma: Explorations in Memory,* Baltimore: The Johns Hopkins University Press, 158-182.

Walker, James W., 1982, *A History of Blacks in Canada.* Hull: Canadian Government Publication Center.

----, 1992, *The Black Loyalists, The Search for a Promised Land in Nova Scotia and Sierra Leone 1783-1870.* Toronto: University of Toronto Press.

Ward, Frederick, 1997, "Dialogue #1: Mama", in: George E. Clarke (ed.), *Eyeing the North Star, Directions in African-Canadian Literature,* Toronto: McClelland & Stewart, 47.

Winks, Robin W., 1997, *The Blacks in Canada: A History.* 2nd ed., Montreal: McGill-Queen's University Press.

Weber, Angelika, 2001, "Autobiographisches Gedächtnis", in: Pethes / Ruchatz, 67-70.

ISABELLE MENSEL

Le débat autour du bilinguisme dans la province canadienne de l'Ontario

La relation de l'anglais et du français commentée par les locuteurs dans les forums virtuels de discussion

Zusammenfassung

Der Beitrag beleuchtet das Verhältnis von Englisch und Französisch in der kanadischen Provinz Ontario. Der erste Teil stellt den aktuellen Stand der Frankophonie in der Region dar sowie die gesetzlichen Rahmenbedingungen. Vor diesem Hintergrund werden im zweiten Teil die Beiträge virtueller Diskussionsforen untersucht, anhand derer sich die Einstellungen und Argumentationsmuster sowohl franko- als auch anglophoner Sprecher aufzeigen lassen. Das Schlusskapitel fasst die herausgearbeiteten Ergebnisse zusammen und stellt sie den Resultaten einer provinzweiten Umfrage entgegen.

Abstract

The study examines the relationship between English and French in the Canadian province of Ontario. The first part explores the present state of the francophonie *in the province as well as the legislation. The second part focuses on the contributions to virtual discussions on Internet forums which permits to analyse the attitudes and argumentation patterns of both francophone and anglophone speakers. The final chapter summarizes the results and compares them with a survey conducted throughout the province.*

La plus grande minorité francophone hors Québec : les Franco-Ontariens

Dans cette contribution, nous nous intéresserons à la relation de l'anglais et du français dans la province canadienne de l'Ontario.

L'Ontario est à la fois la province la plus importante sur le plan économique et la province la plus peuplée avec 11,4 millions d'habitants. Ses 488 815 habitants de langue maternelle française,[1] c'est-à-dire 4,1% de la population de la province, cons-

---

1 Quant aux différentes variétés du français ontarien v. les études de Duncan (2005), Mougeon/ Nadasdi (1998), Roy (2004b), Tennant (1995).

tituent la plus forte minorité francophone hors Québec (v. Erfurt 2005, 58 ; Kadlec/Holes 2003, 92 ; Tetu 1996, 354 ; <http://www12.statcan.ca/francais/census06/data/highlights/language/Table401.cfm>, 21/01/2008 ; <http://www. Office des Affaires francophones>, 24/05/07). La population francophone se concentre sur trois régions : l'Est, le Nord-Est et le Centre. Ensemble ils regroupent 92% de la population francophone de l'Ontario (<http://www12.statcan.ca/francais/census01/products/highlight/LanguageComposition/>, 21/01/2008 ; Picard/Allaire 2005, 14). L'Est et le Nord-Est sont deux régions plus rurales que le Centre : « Les francophones se retrouvent en très faible minorité dans [les] grandes agglomérations urbaines, à l'exception d'Ottawa et de Sudbury-Thunder Bay […] » (Picard/Allaire 2005, 15 ; v. aussi Gilbert 2002, 674, 2005, 59 et Gilbert/Langlois 2006a, 106). Ils représentent 7,7% de tous les Canadiens francophones et 51,8% de tous les Canadiens francophones à l'extérieur du Québec (v. Kadlec/Holes 2003, 92). En Ontario, le nombre de personnes connaissant le français (seulement ou avec l'anglais) a triplé en moins de 50 ans. Environ 1,3 million d'Ontariens savent parler le français, ce qui équivaut à 12% de la population totale ; 42 000 d'entre eux ne maîtrisent pas l'anglais (<http://www.franco.atlas/ francophonie>, 22/05/07).[2] Néanmoins cette province reste – comme les autres – majoritairement anglophone.

Comme le souligne Thim-Mabrey, la langue et son utilisation sont essentielles pour la construction d'identité :

> Sprache bildet eine wesentliche Grundlage des Selbstverständnisses sowohl von Völkern und ethnischen Minderheiten als auch von kleineren und größeren, regionalen und sozialen Gruppen. Sie kann als soziales, kulturelles oder politisches Mittel zur Identitätsstiftung und -vergewisserung oder – im Konfliktfall – zur Identitätssicherung verstanden und instrumentalisiert werden. (Thim-Mabrey 2003, 5)

Après la description de la situation actuelle de la francophonie en Ontario ainsi que du cadre législatif, nous nous concentrerons sur le quotidien des locuteurs dans cette analyse. Cette contribution se propose plusieurs objectifs :
- Comment des locuteurs moyens vivent-ils et perçoivent-ils le bilinguisme ordonné par l'État ? Est-ce qu'ils considèrent possible d'employer le français au quotidien dans une société dominée par l'anglais comme c'est le cas en Ontario ?

---

2 Ces chiffres proviennent du recensement canadien qui ne distingue pas les individus selon leur niveau de bilinguisme. Mougeon (1995, 53) souligne que l'ensemble des individus pouvant converser dans les deux langues officielles n'est pas un groupe homogène et qu'il est possible de distinguer au moins trois groupes de francophones bilingues : 1) les bilingues à dominance française dont la capacité d'expression en français surpasse celle en anglais ; 2) les bilingues équilibrés pouvant s'exprimer avec autant d'aisance en français qu'en anglais ; 3) les bilingues à dominance anglaise ayant de moins bonnes capacités d'expression en français qu'en anglais.

- Quelles attitudes et quels groupes peut-on discerner ? Quels types d'argumentation peut-on démontrer et quelles conclusions peut-on tirer en ce qui concerne l'identité des différents groupes ?

Les contributions aux forums virtuels de discussion ainsi que les réponses à l'enquête virtuelle du journal *La Tribune* composent la base de l'étude.[3]

L'État actuel de la francophonie en Ontario

L'immigration francophone en Ontario s'est produite en deux vagues. En raison de la surpopulation dans les régions rurales du Québec un grand nombre de mineurs et de bûcherons s'est installé entre 1830 et 1920 en Ontario (v. Bernard 1990, 15 ; Dennie 1989, 73 ; Mougeon 1993, 53-54, 1995, 48).[4] A la fin des années 1950 a commencé une deuxième vague migratoire moins importante qui se poursuit jusqu'aujourd'hui (v. Budach 2003, 616). Les immigrants de cette période venant du Québec, d'autres provinces du Canada ainsi que d'autres pays d'expression française se sont établis dans les grands centres urbains du sud de l'Ontario. « Il s'agit d'une population d'origine surtout citadine et socialement diversifiée [...] en quête des emplois offerts par les secteurs public et industriel » (Mougeon 1995, 48).

Sous cet aspect, il convient de distinguer deux 'francophonies' comme le souligne Erfurt (v. 2005, 169-170) en parlant de la « diversification des identités francophones » : la francophonie dite «traditionnelle »[5] et la « nouvelle » francophonie des *Néo-Canadiens*. Ce dernier groupe comprend les minorités ethnoculturelles et raciales dont le nombre a augmenté durant les années 1990. Entre 1996 et 2001 leur nombre a plus que doublé, passant de 29 000 à 58 520. « Ces groupes représentaient moins de 6% des francophones en 1996 ; ils dépassent les 10% en 2001 [...] » (Picard/Allaire 2005, 20). Ces immigrants viennent de l'Algérie, du Congo-Zaïre, d'Haïti, du Liban, du Vietnam, du Burundi, de Djibouti et se concentrent dans les deux centres urbains de l'Ontario : Toronto et Ottawa (v. Erfurt 2005, 169 ; Labrie 2001, 64 ; Gilbert/Langlois 2006a, 106).[6]

---

3 Pour une description détaillée du corpus ainsi que des considérations méthodologiques v. les chapitres 'Présentation du corpus' et 'Méthode'.
4 Pour une analyse approfondie du développement économique de l'Ontario v. les travaux de Erfurt/Heller/Labrie (2001, 52-58), Gaudreau (1990), Tremblay (1990).
5 Elle comprend également les autochtones – Métis, Premières Nations et Inuits – de langue maternelle française qui résident surtout dans le Nord-Est ainsi que dans le Nord-Ouest. « En 2001, 4% de la population francophone du Nord-Est et 5% de celle du Nord-Ouest font partie du groupe métis. Le pourcentage de la population autochtone ayant le français comme première langue officielle parlée atteint les 5% dans le Nord-Est et les 6% dans le Nord-Ouest. L'ensemble de la francophonie ontarienne compte 2,4% d'autochtones [...] » (Picard/Allaire 2005, 21). Malgré le nombre peu élevé de francophones dans le Nord, celui-ci «a sans doute servi la continuité identitaire de la communauté franco-ontarienne » (Moïse 2004, 43).
6 Ils ont créé des associations regroupées selon leur pays d'origine, lesquelles ont pour mission de faciliter l'intégration des nouveaux-venus dans la société canadienne (v. Erfurt 2005, 169).

Afin d'analyser la situation linguistique, il est nécessaire de décrire le maintien du français et le transfert à l'anglais au foyer. Selon le recensement canadien de 1981, 33% des Franco-Ontariens communiquent en anglais au foyer. D'après le recensement de 2001, le maintien de la langue française à la maison s'élève à 58,9% pour toute la Province (cf. Picard/Allaire 2005, 21); ce sont 326 030 personnes affirmant parler le français le plus souvent à la maison (v. <http://www.franco.ca/atlas/ francophonie>, 22/05/07).[7] « En d'autres termes, un tiers des Franco-Ontariens qui ont acquis le français comme langue maternelle, c'est-à-dire au foyer, ont par la suite abandonné cette langue en ce lieu » (Mougeon 1993, 55). Castonguay (1979, 23-31) considère l'exogamie linguistique comme facteur majeur dans l'érosion de la communauté franco-ontarienne. Suite à ses recherches il a constaté que 90% de ceux/celles marié(e)s à un(e) anglophone utilisent l'anglais au foyer tandis que parmi les couples francophones homogènes ce nombre s'élève à seulement 17%.[8] Les études de Mougeon (1977), Mougeon/Beniak (1991) ainsi que ceux de Heller/Levy (1991) et McRoberts ([2]2003, 95) confirment ces résultats :

> [...] l'abandon du français au foyer est nettement plus élevé chez ceux qui déclarent avoir une langue maternelle double ou triple, que chez ceux dont le français est l'unique langue maternelle. En d'autres termes l'apprentissage précoce et simultané du français avec d'autres langues, déclaré par plus de 110000 personnes, n'est guère favorable au maintien de la communauté franco-ontarienne. (Mougeon 1993, 56)[9]

---

7   Il y a des différences notables entre les régions : dans l'Est ce sont 70% tandis que dans le Centre ce sont seulement 34,3% ; dans le Sud-Ouest le taux de 29,6% est le plus faible (v. Picard/Allaire 2005, 21). Ces chiffres montrent que l'Est reste le plus important foyer de concentration avec plus de 200 000 personnes de langue maternelle française, une situation qui s'est affirmée durant les 25 dernières années (v. <www.franco.ca/atlas/francophonie>, 22/05/07).
8   Erfurt (1997b, 161) a constaté que le milieu social joue également un rôle : Ainsi, le français est, dans le milieu ouvrier, plus souvent délaissé au profit de l'anglais. Couture (2001, 15) souligne qu'il serait également important d'étudier les mariages bilingues parlant anglais à la maison et français au travail (institutions fédérales, écoles etc.).
9   Ces résultats sont confirmés par Kadlec/Holes (2003, 92) qui constatent que seul 2,9% des Ontariens parlent français à la maison et que 37% des francophones abandonnent au cour de leur vie le français au profit de l'anglais.
    Le niveau de concentration francophone locale joue un rôle important dans le comportement sociolinguistique des Franco-Ontariens (v. Mougeon 1995, 49-50). Dans les localités de très forte majorité francophone, la communication en dehors du foyer, c'est-à-dire dans le secteur public et partiellement aussi dans le secteur privé, se déroule en français. Bon nombre des francophones y demeurent monolingues ou presque monolingues en français. Par contre, dans les localités majoritairement anglophones, la communication en français ne fonctionne que dans des limites très restreintes, ce qui explique que la quasi-totalité des francophones y est bilingue. Le recensement canadien (1991) a également montré « que dans les communautés franco-ontariennes situées dans des localités majoritairement anglophones, les individus de langue maternelle française ont tendance à abandonner l'emploi du français pour la communication

L'emploi du français au travail dépend de la force démographique des francophones sur place.[10] Mougeon (1993, 56) mentionne la ville de Hawkesbury dans le sud-est ontarien où le taux de francophones s'élève à 85%. Étant donné que l'industrie locale se trouve en grande partie sous contrôle anglophone, de nombreux francophones sont néanmoins obligés de travailler en anglais.[11]

L'éducation est le seul secteur dans lequel on puisse travailler principalement en français (v. Mougeon 1993, 57). Les autres secteurs publics, notamment ceux des gouvernements fédéraux et provinciaux, offrent des postes «bilingues» qui impliquent un certain emploi du français, principalement dans le cadre de la prestation de services à une clientèle francophone. Cependant, cette offre est assez restreinte (v. Mougeon 1993, 57). En ce qui concerne le secteur privé,

> les possibilités en matière de travail en français sont beaucoup plus réduites. En effet, il y a peu d'entreprises privées qui sont possédées et gérées par les francophones[12] ou qui sont situées dans des localités à forte concentration franco-ontarienne où l'on peut estimer qu'il est 'payant' d'offrir des services en français. (Mougeon 1993, 57)[13]

Dans l'ensemble, on peut constater que, par rapport aux secteurs d'emplois, la présence des francophones dans les autres activités tertiaires caractérise le profil de l'emploi franco-ontarien : finance, assurances, commerce, services aux entreprises. Le nombre de francophones travaillant dans le secteur de la production manufacturière est toujours important, notamment dans l'industrie de la construction. Dans le secteur des services (santé, services sociaux, administration publique) la population franco-ontarienne est assez bien représentée (v. <http://www.franco.ca/atlas/ francophonie>, 22/05/07).

---

au foyer [...]. Par contraste, dans les communautés franco-ontariennes très fortement majoritaires, l'anglais ne pénètre pratiquement pas dans les foyers » (Mougeon 1995, 49-50).

10 Kadlec/Holes (2003, 92-93) offrent une vision panoramique des taux de francophones dans les différentes provinces de l'Ontario.

11 Roy (2004a) a mené une étude dans un centre d'appels dans le Sud de l'Ontario afin de décrire les défis pour la communauté francophone face à la nouvelle économie.

12 Le nombre d'entreprises et de sociétés appartenant à des francophones s'élève à 12000 (v. <http://www. Office des Affaire francophones>, 24/05/07). Ils forment près de 10% de la main-d'œuvre francophone (v. <http://www. franco.ca/atlas/francophonie>, 22/05/07). Blatt (1991/1992, 61) note « une vague concentration dans le 'commerce au détail' et dans les 'services personnels et communautaires'».

13 Mougeon (1993, 57) soutient la thèse qu'en raison du niveau de revenu inférieur des Franco-Ontariens comparé à celui de la majorité anglophone (v. Lalonde 1978, 28) les francophones souhaitent améliorer leur statut socio-professionnel et pour cela considèrent la maîtrise de la langue, ou des langues, employées dans le secteur économique où ils travaillent (l'anglais et le français pour la bourgeoisie, l'anglais pour les ouvriers) comme facteur déterminant.

On note un maintien élevé du français dans deux secteurs : l'église catholique canadienne française et le réseau associatif franco-ontarien. Surtout dans le passé, le clergé catholique canadien français a lutté pour le maintien du français (v. Erfurt 1997a, 177, 1999, 60-61 ; Mougeon 1993, 57 ; Pion 1989, 86 ; Rabier 1989, 162) : « […] l'Eglise a historiquement assuré […] presque toutes les institutions d'enseignement, sans lesquelles la survivance culturelle des Franco-Ontariens eût été impossible » (Gilbert 1984, 109).[14]

Dans le mouvement associatif franco-ontarien Mougeon (1993, 57-58) constate deux tendances opposées. D'un côté, le nombre des associations ou regroupements franco-ontariens – surtout ceux à caractère professionnel – augmente, ce qui s'explique par un désir accru d'autonomie se manifestant notamment au sein de l'élite franco-ontarienne. De l'autre côté, il y a, exception faite des regroupements dans le domaine artistique, un manque de relève.[15]

Les écoles de langue française se fixent trois buts :
1) fournir une éducation générale comparable à celle que reçoivent les élèves anglo-ontariens,
2) prodiguer un enseignement de certaines matières dans une optique plus spécifiquement franco-ontarienne ou franco-canadienne (par exemple l'histoire) et
3) endiguer l'assimilation de la communauté franco-ontarienne. (v. Mougeon 1993, 58-59)

Tout enfant ayant au moins un parent de langue maternelle française a le droit de recevoir l'instruction en français. Cela signifie que l'enfant ne doit pas être forcément de langue maternelle française (v. Mougeon 1993, 59). Dans ce cas, bon nombre des écoles franco-ontariennes proposent des classes où les élèves de foyers peu ou non francophones reçoivent un enseignement du français qui est adapté à leur niveau.[16] Mougeon (1993, 59) constate que depuis l'instauration des écoles franco-ontariennes, deux types opposés de reproduction linguistique se sont développés chez les Franco-Ontariens. Dans le premier type, le français est transmis d'abord par le foyer et renforcé ensuite par l'école. Dans le second type, le français est transmis uniquement par l'école.[17]

On compte 358 écoles primaires et secondaires de langue française avec plus de 120 000 élèves inscrits ; à cela s'ajoutent les plus de 122 000 élèves inscrits dans les écoles d'immersion (v. <http://www.franco.ca/atlas/francophonie>, 22/05/07).[18]

---

14 La lutte entre les anglophones (protestants) et les francophones (catholiques) est décrite par Choquette (1975).
15 Erfurt (1998, 2000) a analysé les discours polito-linguistiques des associations franco-ontariennes.
16 Landry/Allard (1996, 76, 81-82) et Mougeon/Beniak/Canale (1984) ont étudié la compétence du français des différents groupes d'élèves.
17 Carrier (1985), Frenette/Churchill/Quazi (1985), Gervais (1985) se sont intéressés à l'enseignement universitaire en Ontario.
18 Cazabon (1996), S. Guillaume/P. Guillaume (2003, 53-72), Heller (1994), Tremblay (1986), Welch (1991/1992) offrent une analyse approfondie du système éducatif. Bordeleau (1987), Bradley

Contexte juridique

En 1969, le Parlement du Canada adopte la *Loi sur les langues officielles* que seront désormais l'anglais et le français.[19] Le gouvernement fédéral est tenu de servir la population dans les deux langues.[20] En cette même année, le Nouveau-Brunswick devient officiellement bilingue. Cette province reste jusqu'à présent la seule à avoir ce statut. D'autres lois et mesures se succèdent, comme par exemple, en 1974, les règlements sur l'étiquetage bilingue des produits de consommation, l'adoption de la *Charte de la langue française* par Le Québec en 1977, qui fait du français la langue officielle de la province.[21] En 1982 a lieu l'adoption de la *Loi constitutionnelle* qui comprend la *Charte canadienne des droits et libertés*.[22] Celle-ci garantit aux minorités l'enseignement primaire et secondaire dans leur langue, là où le nombre le justifie (v. Braën 1988, 40). Quatre ans plus tard, l'Ontario vote la *Loi sur les services en français*, qui garantit le droit de recevoir des services en français de l'administration centrale des ministères et organismes gouvernementaux et de leurs bureaux se trouvant dans l'une des 23 régions désignées.[23] Ces régions sont celles où vivent au moins 5000 francophones ou bien où un pourcentage d'au moins 5% de la population totale est francophone (v. Gilbert/Langlois 2006b, 437). En 2009, les régions désignées seront au nombre de 25 (v. <http://www.radio-Canada.ca>, 03/04/07 ; <http://www. franco.ca/atlas/francophonie>, 22/05/07).

Cette *Loi de 1986 sur les services en français* ne s'applique pas aux municipalités et conseils locaux visés par la *Loi sur les affaires municipales*. Néanmoins, le gouvernement a déjà offert de 1989 à 1997 de l'aide technique et financière aux municipalités dans des régions désignées souhaitant offrir des services en français. « Une trentaine de municipalités, dont Ottawa, se sont déclarées bilingues » (<http://www.franco.ca/atlas/francophonie>, 22/05/07). Environ 44 municipalités offrent officiellement des services en français à la population francophone (v. <http://www. Office des Affaires francophones>, 24/05/07).

En ce qui concerne les services juridiques, il faut mentionner que le français a depuis la *Loi sur les tribunaux judiciaires* de 1984 (articles 125, 126) le statut de langue officielle dans le domaine de la justice en Ontario même si l'anglais demeure la

---

(1987), Lagacé (1987), Mougeon (1987), Size-Cazabon (1987) analysent les enjeux du concept de l'immersion. Foucher (1988) et Frenette/Gauthier (1989) retracent l'histoire des droits scolaires des Franco-Ontariens. Behiels (2005) décrit la division entre Franco-Ontariens laïcisés et Franco-Ontariens catholiques.

19 Pour une description approfondie de cette loi et de ses enjeux v. Beaty (1986, 21-22).
20 En ce qui concerne l'histoire de la législation en Ontario v. Kadlec/Holes (2003, 93-94).
21 La situation linguistique au Québec est décrite par Amyot (1980), Heller (1996, 24-30), Lepicq/Bourhis (1996, 93-105), Martel (2000), Maurais (1993) et Schafroth (2001).
22 Rabier (1983) a analysé les conséquences de la nouvelle constitution pour les Franco-Ontariens. Bastarache (1988, 55-58) se concentre sur la *Charte*.
23 Beauregard (1986, 146) signale l'importante pénurie de spécialistes francophones dans les secteurs de l'activité publique lors de la mise en place de cette loi.

langue ordinairement d'usage (v. <http://www. franco.ca/atlas/francophonie>, 22/05/07 ; http://www. Office des Affaires francophones, 24/05/07).[24]

Présentation du corpus

Le corpus comprend 15 contributions de deux forums canadiens de *Google* ainsi que les réponses à une enquête du journal *La Tribune*.

Les exemples (1)-(3) proviennent d'un forum avec le titre « Le bilinguisme à la canadian [sic] » qui date du 26 octobre 2002. Deux personnes ont participé à cette discussion. Les deux premiers exemples appartiennent à la longue contribution d'un seul participant, l'exemple (3) est la réponse courte à ces propos. Les exemples (4)-(6) font partie d'un forum datant du mois de juillet 2001 qui s'intitule « Est-ce que vous l'avez vu ? ». Les exemples proviennent de trois participants différents.[25] Leur ordre reflète le cours de la discussion.

Chaque internaute est libre de participer à cette communication de groupe et d'y exposer ses opinions. Il est clair que les participants des ces forums ne constituent pas un échantillon représentatif des quelques 11 millions d'Ontariens, mais leur caractère ouvert permet des conclusions relatives aux comportement et à l'attitude d'un locuteur moyen. Polzin-Haumann caractérise les forums de la façon suivante :

> Der fließende Diskussionsstil – jeder Teilnehmer kann sofort zu allen Fragen Stellung beziehen – ermöglicht ein spontanes Kommunikationsverhalten, d. h. es sind tendenziell wenig (etwa durch vorgegebene Formulierungen) gesteuerte Äußerungen zu erwarten. Auch entsprechende gruppendynamische Prozesse lassen sich in den Foren präzise beobachten. (Polzin-Haumann 2005, 286)

Il est clair que nous ne connaissons ni l'âge ni la profession, peut-être même pas le vrai nom des participants de ces forums, nous ne pouvons donc pas définir leur contexte social et culturel. En revanche, leurs prises de position sont moins réfléchies que par exemple lors d'une enquête ; les participants réagissent plus spontanément puisque personne ne les «contrôle» ni leur pose de questions[26].

Les contributions (7)-(15) sont des réponses à l'enquête virtuelle « Comment vivez-vous le bilinguisme au quotidien ? », initiée par le journal *La Tribune* du 6 au

---

24 *L'association des juristes d'expression française de l'Ontario* (*AJEFO* ; <http://www.ajefo.ca>, 21/01/08) se consacre à l'amélioration des services juridiques en français (<http://www. Office des Affaires francophones>, 24/05/07). Le site de l'aménagement linguistique au Canada (<http://www.salic-slmc.ca/>, 21/01/08) offre des informations détaillées sur toutes les lois à incidence linguistique. Pour des analyses spéciales, relatives au domaine juridique, cf. les travaux de Dennie (1988), Pelletier (1988), Saint-Aubin (1988).
25 Les données comprennent prénoms et noms de famille.
26 Dorta (2005) et Beißwenger (2001) offrent une analyse approfondie de la communication sur Internet.

11 février 2007 et présenté par Radio-Canada. Chaque prise de position fait mention du nom complet ainsi que de la province du participant.[27] Les différentes dates de parution du corpus donnent un aperçu des opinions des dernières années.

Méthode

On pourrait caractériser la méthode ici choisie par une « observation participante virtuelle ». Les discussions documentées dans les forums ont été examinées et les contributions sélectionnées dans le but de présenter un échantillon aussi représentatif que possible des différentes opinions. Outre les contributions des forums, j'ai procédé à une analyse des réponses à l'enquête du journal *La Tribune*. Dans ce cas, les participants se prononcent sur une question donnée au lieu de participer à une discussion comme dans les forums.

Le corpus constitué ainsi permet d'avoir un aperçu du comportement linguistique ; il est bien entendu que ce tour d'horizon nous donne un exposé sommaire de la situation linguistique sans vouloir prétendre à une étude approfondie dans le temps et la durée. Au point de vue méthodique, l'accent pèse sur la méthode d'analyse de discours. Il serait souhaitable d'établir un contact direct et intensif avec les groupes et personnes comme le souligne Erfurt (v. 2000, 196) dans son étude sur les politiques linguistiques du monde associatif francophone en Ontario. De cette manière, on pourrait examiner de près le mode de fonctionnement de chaque groupe qui doit faire face quotidiennement aux problèmes linguistiques et qui doit essayer de vivre en se frayant un chemin malgré la société anglophone dominante. Il faudrait également s'intéresser aux problèmes vitaux tels les conflits, respecter les divergences d'opinions et finalement saisir les normes spécifiques aux groupes et comprendre leurs visions (v. Erfurt 2000, 195).

L'analyse des contributions ne tiendra pas seulement compte du contenu mais également des procédés linguistiques (mots, unités syntaxiques, métaphores) « révélateurs des formations discursives et des positionnements » (Labrie et al. 2004, 233) ainsi que de la construction de l'argumentation. Nous définissons le terme « discours » selon Erfurt :

> Diskurse sind sprachlich verfasste soziale Praxis, in der die Verhältnisse in einer Gesellschaft für eine bestimmte Öffentlichkeit inszeniert werden – als bedeutsam, bedrohlich, skandalös oder amüsant, als identitätsstiftend oder solidarisch, mit ihren Hintergründen oder ohne diese, als Pro- und Kontra-Argumentationen oder in der Polyphonie der unterschiedlichen Lesarten. (Erfurt 2005, 161)

---

27 Bien sûr ces données peuvent être aussi fausses que les noms dans les forums, mais le même problème se pose lorsque des personnes remplissent par écrit des questionnaires leur demandant des informations personnelles.

Cette définition montre que les discours ne sont pas des objets bien délimités ou fixes mais, au contraire, « un moyen d'action sociale en même temps qu'un objet social fluide, qui est imbriqué dans les transformations sociales » (Labrie/Heller 2004, 405). Ils sont intimement liés à l'interprétation de la réalité des participants.

Analyse du corpus

En tout premier lieu, il est à constater que le débat autour du bilinguisme au Canada est mené dans de nombreux forums, en partie de façon très véhémente et avec beaucoup d'émotion, ce qui se reflète dans l'usage de gros mots.

Du côté des anglophones radicaux, la peur se fait sentir ; les francophones pourraient prendre le pouvoir au niveau des provinces, ainsi qu'au niveau national:

> (1) Thanks to official bilingualism, Francophones are taking over the federal government. Under bilingual requirements, 71% of all new hires are francophones. (french as first language) To make matters worse: They are pushing to have official bilingualism entrenched in provincial and municipal governments wherever people are complacent enough to allow them to do it, and wherever people can be bullied into it. For example, the province of New Brunswick has been declared officially bilingual, municipalities of Moncton and St. John to follow, with the attendant reclassification of public service jobs and firings at every level. Now they want the Province of Ontario declared officially bilingual, and the opposition liberals have promised to force bilingualism on Ontario's provincial bureaucracy. After that, the municipality of Toronto, Canadas largest and most influential city will go officially bilingual, necessitating costly changes, firings, restructuring etc. at every level of the municipal bureaucracy. Official Bilingualism, as it is applied today, means that most of the highest paid and powerful positions in government and public service go to Francophones.
> (<http://groups.google.de/group/qc.politique>, 13/03/2007)[28]

Le participant juge le bilinguisme ordonné par l'État responsable de la situation menaçante de son point de vue. Il ne la définie pas comme l'emploi égal de deux langues, mais comme l'absorption lente de l'anglais et l'incessante prise du pouvoir par les francophones qui cherchent à s'incruster partout, ce qu'il exprime par le participe *entrenched*. De son point de vue, ils n'agissent pas seulement de façon pacifique, mais, au contraire, ils tracassent les gens. Il signale cela par le participe *bullied*. Les conséquences sur le marché du travail sont d'après lui extrêmement injustes : les hauts postes sont réservés aux francophones. Le participant soutient son argumentation par la donnée d'un chiffre. Par ce biais, il essaie de solidifier les

---

28 L'orthographe ainsi que la ponctuation de l'original n'ont pas été modifiées.

faits mentionnés et essaie de susciter un esprit sérieux ; en même temps, il se tait sur la provenance de ce chiffre. Il émet une opinion défavorable quant aux frais occasionnés par la réorganisation de la bureaucratie.

« L'impérialisme francophone » provient du Québec comme il l'explique dans sa contribution :

> (2) This is part of the gradual process of Quebec's takeover of Canada. Once the militant french [sic] have control of Montreal, Toronto, and Ottawa (and they soon will), they have an overwhelming position of political power and control of this nation. Ottawa is gradually becoming uninhabitable to unilingual English people, just as happened in Montreal. The same process will take place gradually throughout New Brunswick and Ontario if people do not uphold their rights.
> (<http://groups.google.de/group/qc.politique>, 13/03/2007)

Selon lui, l'identité anglophone est menacée. La législation ne protège pas la minorité francophone, mais attaque la majorité anglophone. Ce type d'argumentation correspond à celui de différentes organisations canadiennes et ontariennes luttant pour les droits des anglophones. À titre d'exemple nous en présentons deux. La première, l'*Ontario Confederation of Regions Party* (*CoR*)[29], qui existe depuis 1990, lutte pour un referendum sur la *Loi de 1986 sur les services en français* : « English is the official language of Ontario and CoR would keep it that way. People may use whatever language they wish, but documents relating to business, financial records and licenses would be in English » (<www.home.mountaincable.net/~galloway/cor/policies.htm>, 12/08/2008). Les membres rejettent la reconnaissance officielle de la langue française (et de tout autre langue) reléguant son utilisation au domaine privé.

La seconde, l'Association *Language Fairness National*[30], argumente dans le même ordre d'idées : « [...] the English majority have become disenfranchised by their governments' discriminating language policies » (<www.languagefairness.com>, 07/07/2008). Selon cette organisation, seuls les francophones peuvent être bilingues puisqu'ils vivent dans un environnement anglais ; les anglophones, par contre, ne se retrouvent pas dans la même situation : « The only fluently bilingual people in Canada are the French Canadians because they are in English immersion daily. Without similar French immersion, the English majority are least likely to be bilingual, [....] » (<www.languagefairness.com>, 07/07/2008).

---

29 Ce parti orienté vers la droite existe depuis mai 1990.
30 *Language Fairness National* est un groupe de citoyens qui se décrit comme suit : « We are a web based organization of like-minded citizens whose main office is situated on the Internet to allow representatives, from across the country, access to administrative files and information plus ability to post directly to the site. We believe in empowering individuals and welcome volunteers. » (<www.languagefairness.com/Mission.php>, 12/08/08)

La réaction à cette contribution[31] extrêmement émotionnelle est encore beaucoup moins différenciée :

> (3) ….les anglos sont trop imbéciles et arogants [sic] pour apprendre le français……les seuls bilingues au Canada çe [sic] sont les francophones……[…]
> (<http://groups.google.de/group/qc.politique>, 13/03/2007)

Plus différenciées mais néanmoins aussi émotionnelles sont les contributions de la *Google-Group.soc.culture.quebec* qui datent de l'an 2001. Le forum commence par une contribution qui présente la situation linguistique dans l'Etat du Michigan et la compare à celle en Ontario. L'internaute raconte les principaux évènements historiques et se sert à plusieurs reprises d'exemples personnels de ses connaissances pour montrer à quel point l'importance du français a baissé au cours de deux centenaires :

> (4) Le Français est pas mal disparu dans le nord du Michigan comme d'autres villes ou villages en Ontario. C'est pire par ici car il était interdit d'enseigner le Français dans les écoles. L'Ontario a passé une loi similaire mais grâce à Trudeau l'effet a pas été aussi grand qu'ici.
> (<http://groups.google.de/group/soc.culture.quebec>, 13/03/2007)

Ses déclarations assez modérées sont vivement commentées :

> (5) Cette affirmation est issue de quel roman-fiction? Les conséquences du règlement 17 anti-écoles françaises en Ontario (1912) se font encore sentir!
> En 2001, il n'y a pas encore d'université francophone digne de ce nom en Ontario et le dernier hôpital est en sursis. De plus, lors de la constitution de 1982, l'Ontario, avec l'appui de Trudeau, a refusé le bilinguisme institutionnel …
> Au contraire Trudeau a remplacé le biculturalisme (1971) par le multiculturalisme. Biculturalisme aurait signifié donner aux Franco Ontariens les mêmes services qu'aux Anglo Québecois. De sorte que de recensement en recensement, c'est le désastre…Ainsi au recensement de 1996, il ne restait que 306 788 Franco Ontariens (sur 499 687 de langue maternelle française) parlant encore français à la maison soit seulement 2,9% de la population pour un taux d'assimilation de 39%.
> Les ex bastion [sic] francophones comme Sudbury, et d'autres, sont de moins en moins francophones.

---

31 V. les exemples (1) et (2).

> En Ontario, le français est une langue locale et marginale…gracieuseté de Trudeau et de l'échec de sa politique de bilinguisme!
> (<http://groups.google.de/group/soc.culture.quebec>, 13/03/2007)

Cette réplique évoque plusieurs secteurs: la législation,[32] la politique et l'éducation.

A la différence de l'exemple (1), le participant mentionne la source des statistiques citées : il s'agit du *recensement canadien* de 1996. La contribution (5) nous démontre le contraire des exemples (1) et (2). Les francophones ne se sentent pas protégés par les lois, bien au contraire. La politique du bilinguisme provoque la séparation et non l'intégration. D'un côté se trouvent les anglophones qui n'ont pas besoin d'apprendre le français dans la vie quotidienne et de l'autre côté, les francophones qui sont obligés d'être bilingues. Ce sentiment de défaite se retrouve déjà dans la discussion des années 1980 :

> Le bilinguisme, qui se voulait un outil pour rétablir les inégalités sociétales entre les deux peuples fondateurs, fait partie aujourd'hui des stratégies et des pratiques pour maintenir les positions individuelles et pour consolider les positions des groupes les uns par rapport aux autres. Vingt ans de luttes linguistiques pour voir le bilinguisme, notre cheval de bataille, se transforme tout à coup en pégase aux mains de la majorité. Nous aurions dû savoir qu'une valeur culturelle s'établit dans une relation sociale, et que les Franco-Ontariens minoritaires, c'est-à-dire sans pouvoir symbolique réel, ne pouvaient pas modifier leur position sociale en jouant la carte du bilinguisme. (Bernard 1986, 41)

La métaphore *ex bastions* de la contribution (5) évoque l'image d'un champ de guerre : les villes deviennent des points stratégiques qui sont à défendre. Ainsi, la situation linguistique est représentée comme une guerre ou du moins comme une bataille avec des fronts nets et inconciliables.

Le participant qui répond à la contribution de l'exemple (5) choisit un ton plus modéré :

---

32 « As early as in 1885, Ontario passed an act according to which English had to be taught in all schools in the province, including schools with French as a teaching language. Under the pressure of Irish Catholics and English-speaking Protestants, the […] *Regulation no. 17 (Règlement 17)*, adopted in 1912, cancelled all the schools with French as a teaching language and one year later, Ontario stopped supporting bilingual Catholic schools. […] *Regulation no. 17* was cancelled in 1927, but up to 1969, there was no French secondary school obtaining support from the province of Ontario » (Kadlec/Holes 2003, 93-94) [en italique dans la citation]. L'Institut franco-ontarien a consacré un numéro de sa *Revue du Nouvel-Ontario* (1981) aux lois et idéologies de l'Ontario français.

(6) J'ai de la famille en Ontario et je sais que ce n'est pas le multiculturalisme ni Trudeau qui les forces à se faire assimiler. Les gens veulent que leurs enfants aient une bonne éducation et soit partie de la majorité. La langue prend de moins en moins d'importance face à une bonne job et securité pour l'avenir.
[…] Ce sont les Francos Ontariens qui n'en veulent pas. Les enfants ne regardent que la TV en anglais, n'écoutent que des chansons en anglais. Les parents sont toujours pas pour emprisonner les enfants pour les forcer à garder la langue. Les enfants veulent être comme tout le monde et quand ils sont assez matures pour se rendre compte que cela aurait été important de garder leur langue il est trop tard. Et de toute façon la langue n'est qu'un moyen de s'exprimer. On a beau y mettre un grande importance les nouvelles générations feront bien ce qui leur plait [sic] peu importe les batailles que nous fassions pour garder la langue. Le fait que la majorité du monde en Amérique est anglophone est une évidence qu'il est impossible de cacher aux enfants.
(<http://groups.google.de/group/soc.culture.quebec>, 13/03/2007)

Il voit les raisons pour la baisse du français non pas dans la politique mais dans le comportement des gens. En espérant avoir de meilleures chances sur le marché du travail, les Franco-Ontariens incitent leurs enfants à parler la langue que parle la majorité. Les enfants, de leur côté, sont influencés par un milieu à dominance anglophone et, ainsi, choisissent de passer leur temps libre (télévision, musique) en anglais.[33] En fin de compte, le participant pense que la raison principale du déclin du français se trouve dans la supériorité numérique de l'anglais ; il est impossible de cacher aux enfants ces chiffres incontestables. Le fait qu'il réduise la langue à l'aspect de « moyen de communication » reflète sa résignation presque totale ; il n'évoque même plus la question de l'identité. Cette observation correspond aux recherches d'Erfurt qui en analysant les politiques linguistiques du monde associatif francophone en Ontario a pu constater que

> [l']engagement permanent pour la francophonie est confronté, chez lui [scil. un membre du Conseil d'administration d'une association francophone], avec l'expérience individuelle, qu'il ressent comme défaite personnelle, à un point tel que même ses propres enfants sont victimes de la pression de l'anglicisation. (Erfurt 1998, 161)[34]

---

33 Cette observation est aussi confirmée par Cazabon (1984, 81), Duquette (2001, 106), Gueguen-Charron (1986, 136) et Laflamme/Berger (1988, 627-628).
34 Afin de préserver l'unité syntaxique nous citons d'après la version française. Une version allemande légèrement modifiée a paru en 2000.

Quant à l'argument de la maîtrise des deux langues officielles pour avoir des avantages sur le marché du travail, celui-ci est également avancé par de nombreux participants à l'enquête virtuelle « Comment vivez-vous le bilinguisme au quotidien ? », initiée par le journal *La Tribune*. Les participants à cette enquête jugent cela de façon positive – à la différence des participants de la *Google-Group*. Les exemples suivants proviennent aussi bien d'interlocuteurs anglophones que d'interlocuteurs francophones, ainsi que de différentes provinces :

> (7) De prime abord, je dois vous dire que je suis entièrement en faveur du bilinguisme. En 1973-74, j'ai participé en tant que fonctionnaire fédéral au programme d'échange sur le bilinguisme et le biculturalime [sic]. Durant cette année, j'ai appris beaucoup sur le biculturalisme et j'ai pu parfaire ma connaissance de la langue seconde, ce qui m'a énormément aidé dans ma carrière. Mes enfants sont allés à l'école anglaise et aujourd'hui parlent couramment l'anglais. Nous avons appris à connaitre [sic] et à apprécier l'autre culture et nous en sommes très reconnaissants. A mon humble avis, le bilinguisme au Canada est un must si on veut progresser.
> andré arcand
> cantley, québec (<http://www.radio-Canada.ca>, 03/04/2007)

> (8) J'habite Thunder Bay en Ontario et mes enfants fréquentent une écœl [sic] francophone et je travaille en frnçais [sic] tous les jours. Je peux aussi travailler en anglais si je le désire je n'ai aucune difficulté avec cela. Je suis très fière de tous les efforts que j'ai eu a faire pour être a ce niveau la. Mes enfants bénéficient de notre ouverture d'esprit face au monde et aux différentes langues et cultures. Nous avons un très beau pays a vous de le visiter!!!! Avant de de [sic] partir du Québec je ne comprenais absolument rien en anglais. maintenant je ne peux vivre sans cette langue car je l'utilise a [sic] tous les jours.
> Caroline Gobeil-Vaillancourt
> Thunder Bay Ontario (<http://www.radio-Canada.ca>, 03/04/2007)

> (9) Ma mère est francophone et mon père anglophone. À la maison, nous parlions français avec ma mère mais je refusais de parler anglais avec mon père. Tandis que mon frère, un exemple parfait du bilinguisme, a toujours parlé français avec ma mère et anglais avec mon père. À 10 ans, j'ai réalisé l'importance et la richesse de parler deux langues. Je crois que cela prend de la volonté et il faut absolumment [sic] mettre la politique de côté.
> Maintenant à 26 ans, je parle 4 langues et j'en suis très contente!
> Raffaella Ricci
> Montréal (<http://www.radio-Canada.ca>, 03/04/2007)

(10) Je travaille en anglais et je vis à la maison en français. Je suis content de connaître l'anglais pour l'ouverture au monde et particulièrement au domaine scientifique que je pratique. Je suis aussi content de connaître le français à cause de l'ouverture à la culture française que je préfère à la culture américaine. Si j'avais l'opportunité, j'apprendrais d'autres langues. Je crois que le bilinguisme est une richesse pour les Canadiens qui le pratiquent. On dit que ça prévient la sélénilité [sic].
Marc A. Vallée
Ottawa (<http://www.radio-Canada.ca>, 03/04/2007)

(11) [...] les bilingues et polyglottes ont un avantage marqué sur les unilingues dans le marché du travail de Toronto, surtout dans le secteur du service à la clientèle et autres activités demandant des communications avec le Québec. Une langue et une culture se préservent avant tout à la maison. Nous parlons français, anglais et espagnol à la maison, le plus jeune va à l'école française et est trilingue depuis son plus jeune âge.
François Ouellette
Toronto (<http://www.radio-Canada.ca>, 03/04/2007)

(12) La langue est un outil et avoir plusieurs outils nous permet des garanties de succès. Moi je parle le français et l'anglais et un peu d'espagnol. Ma conjointe parle aussi le français et l'anglais. Une de mes filles parle l'allemand, le français, l'anglais et le russe. Parler d'autres langues aide à garder notre esprit ouvert au reste du monde.
Jean Montminy
London Ontario (<http://www.radio-Canada.ca>, 03/04/2007)

Ces déclarations montrent que les participants ne considèrent pas le bilinguisme uniquement comme atout professionnel mais qu'ils le voient aussi comme un enrichissement sur le plan culturel. Une nouvelle langue permet de découvrir dans la vie des horizons insoupçonnés et des perspectives toutes nouvelles. Le bilinguisme leur ouvre de nouvelles perspectives. Ces locuteurs font preuve d'un certain romantisme face au multilinguisme. Quelques prises de position sont d'un caractère presque euphorique comme le prouve l'exemple suivant :

(13) Le bilinguisme est un choix que je fais à chaque jour. Comme francophile, j'ai toujours l'option de vivre et de travailler en anglais, mais je crois que j'ai aussi une responsabilité personnelle et professionnelle de m'impliquer le plus possible dans les cultures francophones et d'apprendre le plus possible de la langue française. C'est pour cela que, par exemple, je choisi fréquemment de regarder Radio-Canada au lieu CBC, ou de lire un roman dans la langue de Molière au lieu d'un livre

dans la langue de Shakespeare, ou d'aller voir un film/concert/théâtre en français au lieu qu'en anglais. Même si mon français n'est pas parfait, et même si je ne suis pas un francophone de souche, je considère que j'ai bien le droit de faire l'expérience de la francophonie, parce-que, en fin de compte, j'ai le français a cœur!
Joseph Civitella, PhD
Ottawa, ON (<http://www.radio-Canada.ca>, 03/04/2007)

Certains, comme la participante de l'exemple (14), nous disent de ne plus tenir compte de l'aspect politique. Ils veulent adoucir les fronts endurcis décrits plus haut et veulent remplacer les guerres idéologiques par le dialogue.

(14) Je trouve franchement hallucinant le ton de la plupart des messages. Soit, on vit dans un pays théoriquement bilingue. Sauf qu'au lieu que ce bilinguisme soit perçu, comme partout ailleurs, comme un avantage, voire un minimum (vérifiez donc combien de gens parlent plus de deux langues ailleurs qu'en Amérique du Nord), chez nous, ça reste un débat tellement politique et émotif que c'est impossible d'aborder la question de façon rationnelle.
Pour le million de francophones et le milion [sic] et demi additionel [sic] de francophiles à l'extérieur du Québec, et pratiquement le même nombre d'Anglophones [sic] au Québec, est-ce qu'on pourrait travailler à la promotion de la dualité linguistique au lieu de brandir constamment des lois et règlements qui mettent tout le monde sur la défensive? Évidemment que les lois et règlement [sic] sont nécessaires, mais si on abordait la question autrement, juste de temps en temps, on aurait peut-être de meilleurs résultats. Mais bon, j'imagine que c'est trop demander.
marie-josée leclerc
Aylmer (<http://www.radio-Canada.ca>, 03.04.2007)

Cet exemple est le premier dans lequel un participant fait référence à une situation de multilinguisme en dehors de l'Amérique du Nord. En agissant ainsi, l'intervenante essaie d'apaiser le débat échauffé autour du bilinguisme.

Résultats et perspectives

Les forums analysés, dont toutes les contributions ne peuvent être examinées dans ce cadre, montrent que la situation linguistique est loin d'être ressentie comme résolue, malgré les nombreuses règles juridiques en vigueur. En effet, la relation entre les deux langues officielles n'est pas jugée comme égale. Les locuteurs sont très sensibles par rapport à des questions linguistiques dans tous les domaines. Comme on devait s'y attendre, on y retrouve toutes les attitudes possibles : en partant de positions radicales qui soutiennent des propos faux et non prouvés, en passant par des prises de position modérées jusqu'à des contributions différenciées dont les argumentations reposent sur des faits prouvables et qui aspirent à un arrangement entre anglophones et francophones. En tout, les prises de position modérées prédominent ; la radicalité des contributions (1)-(3) est remarquable et ne peut en aucun cas être considérée comme représentative pour la conscience d'une majorité de locuteurs. Ce qui, par contre, n'est également pas représentatif pour les locuteurs anglophones est l'approbation intégrale de la culture francophone ainsi que le fort sentiment de responsabilité de la promouvoir et de la mettre au même niveau que la culture anglaise, comme le fait le participant dans l'exemple (13).

Un résultat marquant indique qu'il n'y a aucun exemple dans lequel un locuteur considère la situation linguistique comme non problématique et entièrement résolue. Même les déclarations de ceux qui rejettent la politisation de la discussion autour des langues et qui mettent en avant des aspects culturels et personnels (exemples (9), (14)) montrent, qu'en inversant leur argumentation, un conflit latent se dessine: une telle attitude est impensable pour la majorité dans la discussion échauffée en Ontario et dans les autres provinces du Canada.

Des déclarations à propos de l'infériorité ou de la supériorité d'une langue n'ont également pas pu être relevées.

Comment peut-on donc décrire le débat autour du bilinguisme dans la province canadienne de l'Ontario ? Les exemples ainsi qu'une enquête de l'entreprise privée CROP (2006), ordonnée par *Radio Canada*, montrent que le bilinguisme est très apprécié et encouragé en tant que but de grande valeur. Ainsi, 41% des anglophones sont très favorables et 36% assez favorables au bilinguisme; parmi les francophones, 61% y sont très favorables et 31% assez favorables (v. CROP 2006, 23). 77% des anglophones et 96% des francophones souhaitent que le Canada demeure bilingue (v. CROP 2006, 24). En outre, 99% des francophones et 81% des anglophones pensent que le Premier ministre doit être bilingue ; presque autant sont d'avis que les ambassadeurs, les hauts fonctionnaires et ministres doivent également être bilingues (v. CROP 2006, 31). Cependant, les chiffres relatifs à la maîtrise des langues démontrent une toute autre réalité. Selon leur propre estimation, seulement 18% des anglophones et 56% des francophones sont bilingues (v. CROP 2006, 36).[35] La situation en Ontario peut d'après cela être considérée comme typique pour l'ensemble du Canada – à l'exception du Québec. Les francophones en tant que

---

35 Les locuteurs francophones définissent le bilinguisme de la façon suivante (v. CROP 2006, 34): être capable de soutenir une conversation en anglais (94%), être capable de lire en anglais (86%), être capable d'écouter la radio et de regarder la télé en anglais (85%), être capable d'écrire en anglais (79%), être capable de parler en anglais sans accent (24%). Les locuteurs anglophones évaluent les mêmes critères comme suit (v. CROP 2006, 35): être capable de soutenir une conversation en français (91%), être capable de lire en français (79%), être capable d'écouter la radio et de regarder la télé en français (70%), être capable d'écrire en français (68%), être capable de parler en français sans accent (27%).

minorité y sont forcés de s'adapter et sont obligés de parler l'anglais assez couramment pour faire face à la vie de tous les jours ;[36] ils n'ont pas le choix. Lorsque les anglophones apprennent le français, c'est de leur libre gré : soit parce qu'ils croient avoir de meilleures chances sur le marché du travail, soit parce qu'ils le considèrent comme un enrichissement culturel. L'exemple suivant décrit ce fait :

> (15) Le bilinguisme, un fait français!
> Le Canada est un pays bilingue car des francophones l'habitent. Le bilinguisme à sens unique. Quand votre langue maternelle n'est pas l'anglais, vous devez être bilingue. Quand votre langue maternelle est l'anglais, vous pourriez apprendre une autre langue, si vous le désirez bien.
> Jean-François Cadorette
> Shawinigan (<http://www.radio-Canada.ca>, 03/04/2007)

Une grande majorité exige de démontrer le bilinguisme, du moins officiellement; mais il n'y a qu'une minorité qui est prête à le vivre au quotidien et qui prend la peine d'apprendre la deuxième langue officielle et de l'utiliser régulièrement.

En résumé, on peut établir les thèses suivantes :
- Le débat autour du bilinguisme ne peut pas être résolu juridiquement.
- Une majorité considérable approuve le bilinguisme ordonné par la loi sans faire pour autant l'effort d'apprendre l'autre langue.
- En Ontario, l'anglais gardera sa dominance. A long terme, l'importance du français restera tout au plus au même niveau (v. Couture 2001, 14). De ce fait, son importance diminuera probablement et le français connaîtra alors le même sort qu'il a connu en Nouvelle-Angleterre où les communautés francophones sont soumises à une forte pression d'assimilation (v. Bollée 1990, 761-762 ; Erfurt 2005, 58 ; Neumann-Holzschuh ²2008, 115).[37]

En ce qui concerne l'approche méthodique, il est à souligner que l'analyse de la communication sur Internet offre de nombreuses possibilités d'étudier l'attitude et la conscience des locuteurs. Elle fournit un complément important à l'exploitation des discussions scientifiques et à l'analyse des enquêtes ; sur la Toile, les participants gardent l'anonymat et ne sont pas influencés par certaines données comme, par exemple, des questionnaires.

---

36 Laflamme (1989, 42) emploie le terme de *langue de la réalité* pour désigner l'anglais.
37 C'est en Louisiane que le français est le plus fort représenté aux Etats-Unis. V. les travaux de Neumann-Holzschuh (2005), Valdman (1996), Wiesmath (2001).

Bibliographie

Amyot, Michel, 1980, *La situation démolinguistique au Québec et la charte de la langue française*. Québec : Conseil de la langue française.
Bastarache, Michel, 1988, « Les difficultés relatives à la reconnaissance constitutionnelle des droits linguistiques en Ontario », *Revue du Nouvel-Ontario*, 10, 51-64.
Beaty, Stuart, 1986, « Constitution, droits et minorités », *Revue du Nouvel-Ontario*, 8, 19-27.
Beauregard, Rémy, 1986, « Le support gouvernemental et l'épanouissement de la communauté franco-ontarienne », *Revue du Nouvel-Ontario*, 8, 145-149.
Behiels, Michael, 2005, *La francophonie canadienne : renouveau constitutionnel et gouvernance scolaire*. Ottawa : Presses de l'Université d'Ottawa.
Beißwenger, Michael (dir.), 2001, *Chat-Kommunikation: Sprache, Interaktion, Sozialität & Identität in synchroner computervermittelter Kommunikation. Perspektiven auf ein interdisziplinäres Forschungsfeld*. Stuttgart : Ibidem.
Bernard, Roger, 1986, « Le rôle social des institutions ethniques », *Revue du Nouvel-Ontario*, 8, 41-48.
----, 1990, « Peuplement du Nord de l'Ontario », *Revue du Nouvel-Ontario*, 12, 15-40.
Blatt, Rena, 1991/1992, « Les entrepreneurs franco-ontariens », *Revue du Nouvel-Ontario*, 13-14, 57-70.
Bollée, Annegret, 1990, « Frankophonie IV. Regionale Varianten des Französischen außerhalb Europas I. b) Vereinigte Staaten und Karibik », dans : Günter Holtus/Michael Metzeltin/Christian Schmitt (dirs.), *Lexikon der Romanistischen Linguistik*, Band V,1, Tübingen : Niemeyer, 754-767.
Bordeleau, Louis-Gabriel, 1987, « Impact de l'immersion sur l'éducation en langue française : perspective et tentative de synthèse », *Revue du Nouvel-Ontario*, 9, 11-27.
Born, Joachim (dir.), 2001, *Mehrsprachigkeit in der Romania: Französisch im Kontakt und in der Konkurrenz zu anderen Sprachen. Akten des 2. Frankoromanistenkongresses, Dresden, 25. bis 27. September 2000*. Wien.
Bradley, Robert, 1987, « Le programme d'immersion française... Boule de neige », *Revue du Nouvel-Ontario*, 9, 117-125.
Braën, André, 1988, « Le compromis de la Cour suprême du Canada en matière de droits linguistiques », *Revue du Nouvel-Ontario*, 10, 39-48.
Budach, Gabrielle, 2003, « Community and Commodity in French Ontario », *Language in Society*, 32, 603-627.
Carrier, Denis, 1985, « Langue d'enseignement et comportement universitaire des Franco-Ontariens », *Revue du Nouvel-Ontario*, 7, 53-68.
Castonguay, Charles, 1979, « Exogamie et anglicisation chez les minorités canadiennes-françaises », *The Canadian Review of Sociology and Anthropology. La revue canadienne de Sociologie et d'Anthropologie*, 16, 21-31.
Cazabon, Benoît, 1984, « Les Franco-Ontariens dans leur regard : Pour une description linguistique du fait français en Ontario », *Revue du Nouvel-Ontario*, 6, 69-93.
----, 1996, « La pédagogie du français langue maternelle en Ontario : moyen d'intervention sur la langue en milieu minoritaire », dans : Erfurt, 295-314.
Choquette, Robert, 1975, *Language and Religion: A History of English-French Conflict in Ontario*. Ottawa : University of Ottawa Press.
Couture, Claude, 2001, « La disparition inévitable des francophones à l'extérieur du Québec : un fait inéluctable ou le reflet d'un discours déterministe ? », *Francophonies d'Amérique*, 11, 7-18.
CROP (dir.), 2006, *Les Canadiens et le bilinguisme : Rapport final*. Montréal.
Dennie, Donald, 1988, « Le français dans la pratique du droit en Ontario », *Revue du Nouvel-Ontario*, 10, 123-135.
----, 1989, « L'étude des réalités franco-ontariennes », *Revue du Nouvel-Ontario*, 11, 69-83.

Dorta, Gabriel, 2005, *Soziale Welten in der Chat-Kommunikation. Untersuchungen zur Identitäts- und Beziehungsdimension in Web-Chats*. Bremen : Hempen.

Duncan, Ryan, 2005, *Pour une description linguistique du fait français en Ontario : Analyse du français parlé en situation minoritaire et sa représentation dans les œuvres littéraires*. Ottawa : Carleton University.

Duquette, Georges, 2001, « Double Minorisation : Intragroup Domination and Cultural Hegemony », *Language, Culture and Curriculum*, 14, 98-111.

Erfurt, Jürgen (dir.), 1996, *De la polyphonie à la symphonie : Méthodes, théories et faits de la recherche pluridisciplinaire sur le français au Canada*. Leipzig : Leipziger Universitäts-Verlag.

----, 1997a, « Identité culturelle et pratiques langagières en milieu minoritaire : le cas des francophones au sud de l'Ontario », dans : Gabriele Budach/Jürgen Erfurt (dirs.), *Identité franco-canadienne et société civile québécoise*. Leipzig : Leipziger Universitäts-Verlag, 171-180.

----, 1997b, « 'Ma langue maternelle c'est l'anglais [....] oui, well, mon père était anglais, pis ma mère était française.' : Sprachkonflikte und sprachliche Identität in der frankophonen Diaspora Kanadas », dans : James Dow/Michèle Wolff (dirs.), *Languages and Lives : Essays in Honor of Werner Enninger*. New York : Lang, 155-169.

----, 1998, « Politiques linguistiques du monde associatif francophone en Ontario », *Etudes canadiennes/Canadian Studies*, 45, 153-167.

----, 1999, « Le changement de l'identité linguistique chez les Franco-Ontariens : Résultats d'une étude de cas », dans : Normand Labrie/Gilles Forlot (dirs.), *L'enjeu de la langue en Ontario français*. Ottawa : Prise de Parole, 59-77.

----, 2000, « Unilinguismus versus Bilinguismus. Sprachpolitische Diskurse frankophoner Assoziationen in Ontario, Kanada », dans : Peter Stein (dir.), *Frankophone Sprachvarietäten: Variétés linguistiques francophones. Hommage à Daniel Baggioni de la part de ses 'dalons'*. Tübingen : Stauffenburg, 191-209.

----, 2005, *Frankophonie: Sprache, Diskurs, Politik*. Tübingen.

Erfurt, Jürgen/Monica Heller/Normand Labrie, 2001, « Sprache, Macht und Identität im französischsprachigen Kanada – ein Forschungsbericht », *Zeitschrift für Kanada-Studien*, 39, 44-67.

Foucher, Pierre, 1988, « Le droit à l'instruction en français en Ontario en dépit de la loi ou avec la loi », *Revue du Nouvel-Ontario*, 10, 67-81.

Frenette, Normand/Stacy Churchill/Saeed Quazi, 1985, « Les écoles franco-ontariennes et la préparation aux études postsecondaires », *Revue du Nouvel-Ontario*, 7, 91-108.

Frenette, Normand/Lise Gauthier, 1989, « Luttes idéologiques et culturelles institutionnelles en éducation franco-ontarienne », *Revue du Nouvel-Ontario*, 11, 49-67.

Gaudreau, Guy, 1990, « Le développement des activités forestières en Ontario (1855-1900) : une prise de vue quantitative », *Revue du Nouvel-Ontario*, 12, 65-90.

Gervais, Gaétan, 1985, « L'enseignement supérieur en Ontario français (1848-1965) », *Revue du Nouvel-Ontario*, 7, 11-52.

Gilbert, Angus, 1984, « La perception des Franco-Ontariens par un Anglo-Ontarien », *Revue du Nouvel-Ontario*, 6, 107-112.

Gilbert, Anne, 2002, « Entre l'école et l'hôpital : le développement de la francophonie canadienne », dans : Michel Venne (dir.), *Québec 2003 : annuaire politique, social, économique et culturel*. Montréal : Fides, 673-678.

----, 2005, « La diversité de l'espace franco-ontarien : un défi au développement », dans : Jean-Pierre Wallot (dir.), *La gouvernance linguistique : le Canada en perspective*. Ottawa : Presses de l'Université d'Ottawa, 57-75.

Gilbert, Anne/André Langlois, 2006a, « Organisation spatiale et vitalité des communautés francophones des métropoles à forte dominance anglaise du Canada », *Francophonies d'Amérique*, 21, 105-129.

----, 2006b, « Typologie et vitalité des communautés francophones minoritaires au Canada », *The Canadian Geographer/Le Géographe canadien*, 50, 432-449.

Gueguen-Charron, Laura, 1986, « La minorité dans la société ontarienne », *Revue du Nouvel-Ontario*, 8, 131-138.

Guillaume, Sylvie/Pierre Guillaume, 2003, *Nouveaux regards sur les francophonies torontoises*. Pessac : Maison des Sciences de l'Homme d'Aquitaine.

Heller, Monica/Laurette Levy, 1991, *Les mariages linguistiquement mixtes: créativité et contradictions*. Toronto : Conseil de recherche en sciences humaines du Canada.

----, 1994, *Crosswords: Language, Education and Ethnicity*. Berlin/New York : Mouton de Gruyter.

----, 1996, « Langue et identité : l'analyse anthropologique du français canadien », dans : Erfurt, 19-36.

Heller, Monica/Normand Labrie (dirs.), 2004, *Discours et identités : la francité canadienne entre modernité et mondialisation*. Bruxelles : Éditions modulaires européennes.

Institut franco-ontarien (dir.), 1981, *Les idéologies de l'Ontario français : un choix de textes (1912-1980)*, in : *Revue du Nouvel-Ontario* 3, Sudbury : Université Laurentienne.

Kadlec, Jaromír/Jan Holes, 2003, « Language Laws, Linguistic Situation and Position of French-Speaking Population in Canadian Province of Ontario », *Brno Studies in English*, 29, 91-98.

Labrie, Normand, 2001, « Mondialisation et conditions de viabilité de la langue française en Amérique du Nord », *Présence francophone*, 56, 55-71.

Labrie, Normand/Monica Heller, 2004, « La francité ré-imaginée », dans : Heller/Labrie, 403-419.

Labrie, Normand et al., 2004, « La Rencontre provinciale de 1998 : de la fragmentation à l'éclatement ? », dans : Heller/Labrie, 229-267.

Laflamme, Simon/Jacques Berger, 1988, « Compétence linguistique et environnement social », *The Canadian Modern Language Review. La revue canadienne des langues vivantes*, 44, 619-638.

Laflamme, Simon, 1989, « Eléments pour une analyse de la conscience franco-ontarienne », *Revue du Nouvel-Ontario*, 11, 35-46.

Lagacé, Michel, 1987, « L'immersion française au secondaire dans les écoles de Sudbury », *Revue du Nouvel-Ontario*, 9, 127-139.

Lalonde, Francine, 1978, *Deux poids, deux mesures : Les francophones hors Québec et les anglophones au Québec. Un dossier comparatif*. Ottawa : Fédération des francophones hors Québec.

Landry, Rodrigue/Réal Allard, 1996, « Vitalité ethnolinguistique : une perspective dans l'étude de la francophonie canadienne », dans : Erfurt, 61-87.

Lepicq, Dominique/Richard Bourhis, 1996, « Attitudes et comportements linguistiques dans les zones bilingues du Canada », dans : Erfurt, 89-117.

Martel, Pierre, 2000, « Le bon usage au Québec », dans: Elmar Schafroth/Walburga Sarcher/Werner Hupka (dirs.), *Französische Sprache und Kultur in Québec*. Hagen : ISL, 11-40.

Maurais, Jacques, 1993, « Etat de la recherche sur la description de la francophonie au Québec », dans : Robillard/Beniamino, 79-99.

McRoberts, Kenneth, ²2003, « Conceiving Diversity : Dualism, Multiculturalism, Multinationalism », dans : François Rocher/Miriam Smith (dirs.), *New Trends in Canadian Federalism*. Peterborough : Broadview Press, 85-109.

Moïse, Claudine, 2004, « Le nouvel Ontario : nordicité et identité », dans : Heller/Labrie, 43-88.

Mougeon, Raymond, 1977, « French Language Replacement and Mixed Marriages: The case of the Francophone Minority of Welland, Ontario », *Anthropological Linguistics*, 19, 368-377.

----, 1987, « Impact de l'essor de l'immersion sur l'éducation et le devenir des Franco-Ontariens », *Revue du Nouvel-Ontario*, 9, 31-48.

----, 1993, « Le français en Ontario : bilinguisme, transfert à l'anglais et variabilité linguistique », dans : Robillard/Beniamino, 53-77.

----, 1995, « Diversité sociolinguistique au sein d'une communauté francophone minoritaire : les Franco-Ontariens », *Linx*, 33, 47-69.

Mougeon, Raymond/Edouard Beniak/Michael Canale, 1984, « Acquisition du français en situation minoritaire : Le cas des Franco-Ontariens », *Le français dans le monde*, 185, 69-76.

Mougeon, Raymond/Edouard Beniak, 1991, *Linguistic Consequences of Language Contact and Contraction: The Case of the French in Ontario, Canada*. Oxford : Oxford University Press.

Mougeon, Raymond/Terry Nadasdi, 1998, « Sociolinguistic Discontinuity in Minority Language Communities », *Language. Journal of the Linguistic Society of America*, 74, 40-55.

Neumann-Holzschuh, Ingrid, 2005, « Si la langue disparaît…: Das akadische Französisch in Kanada und Louisiana », dans : Ingo Kolboom/Roberto Mann (dirs.), *Akadien: Ein französischer Traum in Amerika*. Heidelberg : Synchron, 795-821.

----, ²2008, « Das Französische in Nordamerika », dans : Ingo Kolboom/Thomas Kotschi/Edward Reichel (dirs.), *Handbuch Französisch: Sprache, Literatur, Kultur, Gesellschaft*. Berlin : Erich Schmidt, 109-119.

Pelletier, Jean-Yves, 1988, « Les juges de l'Ontario français », *Revue du Nouvel-Ontario*, 10, 99-111.

Picard, Louise/Gratien Allaire, 2005, *Deuxième Rapport sur la santé des francophones de l'Ontario*. Sudbury : Université Laurentienne.

Pion, Denis, 1989, « Les changements culturels dans la religion des Nord-Ontariens », *Revue du Nouvel-Ontario*, 11, 85-98.

Polzin-Haumann, Claudia, 2005, « Zwischen *unidad* und *diversidad*: Sprachliche Variation und sprachliche Identität im hispanophonen Raum », *Romanistisches Jahrbuch*, 56, 271-295.

Rabier, Christiane, 1983, « Les Franco-Ontariens et la constitution », *Revue du Nouvel-Ontario*, 5, 37-49.

----, 1989, « Les Franco-Ontariens et l'idéologie dominante », *Revue du Nouvel-Ontario*, 11, 159-169.

Robillard, Didier de/Michel Beniamino (dirs.), 1993, *Le français dans l'espace francophone : Description linguistique et sociolinguistique de la francophonie*. Vol. 1, Paris : Champion.

Roy, Sylvie, 2004a, « La mondialisation et la nouvelle économie : un centre d'appels dans le Sud de l'Ontario », dans : Heller/Labrie, 365-399.

----, 2004b, « Language Varieties as Social Practices: Evidence from Two Minority Francophone Communities in Canada », *Canadian Journal of Linguistics/Revue canadienne de linguistique*, 49, 353-373.

Saint-Aubin, Étienne, 1988, « Les droits linguistiques des justiciables et témoins en Ontario », *Revue du Nouvel-Ontario*, 10, 83-94.

Schafroth, Elmar, 2001, « Das Englische im Meinungsspektrum der frankophonen Presse Québecs », dans : Born, 129-150.

Size-Cazabon, Judy, 1987, « Les aspects politiques et culturels du programme d'immersion », *Revue du Nouvel-Ontario*, 9, 93-114.

Tennant, Jeff, 1995, *Variation morphonologique dans le français parlé des adolescents de North Bay (Ontario)*. Toronto : University of Toronto.

Tetu, Michel, 1996, « Le français au Canada et le monde francophone », dans : Erfurt, 351-363.

Thim-Mabrey, Christiane, 2003, « Sprachidentität – Identität durch Sprache: Ein Problemaufriss aus sprachwissenschaftlicher Sicht », dans : Nina Janich/Christiane Thim-Mabrey (dirs.), *Sprachidentität – Identität durch Sprache*. Tübingen : Narr, 1-18.

Tremblay, Martine, 1990, « Peuplement et colonisation du Québec et du Nord de l'Ontario : connaissances actuelles et perspectives de recherche », *Revue du Nouvel-Ontario*, 12, 43-63.

Tremblay, Onésime, 1986, « L'éducation et l'épanouissement de la minorité franco-ontarienne », *Revue du Nouvel-Ontario*, 8, 139-144.

Valdman, Albert, 1996, « Le français en Louisiane », dans : Denis de Robillard/Michel Beniamino (dirs.), *Le français dans l'espace francophone*. Vol. 2, Paris : Champion, 633-650.

Welch, David, 1991/1992, « Les luttes pour les écoles secondaires franco-ontariennes », *Revue du Nouvel-Ontario*, 13-14, 109-131.

Wiesmath, Raphaële, 2001, « *Français acadien traditionnel*, chiac und *français cadien* in Neubraun-schweig und Louisiana: drei Spielarten des akadisch-englischen Sprachkontakts », dans : Born, 151-173.

Internet

Association des juristes d'expression française de l'Ontario, (<http://www.ajefo.ca>), 21/01/2008.
Atlas de la francophonie : Provinces et territoires, (<http://www. franco.ca/atlas/francophonie>), 22/05/07.
La communauté francophone, (<http://www. Office des Affaires francophones>), 24/05/07.
Language Fairness National Philosophy, (<http://www.languagefairness.com/Mission.php>), 12/08/08.
Langue maternelle, chiffres de 2001 pour les deux sexes, pour le Canada, les provinces, les territoires et les divisions de recensement, (<http://www12.statcan.ca/francais/census01/products/highlight/LanguageComposition>), 21/01/08.
Le Bilinguisme est plus présent à Québec qu'à Ottawa, (<http://www.imperatif-francais.org/ bien-venu/articles/2001/le-bilinguisme-est-plus-present-a-quebec-qua-ottawa.html>), 09/02/08.
Les Canadiens et le bilinguisme, (<http://www.radio-canada.ca/actualite/desautels/2007/02/01/002-bilinguisme-accueil.asp>), 03/04/07.
Lois à incidence linguistique, (<http://www.salic-slmc.ca>), 21/01/08.
Population selon la langue maternelle et les groupes d'âge, chiffres de 2006, pour le Canada, (<http://www12.statcan.ca/francais/census06/data/highlights/language/Table401.>), 21/01/2008.
The Ontario Provincial Confederation of Regions Party. Policies. English official language of Ontario, (<http://home.mountaincable.net/~galloway/cor/policies.htm>), 12/08/08.

Marion Stange

Urban Governance in French Colonial North America: Hospital Care in Québec City and New Orleans in the 17th and 18th Centuries

Zusammenfassung

Anders als in den britischen Kolonien in Nordamerika, wo erst 1751 das erste Krankenhaus im modernen Sinne des Wortes gegründet wurde, existierten Einrichtungen dieser Art in Neufrankreich bereits ab der Mitte des 17. Jahrhunderts. Während diese Krankenhäuser anfangs noch ausschließlich auf die Initiative religiöser Orden und privater Gönner im Mutterland zurückgingen, engagierte sich ab den 1660er Jahren auch die französische Krone verstärkt in diesem Bereich. Die Erfahrungen der ersten Jahrzehnte in Nordamerika hatten den französischen Kolonialherren gezeigt, dass eine erfolgreiche Kolonisierung nicht zuletzt auch von der Gesundheit der Siedler und Soldaten abhing und daher die medizinische Versorgung in der Kolonie zentraler Bestandteil der königlichen Kolonialpolitik sein musste. Um die hierfür anfallenden Kosten möglichst gering zu halten, war die Krone bestrebt, religiöse Orden und Siedler in die Verwaltung und Finanzierung von Krankenhäusern einzubeziehen. Anhand der Beispiele des Hôtel-Dieu *in Québec City sowie des* Hôpital du Roi *und des* Hôpital des Pauvres de la Charité *in New Orleans wird in diesem Aufsatz der Frage nachgegangen, auf welche Art und Weise königliche, religiöse und private Akteure kooperierten, um die Pflege und Behandlung von Siedlern und Soldaten in kolonialen Krankenhäusern zu gewährleisten.*

Résumé

Tandis que, dans les colonies britanniques en Amérique du Nord, le premier hôpital au sens moderne du terme ne fut fondé qu'en 1751, la Nouvelle-France détenait des institutions de ce genre déjà depuis le milieu du dix-septième siècle. Au début, ces hôpitaux se basaient exclusivement sur l'initiative des ordres religieux et des donateurs privés. Cependant, à partir des années 1660 la couronne française s'engagea aussi de plus en plus dans ce domaine. Les expériences des premières décennies en Amérique avaient montré clairement aux colonisateurs français qu'une colonisation ne pouvait avoir de succès que si la santé des soldats et des colons pouvait être assurée. En conséquence, des soins médicaux devaient constituer un élément central dans la politique coloniale du roi. Voulant maintenir au plus bas les coûts de cette entreprise, la couronne était intéressée par une intégration des ordres religieux et des acteurs privés dans l'administration et le financement des hôpitaux. En s'appuyant sur l'exemple de l'Hôtel-Dieu à Québec ainsi que de l'Hôpital du Roi et de l'Hôpital des Pauvres de la Charité à la Nouvelle Orléans, cet article veut montrer de quelle manière des acteurs royaux, religieux et privés coopéraient afin de garantir le soin et le traitement des soldats et des colons dans les hôpitaux coloniaux.

Diseases were omnipresent in European colonies in North America during the 17th and 18th centuries. Malaria, dysentery, respiratory sicknesses and epidemic diseases like smallpox and yellow fever represented a serious threat to the settlers' health. Effective care of the colonies' sick civilians and soldiers was of paramount importance for the success of the European powers' colonization efforts. In the French colonies of Canada and Louisiana,[1] religious orders, colonial officials, and the settlers themselves realized the necessity of providing proper medical care to the inhabitants at an early stage of the colonization process. The establishment and maintenance of colonial hospitals constituted a decisive part of this care.

Eager to improve the medical situation in the recently established town of New Orleans (Nouvelle-Orléans), Abbé Raguet, the ecclesiastical director of the Company of the Indies, suggested recruiting Ursuline nuns from France as nurses for the town's royal hospital. In a letter to the bishop of Québec he wrote in May 1726:

> Je me suis appliqué a [...] l'Etablissement de l'hopital de la nouvelle Orleans. Les Malades y sont quelquefois nombreux, et toujours mal, soit pour la subsistence, soit pour les medicamens qu'on detourne trop impuremt. Les Urselines aiant reussi dans le soin quelles ont des Malades en Canada, j'ai pensé quelles reuissiroient aussi a la nouvelle Orleans.

---

[1] During the first half of the 18th century, the territory claimed by the French Crown on the North American continent extended from the area around the Saint Lawrence River (colony of Canada) over the Great Lakes region all the way down the Mississippi River to the Gulf of Mexico (colony of Louisiana). While settlement along the Saint Lawrence River already began during the early 17th century – Québec City as Canada's first permanent settlement was established in 1608 –, the Lower Mississippi Valley was not settled until the beginning of the 18th century after Louisiana had been founded as a French colony by Pierre Le Moyne d'Iberville in 1699. The colony's early settlements Mobile and Biloxi soon proved to be poorly located to serve the economic and strategic needs of a colony which extended from the Gulf of Mexico to the Illinois Country. In order to remedy this situation, the settlement of New Orleans was established in 1718. It was located on the banks of the Mississippi River, close to Lake Pontchartrain, making it possible for ship captains to reach the settlement either from the river or from the lake which in turn was connected to the Gulf of Mexico. The economic and strategic advantages of the site stood in stark contrast to the climatic and environmental features of the location. The swampy, low-lying region was a perfect breeding-ground for diseases, especially malaria and yellow fever, resulting in large numbers of sick settlers and soldiers in need of medical treatment and hospital care every year during the hot and humid summer months.

[…] Les Religieuses prendront l'hopital tel quil est, et y trouveront un Logement convenable. (Centre des archives d'outre-mer (CAOM), Archives des colonies (AC), C13A, vol. 10, 54)

Raguet's efforts to solicit the help of the Ursuline nuns for the management of the hospital in New Orleans soon proved to be worthwhile. In September 1726, the Ursulines of Rouen entered into a contract with the Company of the Indies, which was in charge of the French colony at that time. In this agreement the nuns consented to dispatch a number of their sisters to Louisiana where they would assume control of the king's hospital and provide nursing care for the sick (cf. CAOM, AC, C13A, vol. 10, 88). As Raguet mentions in his letter, this was not the first time that nuns of the Ursuline order engaged in health care in French North America. Almost thirty years before, in 1697, Ursuline sisters had been recruited for the administration of the then newly-founded *Hôtel-Dieu* in Trois-Rivières. Even earlier than that, in 1639, Augustinian nuns from Dieppe had arrived in New France to establish a hospital in the town of Québec. In Louisiana, as in Canada, these nuns played a key role in shaping and organizing the sector of medical care within the *Hôtels-Dieu* or the *Hôpitaux du Roi*. During this time, the sisters benefited to a large extent from the knowledge and experience they had acquired in France before coming to the colonies. However, the completely new environment and the unfamiliar living conditions in North America made new demands on the sisters. They faced a heterogeneous population, unknown diseases, different climatic conditions and, above all, the long distance between colony and home country that made communication as well as the frequent supply of medicine, surgical instruments, and other necessities quite difficult.

The inhabitants of the French colonies in North America had to find their own individual ways of dealing with these new demands and the problems arising in the unfamiliar environment of the New World. Although the strategies adopted by the colonists in response to these challenges could be based on established forms of organization used in the mother country, the settlers nevertheless had to adapt them to their particular needs. Thus, not even the solutions found in the different French colonies in North America were identical. The inhabitants of Canada were faced with different problems than their counterparts in Louisiana.

Taking the relatively small field of hospital care as an example this article wants to look at the ways in which colonial towns in French North America were organized during the 17th and 18th centuries. Of particular interest in this context is the question of which actors were involved in the organization of hospital care in Louisiana and Canada and of how these different actors cooperated in finding solutions to all problems arising in the colonial centers Québec City and New Orleans with regard to the financing and administration of hospitals. The method of comparison that was adopted here serves to identify the peculiar features of hospital organization in the two colonies and thus enables us to understand the actors' opportunities to creatively influence the organization of their community.

The *Hôtel-Dieu* of Québec City: From Religious Initiative to Royal Funding

The *Hôtel-Dieu* in Québec City was founded by Madame de Combalet, the Duchesse d'Aiguillon, a niece of Cardinal Richelieu, in 1639. The duchess had read with excitement the reports of the Jesuit priest Le Jeune about the Jesuits' missionary work in New France. In his narrative for the year 1635, Le Jeune talked about the advantages of a hospital for the Christianizing efforts of the missionaries among the indigenous population of Québec:

> Le deuxiesme iour de Feurier, la petite Sauuage qu'on porta en France l'an passé, fut baptisée au Monastere des filles de la Misericorde, c'est à dire, en l'Hospital de Dieppe [...], l'vn des mieux reglez de l'Europe. Il ne faut qu'entrer dans al salle des pauures, contempler la modestie des filles qui les seruent, considerer leur charité dans les plus fascheuses maladies, ietter les yeux sur la netteté des ceste maison, pour en sortir tout affectionné, et donner mille loüanges à nostre Seigneur. Si vn Monastere semblable à celuy-là, estoit en la Nouuelle-France, leur charité feroit plus pour la conuersion des Sauuages, que toutes nos courses et nos paroles. (Côté 1858, Year 1635, 7sq.)

Inspired by Le Jeune's suggestion, the duchess decided to fund – with her own money – the establishment of an *Hôtel-Dieu*, similar to that in Dieppe, in Canada. Not only did she succeed in convincing the Company of New France to grant her land for the purpose, but she was also able to secure the support of the hospital sisters of Dieppe. In 1636 she wrote to Le Jeune:

> Dieu m'ayant donné le désir d'aider au salut des pauures Sauvages, après auoir leu la Relation que vous en avez faicte, il m'a semblé que ce que vous croyez qui puisse le plus seruir à leur conuersion, est l'establissement des Religieuses Hospitalieres dans la Nouuelle France: de sorte que ie me suis resoluë d'y enuoyer cette année six ouuriers, pour défricher des terres, et faire quelque logement pour ces bonnes Filles. (Côté 1858, Year 1645, 5)

The nuns whom the duchess had managed to recruit for her charitable undertaking in Québec belonged to the order of *Les Religieuses Hospitalières de la Miséricorde de Jésus*, an Augustinian order. They set out for New France in 1639 and, after spending the first years nursing sick Native Americans in the Jesuit missionary settlement of Sillery, the nuns finally settled in Québec City where the first hospital was built in 1644 (cf. Goulet/Paradis 1992, 55sq.). Besides the Christianization of the indigenous population, the main objective of the *Hôtel-Dieu* of Québec City was – as it was the case with the *Hôtels-Dieu* in France – to provide medical care for the sick poor.

During the first decades of the hospital's existence, its funding was largely the responsibility of its foundress, the Duchesse d'Aiguillon. In 1637 she had granted the sisters an annuity of 1,500 pounds for the maintenance of the hospital. Three years later, in 1640, she had agreed to forward them the sum of 40,000 pounds for the construction and maintenance of the institution. When in 1654 the wooden structure of the first hospital building became too small to accommodate the growing number of sick people, the nuns again turned to the duchess and other charitable persons in France and successfully raised funds for a newer and larger building. In 1672, almost ten years after New France was taken over by the French crown, the royal *intendant*, Jean Talon, again enlarged the hospital out of his own funds (cf. Heagerty 1928, 148-155).

Beyond these extraordinary funds designated for constructional purposes, the hospital received annual payments from various sources, which were used for the maintenance of the hospital. After 1663, the hospital's principal income consisted of royal support, revenues from the *biens fonciers des Pauvres* – real estate property that had been bequeathed by private persons for the benefit of the poor –, donations from France, and the fees that some of the patients had to pay for the nursing services provided to them. The share each of these different revenues had of the total amount of income varied over time. While private donations from France were the most important source of income during the first decades, royal subsidies made up the largest part of the hospital's funds from the end of the seventeenth century onwards. This large financial commitment by the Crown was not without self-interest: the sisters were expected to provide medical care for troops and Crown employees that came to the colony in ever-growing numbers. The treatment of these individuals was a lucrative business for the nuns: apart from the pensions that soldiers had to disburse out of their own wages, the religious sisters also received an additional royal subsidy for each day such a patient was treated and accommodated at the hospital.

During the eighteenth century, this royally funded care was extended even further to include French prisoners of war, militiamen, seamen, deckhands on the king's ships, and even salt smugglers (cf. Lessard 1994, 298). The growing number of people eligible for royal support in case of sickness is reflected in the share this kind of revenue had of the *Hôtel-Dieu*'s total income: while it made up only 7-11% between 1666 and 1723, it increased in the following years, accounting for approximately 18% of the nuns' revenues for the time period between 1724 and 1753. This increase was accompanied by a decline of donations from France, the revenue that had been so important in ensuring the maintenance of the hospital during the early years of its existence. Between 1724 and 1733, these payments amounted to just 6% of the hospital's total revenues, declining further in the following three decades (cf. Rousseau 1983, 90). The nuns accepted this situation with mixed feelings: While they needed the annual royal support in order to maintain the hospital and provide care for the sick poor, the hospital's capacity was often completely exhausted with the soldiers alone, meaning that the nuns could not take in any indigent sick.

Besides financial aspects, the establishment of Canada as a royal colony brought with it another consequence for the *Hôtel-Dieu*: The Crown sent a large number of medical practitioners to Quebec, physicians, surgeons and assistant-surgeons, midwives and pharmacists. The *médecin du roi*, the royal physician, as well as the *chirurgien du roi*, were employed by the French Crown to take care of the sick at the *Hôtel-Dieu*. As professional medical practitioners, often educated at universities and schools in France, doctors and surgeons felt superior to the religious sisters and treated them as subordinates. The nuns, in turn, did not accept the doctors and surgeons as their superiors and insisted, as much as possible, on their autonomy. There was little cooperation between the nuns and the lay medical personnel, and complaints came from both sides. In 1736, for example, the surgeon Michel Bertier complained to the minister of marine that the sisters received large numbers of wealthy patients in their institution. Because he was only paid for treating soldiers and poor settlers, he demanded extra pay, if he was to extend his services to the prosperous colonists who came from places as far away as Louisbourg to enjoy the sisters' services (cf. CAOM, AC, C11A, vol. 66, 134-136^v). Seven years later, the Mother Superior of the nuns complained in a letter to a vendor of medicine based in France about the doctor and the surgeon recently arrived from France:

> [Le médecin] qui nous est venu lannée passée paroit jaloux de son metier il si applique mais Comme il na pas lusage du pays il no[us] fait bien de la dépense et no[us] taille de louvrage, il est extreme[men]t susceptible et délicat aimant son point d'honneur, nous ne no[us] accostons pas trop, il no[us] faut de la franchisse, po[ur] nôtre chirurgien il na pas dexperience n'aime pas son ard, nest pas assidu a ses playes ny a louvrage d lhopital que des apprentis font ordinairem[en]t il cest mariez a une jolye demoiselle qui a du bien, par la vous voyez bien Monsieur que no[us] ne voyons notre hopital servi si avantageusem[en]t que parle passé, ou le Roy dépensoit moin ne payant pas tant de gage, ny dapointem... (Lettres de Mère Marie-Andrée Duplessis de Sainte-Hélène 1930, 369)

The *Hôpital du Roi* of New Orleans: A Royal Institution Under Religious Administration

While the *Hôtel-Dieu* of Quebec originally started as a hospital for Native Americans and the sick poor, and then only gradually evolved into a de facto military hospital, the *Hôpital du Roi* in New Orleans was designated as such right from the beginning. Established in the early 1720s, just after the founding of New Orleans, it was intended to serve as a hospital for soldiers and the official administrative personnel of the Company of the Indies that was in charge of the colony during the 1720s. Due to the lack of alternative medical care, however, the hospital also provided treatment for sick civilians, at least during the first decades of the town's existence. The explicitly military character of the hospital can be attributed to the fact that the establishment of Louisiana was primarily a strategic enterprise aimed at securing the region from British and Spanish appropriation. The hospital's administration was formally placed in the hands of the colony's *commissaire-ordonnateur*. This official, analogous to the *intendant* in New France, was in charge of justice, finance, and police, part of which were also matters of health policy. In order to ensure the functioning of the hospital and its adequate supply of food and medicine, the *commissaire-ordonnateur*, in turn, commissioned one of the members of the Superior Council, the administrative body of the colony, with supervising all matters concerning the hospital.

During the first years of the hospital's existence, the care of the sick was carried out by surgeons and doctors sent from France and a small number of male nurses who were appointed by the council (cf. CAOM, AC, C13A, vol. 9, 99^v-100). As the colony grew, it became evident that the nursing care had to be put on a more professional basis. In 1723, during an especially sickly summer, the hospital had to accommodate up to 900 patients at a time, even though the actual capacity was only 80 persons (cf. Giraud 1987, 220). Apart from the lack of space to shelter all the sick settlers and soldiers, there was also not enough personnel to care for the large number of patients. This is why, in 1726, the Company of the Indies entered into a contract with the Ursuline nuns of Rouen to take over the management of the hospital and the care of the sick. Although the Ursulines arrived in Louisiana shortly after the contract was signed, they could not formally attend to their nursing duties, because the new hospital and convent that had been promised to the nuns by the Company were not finished until the early 1730s. In the meantime, the Ursulines focused on the education of girls and the care of orphans and only marginally ministered to the sick.

During the 1720s, it was primarily the Company of the Indies that, in exchange for the trading monopoly it held for Louisiana, oversaw the financial maintenance of the colony including that of the hospital and its personnel. The payments of the Company were completed by funds that originated from taxes on slaves and from fines imposed on settlers for misdemeanors (cf. Duffy 1958, 94). In the treaty with the Ursulines the directors of the Company specified how admission to the hospital was to be regulated:

> Tous malades de maladies ordinaires et non incurables seront recus a l'hopital sur un billet du Medecin et en son absence du Chirurgien major, et s'ils sont pauvres ils seront traités gratis en raportant un Certifficat de leur Curé visé du Procureur general, comme ils n'ont pas le moyen de payer. (CAOM, AC, C13A, vol. 10, 88-100^v)

Employees of the Company were given preference with regard to admission to the hospital, but the Company agreed to pay extra fees for their treatment. Regular colonists who could afford to do so also had to pay for the medical care provided for them (cf. CAOM, AC, C13A, vol. 10, 88-100^v).

The generosity of the Company with respect to the funding of the hospital and the admission of the sick poor was not continued by the Crown when it took over the colony in 1731. Although the king expressed his appreciation for the work of the religious sisters and the hospital's lay medical personnel, he made it clear that the hospital was supposed to serve primarily as a hospital for sick soldiers and workmen in the service of the Crown. Being familiar with the disastrous effects of the Crown's indifferent attitude toward the sick poor in Louisiana, royal officials repeatedly pointed out the inadequacy of the funds available for indigent colonists. In December 1731, for example, *gouverneur* Périer and *commissaire* Salmon wrote to the Comte Maurepas, the French minister of marine, that "the funds assigned for the maintenance of the poor of the hospital appear very moderate when one takes into account the number of sick soldiers and inhabitants to whom this assistance cannot be refused without leaving them to perish" (Rowland/Sanders/Galloway 1984, 93). Unimpressed by these complaints, the Crown insisted that the funds designated for the maintenance of the hospital were more than sufficient, provided that the Ursulines managed their accounts economically. In a memoir to his officials the king instructed them to keep watch over the sisters and to ensure that they took due care of the hospital patients (cf. CAOM, AC, B, vol. 57, 824^v-837^v). Underlining the Crown's unaccommodating position once more, Maurepas wrote in a letter to Salmon in October of 1732:

> Je vous ay deja mandé que le Roy ne vouloit point augmenter le nombre des Lits ny la dépense de l'hopital. Je souhaiterois pouvoir procurer aux habitans ce soulagement dans leurs maladies, mais les fond ne permettent pas de faire cette augmentation de dépense ainsy conformes vous a ce que je vous ay prescript sur cela et ne vous en departez point pour quelque cause que ce puisse estre. (CAOM, AC, B, vol. 57, 855^v)

The order Maurepas refers to here was clear: Civilian inhabitants of the colony were only to be admitted to the hospital if there was room to be spared. The Crown would by no means provide additional funds for the medical care of sick civilians, let alone of the sick poor who were not able to pay for their treatment. Apparently, however, the funds granted by the king did not even suffice to ensure the adequate treatment and accommodation of soldiers and Crown personnel. In May of the following year, Salmon and the recently established governor Bienville again underlined the financial difficulties of the hospital in New Orleans:

...the five thousand livres ordered for the maintenance of the hospitals is hardly sufficient to supply them with the medicines which must be considered a much less considerable expense than the food of the sick [...], much less still than the maintenance of the beds, linen and the other equipment necessary for the hospital. If your Lordship is so good as to notice that the King maintains eight hundred troops in the colony and that half and often two-thirds of these troops suffer every year from fever and dysentery which oblige us to admit them to the hospital, you will see that five thousand livres is not nearly enough to treat so many patients. We are not including in this number many unfortunate inhabitants exhausted by hardship whom charity does not permit us to abandon. (Rowland/Sanders/Galloway 1984, 89sq.)

The *Hôpital des Pauvres de la Charité* of New Orleans: Private Initiative for the Sick Poor

The royal decision left the colony's poor with no place to turn to when sick. The Capuchin priests who were responsible for the colony's poor relief were not able to provide medical care for them due to their limited resources. Relief finally came to the indigent sick in 1736, when a resident of New Orleans, the boat builder Jean Louis, bequeathed his entire estate to the colony, on condition that a hospital would be built for the indigent sick. In his will, Louis appointed a member of the Superior Council by the name of Raguet as executor and administrator of the hospital. Raguet together with the rector of the parish, Father Philippe, and *commissaire* Salmon purchased a building to accommodate the new hospital. By 1737, the first patients were admitted to the institution, which came to be known by the name of *Hôpital des Pauvres de la Charité*. Although Jean Louis had explicitly called for a "hospital for the sick of the city of New Orleans" (Cruzat 1918, 94sq.), the institution funded out of his estate not only served as a place for the indigent sick, but also, analogous to the *Hôpitaux Généraux* in France or the work houses in England, functioned as a house of confinement for beggars who were locked up and put to work in the hospital (cf. CAOM, AC, C13A, vol. 22, 30; Salvaggio 1992, 11).

The funding of the hospital was provided by different sources. Since the initial sum of 10,000 pounds bequeathed to the colony by Jean Louis had been largely consumed by the establishment of the hospital – for the expenses of the building itself, the furniture and medical equipment – it was necessary to find other sources of income. Funds provided by the French Crown were out of the question. The minister of marine, Maurepas, made it clear that the colony had nothing to expect from the royal coffers. In a letter in September 1737 to the colony's highest officials, Bienville and Salmon, he wrote:

[…] J'aurois souhaité que vous m'eussiés expliqué si le montant de cette succession suffira pour l'Entretien de cet hopital, sur quel pié il est Etabli, comment ceux qui y sont recus doivent y estre traittés, de quelle manière il est gouverné, que est ce qui est chargé d'administration de ses biens, en un mot quels sont les arrangemens qu'ont esté pris pour cet Etablissement. Vous aurés agréable de m'envoyer ces Eclairemens. Mais je dois vous prevenir que le Roy n'entrera ny pour le présent n'y pour l'avenir dans aucune dépense pour ce second hopital. (CAOM, AC, B, vol. 65, 519^v)

The Crown remained true to its word. There is no reference to any royal aid extended to the *Hôpital des Pauvres* except for the donation of a new site for the hospital in 1743. The costs of the institution's maintenance were mostly paid out of private donations. Additionally, limited public funds were provided by the colony's administration. They stemmed from fines imposed upon inhabitants for misdemeanors. An example of this can be found in the records of the Superior Council, the highest judicial court of the colony. In 1746, the justices found one Nicolas Judice guilty of assaulting and severely injuring another colonist. The fine of 1,000 pounds that he was sentenced to pay was to be forwarded to the Hospital for the Poor of New Orleans (Cruzat 1933, 136-137).

Although the Crown refused to support the indigent hospital through direct financial aid, the indigent sick benefited from the royal subsidiaries indirectly. The royal physician who was responsible for providing medical care to patients at the royal hospital also visited the sick at the *Hôpital des Pauvres* without charging extra fees. The institution's administrators also found a way of supplying nursing care for the sick in spite of the hospital's limited financial resources. During the first years of the hospital's existence, the work was carried out by a Senegalese black named François Tiocou and his wife Marie Aram, an African slave. Tiocou signed on to work for the hospital for seven years without pay, except for food and clothing. In exchange for their work, Marie would gain her freedom at the end of the term and "enjoy all the privileges of the other legitimate wives married to the subjects of the King" (Dart 1920, 551-553)

The administration of the hospital was carried out by a board of directors that consisted of prominent citizens of the town, government officials and the parish vicar. Every three years these directors elected two executive officers, a general director and a treasurer, to take charge of the management of the institution (cf. Duffy 1958, 108).

Different Paths, Same Result?

As the examples from Québec City and New Orleans show, governance of medical care in French colonial towns in North America was shaped by various actors who contributed in various ways, even if this cooperation was not always harmonious.

Government officials, representatives of the church and private individuals worked together to provide hospital care for the colonies' inhabitants. The organization of the hospitals was adapted to the specific conditions in the respective settlements. In Québec City, the *Hôtel-Dieu* was started by religious sisters with the financial help of a private individual. When the Crown took over New France in 1663, the royal administration took advantage of already existing institutions, like the *Hôtel-Dieu*, and adapted them to its purposes. The resulting cooperation between the Augustinian sisters and the Crown provided a sound financial and organizational basis of medical care in the town of Québec from which both sides, in spite of friction, benefited.

The *Hôpital du Roi* in New Orleans was started by the *Compagnie des Indes* as a hospital for the military and company personnel residing in Louisiana. Not until it became evident that the lay personnel of the hospital were unable to provide effective management of the institution did the company solicit the help of the Ursuline sisters who, from the 1730s onwards, successfully took care of the administration of the hospital and the nursing of the sick. Unlike the *Hôtel-Dieu* in Québec City, the Royal Hospital in New Orleans provided inadequate care for the sick poor. Convinced that there had to be a place in the colony the indigent could turn to in case of sickness, a private person bequeathed his estate to the town of New Orleans, so that a hospital for the poor could be started. After the Crown's refusal to finance the institution, other private individuals, Capuchin priests and government officials residing in the colony stepped in to ensure the proper functioning of the *Hôpital des Pauvres*.

References

Centre des archives d'outre-mer, Aix-en-Provence (CAOM), Archives des colonies (AC), series B, C11A, C13A.

Côté, Augustin (ed.), 1858, *Relations des Jésuites: contenant ce qui s'est passé de plus remarquable dans les missions des pères de la Compagnie de Jésus dans la Nouvelle-France*, vol. 1, Québec City.

Cruzat, Heloise Hulse, 1918, "Sidelights on Louisiana History", *Louisiana Historical Quarterly*, 1.3, 87-153.

Cruzat, Helois Hulse/Henry P. Dart (eds.), 1933, "Records of the Superior Council of Louisiana", *Louisiana Historical Quarterly* 16.1, 135-150.

Dart, Henry P. (ed.), 1920, "Cabildo Archives, French Period", *Louisiana Historical Quarterly*, 3.4, 543-553.

Duffy, John (ed.), 1958, *The Rudoph Matas History of Medicine in Louisiana*, vol. 1, Baton Rouge, LA: Louisiana State University Press.

Giraud, Marcel, 1987, *A History of French Louisiana*, vol. 5, Baton Rouge, LA: Louisiana State University Press.

Goulet, Denis/André Paradis, 1992, *Trois siècles d'histoire médicale au Québec. Chronologie des institutions et des pratiques, 1639-1939*, Montréal, QC: VLB.

Heagerty, John, 1928, *Four Centuries of Medical History in Canada and a Sketch of the Medical History of Newfoundland*, vol. 2. Bristol: Wright.

Lessard, Rénald, 1994, *Pratique et praticiens en contexte colonial: Le corps médical canadien aux 17e et 18e siècles*, PhD Thesis, Université Laval, Québec City.

"Lettres de Mère Marie-Andrée Duplessis de Sainte-Hélène, Supérieure des Hospitalières de l'Hotel-Dieu de Québec", 1930, *Nova Francia,* 5.6, 359-379.

Rousseau, François, 1983, *L'oeuvre de chère en Nouvelle-France. Le régime des malades à Hôtel-Dieu de Québec*, Québec City: Presses de l'Université Laval.

Rowland, Dunbar/A. G. Sanders/Patricia Galloway (eds.), 1984, *Mississippi Provincial Archives*, vol. 4, Baton Rouge, LA/London: Louisiana State University Press.

Salvaggio, John E., 1992, *New Orleans' Charity Hospital: A Story of Physicians, Politics, and Poverty*, Baton Rouge, LA: Louisiana State University Press.

PAUL VILLENEUVE

Societal Change in Quebec and Canada: The Roles of Quebec City and Montreal

Zusammenfassung
Ähnlich wie im Falle Wiens, wenn auch aus anderen Gründen, haben die Städte Québec und Montréal Teile ihres Umlands verloren. In der zweiten Hälfte des 19. Jahrhunderts wurde Québec zur Provinzhauptstadt, nachdem es zuvor die Hauptstadt von Nouvelle France und British North America gewesen war. In der zweiten Hälfte des 20. Jahrhunderts verlor Montréal viel von seiner Bedeutung – es blieb die Wirtschaftsmetropole der Provinz Québec, während sich Toronto zum ökonomischen Zentrum für ganz Kanada entwickelte. Das Schicksal der beiden Städte Québec und Montréal spiegelt eine Reihe wichtiger sozialer Veränderungen in der Provinz und in Kanada. So ist die quiet revolution *in den 1960er Jahren in dem Spannungsfeld zwischen dem turbulenten Montréal und dem ruhigen Québec entstanden. Die zivilgesellschaftlich inspirierte Veränderungsdynamik aus Montréal wurde durch die Regierung in Québec umgelenkt und institutionalisiert. Der Text untersucht die verschiedenen Spannungsbögen zwischen den beiden Städten und ihre Auswirkungen auf die Provinz Québec und auf Kanada insgesamt. Die Betonung der Kultur und Identität der Provinz vertieft die Unterschiede zwischen ihr und dem Rest von Kanada. Jedoch trägt sie auch dazu bei, die Unterschiede zwischen Kanada und den Vereinigten Staaten zu verdeutlichen. Nicht zuletzt aus diesem Grund haben Regierung und Parlament in Ottawa kürzlich den Status von Québec als den einer Nation anerkannt.*

Résumé
Un peu comme Vienne, mais pour des raisons différentes, les villes de Québec et Montréal ont vu leurs hinterlands se rétrécir alors que le Canada passait du statut de colonie à celui de pays indépendant. Au cours de la seconde moitié du 19ième siècle, la ville de Québec devint une capitale provinciale après avoir été la capitale de la Nouvelle-France et de l'Amérique du Nord britannique. Pendant la seconde moitié du 20ième siècle, Montréal perdit son statut de métropole économique du Canada pour devenir métropole du Québec. Le destin historique de ces deux villes est indissociable d'un certain nombre de transformations sociétales vécues par le Québec et le Canada. Par exemple, on peut penser que le premier terme de l'expression «révolution tranquille» renvoie à Montréal

alors que le second évoque Québec, la société civile montréalaise appelant alors de tous ces vœux un changement de société, qui se produisit, mais au rythme d'une modernisation graduelle de l'État localisé à Québec.

Le texte illustre les tenants et aboutissants de cette dynamique territoriale qui est au cœur du processus de construction de l'identité québécoise et qui, se faisant, contribue à différencier le Québec du Canada et, de façon tout à fait paradoxale, à différencier ce dernier des États-Unis. Ceci n'est-il pas devenu manifeste, du moins symboliquement, lorsque tout récemment le Parlement canadien a reconnu le Québec comme nation?

Quebec City celebrates in 2008 its four hundredth anniversary[1]. In European terms, this is not very old but in North American terms, this makes Quebec City one of the oldest cities on the continent. Montreal, founded in 1642, is not much younger chronologically, although it projects an image of modernity which contrasts with the image of heritage and tradition projected by Quebec City, an image that its present leaders would very much like to rejuvenate as we have heard in the Fall of 2007, during the last municipal election campaign. The central question dealt with in this paper pertains to the roles played by Quebec City and Montreal in society-wide processes of change in Quebec and Canada.

Notions about the cultural role of cities (Redfield / Singer 1954) may be helpful in this regard. Cities can be seen as collective actors in the territorial construction of the larger social entities to which they belong, from the regional scale to the world scale. As will be detailed below (fourth section), cities may be located on a continuum with regard to the role they play in society-wide processes of change. At one end, cities may formalize the living culture of their immediate surroundings. This is their "orthogenetic role" which builds on strong continuities between the city and its *umland*. At the other end, cities may be the crucible where immigrants with different cultural backgrounds interact, often producing discontinuous change. This is their "heterogenetic role". The paper seeks to explore the roles of Quebec City and Montreal in the social and territorial construction of Quebec and Canada. This requires an investigation of the ways in which the specific character of each city was formed over time, thereby shaping their particular contribution to the nation-building process.

The geographical notion of "spatial interaction" is relied upon to conduct this investigation. This notion is sketched in the next section. Then, the paper shows how the complex relationship between two frameworks of spatial organisation, namely

---

1   The help of Yvon Jodoin with data analysis and the financial support of the *Social Science Research Council of Canada* and the *Fonds québécois de la recherche sur la société et la culture* are acknowledged.

provinces and metropolises, is at the heart of the social construction of Canada. In the following sections, this relationship is detailed with regard to Quebec as a province and Quebec City and Montreal as its two main urban centers. Finally, the paper suggests that the constructive tension linking the two cities is at the earth of the territorial construction of society in Quebec.

Fields of Spatial Interaction

Studies in human geography have been dominated, during the second half of the last century, by the twin notions of "areal differentiation" and "spatial interaction" (Bunge 1966). Areal differentiation is a condition for spatial interaction, but not a sufficient one. Two other conditions have to operate, besides complementarity resulting from differentiation, for spatial interaction to take place: absence of intervening opportunity and transferability (Ullman 1980). Functional relationships over space take the form of flows of goods, people and data. The structure of these flow patterns provides fundamental information on the characteristics of processes of territorial integration and disintegration. Here, scale is of the utmost importance: growth at one scale may translate into redistribution at a higher scale; increasing interaction at one scale may entail greater areal differentiation at the scale above.

Up until about fifteen years ago, the geographical study of spatial interaction was dominated by the metaphor of gravitation borrowed from Newtonian physics. This approach yielded a number of insights into a variety of theoretical and practical issues ranging from abstract notions of social space to methods of transportation planning (Fotheringham / O'kelly 1989). However, a view that considers persons as aggregates of molecules leaves out human agency which, to be sure, constitutes the defining substance of social systems. Prior to about 1980, many geographers tended to overlook the important connections between their notion of spatial interaction and the sociologists' notion of social action. Authors such as Giddens (1984) have partly filled the gap. Structuration theory opens up a rich context of interpretation in which to think about spatial interaction, which also gains from being related to the perspective of symbolic interactionism (Becker / McCall 1990).

Myriad of single interactions continuously take place. These polymorphous, but sometimes denumerable events form a space-time continuum which, if properly analyzed, can yield insights into the temporality and spatiality of social processes, taking us much beyond chronological time and Cartesian space. Days, weeks and years categorise time arbitrarily. Meridians and parallels do the same for space. Starting with the most disaggregate information available on interactional events, and gradually aggregating this information in space-time, according to categories allowed to emerge from the data themselves, should help uncovering the temporality and spatiality of processes, since interaction does not take place randomly in space-time. And it is non-random spatial patterns – direction biased and distance biased patterns – that can be called fields of interaction.

Spatial interactions construct and deconstruct places. Some authors may think that flows are destroying places: "The historical emergence of the space of flows supersedes the meaning of the space of places" (Castells 1989, 348). But flows are forms of interaction, and places, or for that matter regions, have to be seen as "strong bundles" of interactions in space-time. Places acquire their identity through the accumulation of interactions taking place at a given geographical scale, and may loose their identity through interactions at larger, or smaller, scales. For example, a village builds its identity through the local interactions between its inhabitants over the years. If a freeway passes by the village and incites the villagers to interact with the cities located at some distance, the identity of the village may suffer but a new identity, associated with a larger region, may emerge.

For a number of decades, Canada was being constituted as an East-West field of interaction, first under the guidance of British rule and, later on, in the context of MacDonald's National Policy. It is arguable whether Canada ever became a "place". It remained, rather, throughout its history, a collection of places, the "island societies" of Richard Cole Harris (1987). However, the transportation landscape of the past, especially pan-Canadian railways, as well as a whole range of federal institutions, testifies to the attempt to turn Canada into a nation-state. Now, a variety of factors are putting this attempt under renewed and severe strain, including: Québec's desire for political autonomy; the crisis of public finances that tends to force state decentralization; and continental integration: "greater economic inter-dependence within the Western Hemisphere will test the viability of the East-West links" (Gunderson 1996, 2).

Provinces Differentiate, Metropolises Integrate

Provinces and metropolises are two forms of organisation that shape the dynamics of Canada as a spatial entity (Villeneuve 1990). All through Canadian history, metropolises have first and foremost been poles in an urban system favouring territorial integration, while provinces have primarily been frameworks favouring the differentiation of Canadian space. The very notion of "province" has a vernacular ring. It evokes traditions and customs. Harold Innis (1956) saw provinces as remnants of feudal times, especially in their role as collectors of royalties on natural resources. In the United States, the country is divided into "states", a term evoking modernity, while in Canada, the land is divided into "provinces", a term in continuity with the colonial experience. When Quebeckers wanted to affirm their collective identity in the 1960s they started to refer to the "State of Quebec" rather than the "Province of Quebec".

Cole Harris (1987), in a piece on Canadian regionalism, shows that provincial frontiers, when they were drawn, corresponded only slightly to the *umlands* of the main Canadian cities. In Western Canada, provincial boundaries were arbitrary lines drawn even before substantial settlement. In the East, boundaries corresponded roughly to previous colonial territories (e.g. Upper Canada, Lower Canada, New

Brunswick, Nova Scotia) but, with the exception of a small section of the frontier of Southern Quebec, boundaries were not drawn to correspond to "cultural regions". Subsequent settlement, however, took place within the provincial framework and, with time, provincial identities were formed. The strength of these identities varies considerably, at least it did in 1977 when Matthews and Campbell Davis (1986) asked a random sample of 3 165 Canadians whether they regarded themselves as Canadian first, provincial residents first, or both equally (*Table 1*). High percentages were found west of the Ottawa River for those who answered "Canada first". As could be expected, provincial identity was at a maximum in Quebec but, if we include those who shared equal Canadian and provincial identities, it was also quite pronounced in Newfoundland and in Prince Edward Island, probably due to insularity, while it was somewhat less affirmed in other provinces although isolationist sentiments often surface in Alberta and British Columbia. All in all, provinces crystallize Canada's level of fragmentation, a level which varies considerably from east to west. Nevertheless, the territorial boundaries of provinces are clear and they somewhat simplify the complexities of multilevel identities.

Metropolises, on the other hand, evoke the possibility of constituting an integrated Canadian polity. Canadian metropolises were built around the relationship between technology and empire, including: railways, the Intercontinental in the East and the Canadian Pacific in the West; manufacturing in the central axis from Quebec City to Windsor; markets being unified from coast to coast; later on Air-Canada, Radio-Canada, the Trans-Canada Highway. Builders of the Canadian Federation needed this technological arsenal. Continent-wide Canada was not conceivable in the pre-industrial era. It is from the metropolises, first from Montreal and Toronto, that this process of spatial integration was conducted. Finance capital, concentrated on Saint-Jacques street in Montreal and Bay street in Toronto, created the necessary institutions. The railway got Vancouver started and, as soon as 1900, it was the third city in Canada, while for the first half of the 20th century, Winnipeg was the Prairie metropolis and the fourth city in Canada, now passed by Calgary and Edmonton. In the Maritimes, due to provincial and local fragmentation, Halifax has not really emerged as the uncontested regional metropolis, cities such as Saint John's in Newfoundland and Moncton and Saint-John in New Brunswick also polarizing noteworthy *umlands*.

Ottawa-Gatineau symbolizes quite well the complex relation between provinces which differentiate and metropolises which integrate. These two modes of spatial organisation collide on its territory. The city is crossed by the Ottawa River, a corridor of penetration which played a major role in the formative years of the Canadian territory at the time of the fur trade, a river which also forms the frontier between Quebec and Ontario. At the beginning, in 1857, before Confederacy, the federal capital was placed in Ontario by Queen Victoria, but near the province of Québec. This decision was a consequence of the distribution of power between Upper and Lower Canada, although at the time, the country was under the Union regime.

Prime Ministers installed, however, their summer residence on the Québécois side, in the Gatineau Hills. More recently, a part of the federal administration was relocated in Hull (now Gatineau), under the pressure of what was called "French Power" in Ottawa. There is now an administrative entity, the National Capital Commission, which manages the federal presence in the territory straddling both provinces, but there is no autonomous federal district, as in the United States or in Australia, Quebec as well as Ontario being strongly opposed to it, thus perpetuating the principle according to which provinces differentiate Canadian space.

Table 1. Dominant Identity in Percent by Province of Residence, Canada, 1977

Province	Canadian First	Both Equally	Provincial First
NFLD	32	57	11
PEI	53	42	5
NB	61	29	10
NS	63	28	9
QC	48	27	25
ON	91	5	4
MAN	85	9	6
SAS	83	9	8
ALB	70	16	14
BC	82	10	8
CDN	72	16	12

Source: Matthews / Campbell Davis, 1986, p. 103

Montréal and the Conquest of the West

A century ago, associating Montreal to the conquest of the West would have immediately brought images of prairies covered with wheat that was brought East by railways and lakers and stored in grain elevators in the city's harbour, a system whose operations were run from Montreal and London. Today, conquering the West means, for francophones, conquering the Western part of the island of Montreal. The challenge is perhaps less grandiose but the stakes certainly worth the trouble. Thus, in the heart of the business district traditionally English-speaking, a succession of large buildings from the 1980s, erected in the shadow of Mount-Royal, bear names of francophone firms: Banque nationale, L'Industrielle - Vie, La Laurentienne, Les Coopérants. This last one illustrates the architectural style and spirit of postmodernism as it reproduces the forms of the small neighbouring church while crushing it under its mass. Thus is molded into concrete the rather remarkable development, since the 1960s of the francophone business class. In the early 1960s, Quebec's economy was still dominated by corporations or families from the anglophone community. The emerging economic forces of francophones relied heavily on the state of Quebec. They filled, in part, the void left by the departure for Toronto of several corporate headquarters. Since then, the new financial power of francophones transforms the face of downtown Montreal. This new conquest of the West does not affect only the city's business district. The residential areas of the "West Island" are also touched. Notre-Dame de Grâce, Ville Mont-Royal, and even Westmount receive francophone households, often double career couples who combine their incomes to have access to prestigious neighbourhoods, thereby demonstrating their social advancement. Some are replacing the anglophone executives who left Montreal for Toronto following the relocation of a number of corporate headquarters. Hence, this new conquest of the West is a reflection of the shrinking of Montreal's hinterland. This is going on even as Montreal is acquiring an international reputation in several areas, including aeronautics and jazz. Consequently, we have witnessed a strengthening of the status of Quebec as a cultural region and of the international status of Montreal, while at the same time observing a weakening of its status in Canada.

Quebec City the Orthogenetic and Montreal the Heterogenetic

Provincial differentiation and metropolitan integration involving Quebec City and Montreal have interacted in a peculiar way, during Canadian history, thereby shaping Quebec's societal dynamics. There are at least four ingredients forming this territorial process.

Firstly, the inexorable westward movement of the center of gravity of population and activities on the North American continent has contributed to the modification of the Canadian urban hierarchy over the centuries. Around 1765, the three main cities were Halifax (3 000 inhabitants), Quebec City (8 000) and Montreal (6 000). Montreal passed Quebec City around 1830 (each had about 30 000 then) and Toronto passed Montreal around 1975 (each had about 2,8 million then). Also, Quebec City lost to Ottawa the status of Capital of British North America at Confederation. It then became a provincial capital and the main urban center of Eastern Quebec. Montreal lost the status of metropolis of Canada to Toronto during the 1970s. But, as Polèse and Shearmur (2004) note, the movement westward of the center of gravity of the Canadian population and economy does not suffice to explain the shift in the urban hierarchy since a similar westward movement takes place in the United States without New York loosing its supremacy. The fact that Southern Ontario, inserted as it is into the United States space economy, has experienced a strong sequence of development since the first half of the 19th century is part and parcel of the westward movement. Ontarian economic development was triggered by wheat as a staple which, as shown by McCallum (1980), generated through backward linkages an industrialisation based on farm equipment, also used in the opening up of the Prairies, which required iron and steel, which eventually supported the car industry, which, in turn backed up sustained population growth and rapid urbanisation. This interpretation is congruent with the fact that throughout the 20th century, Toronto has grown at a faster rate than Montreal, except for the 1921-1941 period (Stone 1967, 278; Simmons / McCann 2006, 53).

Secondly, the culturally-based spatial differentiation between Quebec and the rest of Canada, which intensified with the quiet revolution of the 1960s, produced a disadvantage for Montreal, in its competition with Toronto for higher order service functions, principally finance and headquarters of firms (Polèse / Shearmur 2004). The outmigration of native-English speakers and the increase in the percentage of English Quebeckers who are bilingual produced a fast decreasing share of Quebec's population that speaks English only. The increasing use of the French language in the Montreal advanced service economy made it more difficult for higher order service firms to compete on the Canadian market and, conversely, made it easier for them to serve the Quebec market, especially in the cultural industries. This corresponded with a shrinking of Montreal's *umland*.

Thirdly, the Province of Quebec in the 1950s and 1960s was rapidly becoming a "wired urban region" after having been, for three and a half centuries, a homogenous and fairly stable cultural area with a strong oral tradition. Phrased in the words of McLuhan, it would seem that French Canadians, or more recently "Québécois", have almost by-passed Gutenberg's Galaxy on their way from the "catholic tribe" to the "global village". The new identity emerging in Quebec in the 1960s may well result from strong urbanisation forces operating in a singularly homogeneous cultural matrix. A common culture, as well as group identity and group consciousness, are the result of shared memories and a greater volume of within-group interactions as opposed to interactions conducted with others, outside the group. In this respect, because of language, French Canadians have always interacted much more among themselves than with others, and urbanisation by bringing people closer together favoured such interaction, even before the advent of electronic media. By 1921, already more than half of the Quebec population was urban, even though the economy was still clearly dominated by primary and secondary activities. Television arrived in Quebec in the early 1950s. It rapidly became a vehicle for the diffusion throughout Quebec of the cultural products generated by the new forms of interaction between Montreal and Quebec City. For example, *La famille Plouffe*, a television series produced in Montreal, was an adaptation of Roger Lemelin's novel *Les Plouffe*, in which the action took place in Saint-Sauveur, the Quebec City neighbourhood where Lemelin was born. With Gabrielle Roy (*Bonheur d'occasion*), he is among the very first urban novelists in Quebec. The protagonists in *Les Plouffe*, published in

1948 (the same year as the *Refus Global,* a manifesto published by a group of Montreal's artists) are urban but their rural roots are still nourishing their values and attitudes. These two works illustrate well the rebellious tendencies present in Montreal and the rural streak still present in Quebec City.

Table 2. Regional Penetration of Mass Media, Quebec, 1970				
	Gutenberg Galaxy		Global Village	
Regions	**Dailies****	**Weeklies****	**Radio****	**Television****
Gaspésie	276	310	17	28
Lac Saint-Jean	559	315	15	29
Québec	631	319	18	28
Mauricie	648	373	16	27
Estrie	546	347	15	26
Montréal	470	572	17	26
Outaouais	257	363	16	27
Abitibi	243	322	16	27
Côte-Nord	404	276	13	30
COV*	**0,79**	**0,73**	**0,29**	**0,15**

* Coefficient of variation = standard deviation of penetration rate/average penetration rate, with n = 9 regions. The higher the coefficient, the stronger is the variation among regions.
** Penetration rate for 1 000 households: based on 1970 surveys made by the Audit Bureau of Circulation of Chicago which provided the count of dailies and weeklies distributed in each region. The penetration rate divides this count by the number of households (ratio multiplied by 1 000) in the region.
*** Average number of hours per week per person > 18 years old : based on 1970 surveys administered by the Bureau of Broadcasting Measurement of Canada using a random sample of about 25 000 households located across the nine regions. Members of households kept a diary of their radio and television listening during a period of two weeks.
Source: SORECOM Inc., 1972, *Enquête sur la diffusion de l'information au Québec* (Québec, Parlement du Québec, Commission parlementaire spéciale sur les problèmes de la liberté de presse), 49-56.

In the pre- and early industrial periods, cultural homogeneity in Quebec, and the easy verbal and non-verbal exchanges that go with it, did not promote much social change because the group was not markedly exposed to significant outside ideas and innovations. The new media completely changed this situation. Innovations and external influences now could break in much more easily, and once they did, they swept through the whole group extremely rapidly precisely because of marked cultural homogeneity. One of the most noticeable correlates of the urban implosion then going on in Quebec is the contraction of the agricultural domain since the 1940s (Clibbon 1972). Less fertile parts of the Laurentian and Appalachian plateaus were reforested. The safety valve mechanism of the pioneer front did not exist any longer in its original form, and the planning of dense urban environments required rather different skills than the ones needed in the opening up of new agricultural land. Also, the circulation of information was becoming less "place dependent", as can be seen in *Table 2* where interregional behaviour is much more homogeneous with respect to the electronic media than it is with respect to the written press. Indeed, coefficients of variation, which measure the interregional homogeneity of media penetration rates, show that electronic media have much lower coefficients than the written press. This suggests that the urban-rural opposition was becoming less and less relevant and that the pre-industrial cultural homogeneity based on face-to-face contacts might have been heightened and brought to a much higher scale by the mass media, which now, of course, include the Internet.

Fourthly, increased spatial interaction between Montreal and Quebec City was observed during the 1950s and 1960s. Was this related to the province developing more autonomously, within its linguistic border, and were these intensified interactions within the province helping to shape the quiet revolution? An article by Redfield and Singer (1954) on the cultural role of cities offers an approach to try and understand these dynamics. The goal of the two Chicago anthropologists was not to show, as is often done now, that cultural industries play a key role in the economy of cities, but rather to reflect on the role of cities in the development of "culture" in an anthropological sense. Much in line with urban ecological concepts, culture for them is grounded in communication and symbolism. They see two very different cultural roles held by cities.

Cities may be, on the one hand, venues for contacts between groups of people of very different language, ethnicity or religion. The resulting ebullient intercultural activity produces discontinuous social change, with much friction and controversy, hence the name "heterogenetic" to qualify this role. On the other hand, cities may also be places where the oral traditions of the cultural regions where they are located are synthesized and systematized. Here, social change is taking place in continuity with the immediate region, hence the name "orthogenetic" to designate this role. Usually, both roles are present in any city but in varying proportions.

In Quebec, Montreal's role is clearly perceived as heterogenetic, the metropolis being the gateway city through which outside influences are introduced in the province as a cultural region. Quebec City, by contrast, is clearly perceived as orthogenetic, a city of heritage, where is formalised and codified the living culture of surrounding rural Quebec. A social revolution began in heterogenetic Montreal during the 1940s and 1950s, with such events as the publication of the art manifesto *"Refus global"* in 1948 and the riots provoked by the suspension of hockey player Maurice Richard in 1955. This form of turbulent social change became more quiet (read "institutionalised") in contact with the orthogenetic milieu of Quebec City when Jean Lesage's liberal party took power in 1960 and began a profound but gradual modernisation of state institutions (Villeneuve 1981, 1988).

This is an interactionist hypothesis. Until the mid-20th century, the exchanges were limited between Eastern Quebec focused on Quebec City and Western Quebec polarised by Montreal which is then, as we have seen, Canada's metropolis. Levels of interaction are higher then within Eastern Quebec and within Western Quebec than they are between them. In Eastern Quebec, Quebec City is becoming totally French as anglophones are departing westward, following the end of the sail boat era and the loss of colonial capital status. The city's demographic growth is then nourished by its rural surroundings. Meanwhile, in Western Quebec, both international immigration and rural-urban migration from the surrounding countryside fed the rapid population growth of Montreal and the distinctive residential segregation pattern where immigrants occupied a South-North corridor along Saint-Laurent Street with francophones to the East and anglophones to the West. Residential segregation was at the time compounded by pronounced income disparities along ethnic lines. As late as 1961, the average income of persons of British origin was 55% higher than that of persons of French origin (Polèse / Shearmur, 2004, p. 334) with only persons of Italian origin and members of First Nations earning less than them, and with persons of other European origins ranging between 11% and 53% higher than them (Raynauld et al. 1966, 3.13).

The Quiet Revolution: from Montreal to Quebec City ... and Back

In the 1950s, interactions of all kinds between Montreal and Quebec City started to increase dramatically. The strongest air link in Canada may be between Montreal and Toronto, but the strongest surface link is between Quebec City and Montreal. The Trans-Canada highway was then put into service. With time, it will not only become a strong functional link between the two cities but also a symbolic bond which, for example, serves as a backdrop for movies such as the popular road-movie "Quebec-Montreal" where various intrigues evolve during the journey between the two cities. The province of Quebec is large enough for a wide variety of movies, radio and television shows to be produced in French. These become formidable vehicles of self-perception and awareness in "real time", without the filter of traditional elites. This explosion of internal interactions in Quebec occurs even though (perhaps because) Montreal is replaced by Toronto as Canada's metropolis, Quebec City having already been reduced to the rank of provincial capital at Confederation.

From a geographical point of view, it would seem that the tremendous social and economic progress of Quebec since the 1960s is somehow correlated, through some form of compensation, with the reduced Canadian role of Montreal.

More recently, the Quebec City region stands out in the political arena by supporting the Conservative Party at the federal level in 2006 and the Democratic Action of Quebec (ADQ) (also perceived as rightist) in 2003, and even more strongly in 2007. A spatial analysis of the vote shows that it is the suburbs of the metropolitan area and surrounding rural areas which have elected candidates from these parties (Villeneuve et al. 2007). This electoral behaviour has a history running at least over the last half century. It is possible to relate this behaviour to the territorial dynamics of the evolving political culture of Quebec. Since the 1940's, it is as if political expression has been oscillating in geographical space between Western Quebec polarised by Montreal and Eastern Quebec largely centered on Quebec City, as if for certain periods, values originating in Eastern less urbanised Quebec were gaining ground in Western metropolising Quebec and, then, for other periods, the reverse spatial process were taking place, with values originating in metropolitan Montreal diffusing toward Eastern Quebec.

Territorial measurements of this pendular movement have been tried, using as an indicator the changing geographical distribution of the electoral support given to the four main political parties concerned, for the elections when these parties were roughly in their ascending phase. More specifically, the average distance of voters from the Montreal central business district (CBD) (corner of Peel and Sainte-Catherine) was computed for the elections when a given party was progressing and/or winning (*Table 3*). This is a weighted average obtained by measuring the distance between Montreal's CBD and the centroids of ridings weighted by the number of voters in each of these. Based on the hypothesis stating that, in general, rural areas tend to be more conservative and urban areas less conservative (Cutler / Jenkins 2000), we should expect, firstly, that supporters of the two most conservative parties, UN (Union nationale) and ADQ, should show larger distances from Montreal's CBD than supporters of the two parties, PLQ (Parti libéral du Québec) and PQ (Parti québécois), deemed less conservative; secondly, we should also expect that more conservative parties, during ascending phases, may enlarge their original base, and diffuse towards Montreal, which would translate into shorter average distances to the Montreal CBD, with the reverse movement for less conservative parties.

Table 3. Territorial Movements of Ascending Political Parties, Province of Quebec, 1944 - 2007

Political Party	Election year	Distance* from Mtl	% of the vote
Union nationale (UN)	1944	216	38,0
	1948	189	51,2
	1952	200	50,5
	1956	187	51,8
Liberal Party of Quebec (PLQ)	1960	174	53,9
	1962	158	56,4
	1966	165	47,3
	1970	135	45,4
	1973	148	54,7
Parti Québécois (PQ)	1970	134	23,1
	1973	141	30,2
	1976	159	41,4
	1981	165	49,3
Action Démocratique du Québec (ADQ)	1998	143	11,8
	2003	168	18,2
	2007	146	30,8

*   Average distance (km) from downtown Montreal of centroids of ridings weighted by the number of voters. Source: computed by Yvon Jodoin at CRAD with data from Direction des élections, Gouvernement du Québec.

Table 3 partly supports this hypothesis. Union nationale shows the largest distances, while ADQ has slightly larger distances than the PQ, but not the PLQ. Actually, the PLQ shows two distinct patterns: for the three elections of 1960, 1962 and 1966, distances are much higher than for the elections of 1970 and 1973. To be sure, the average distances presented in this table are influenced by the general movement of metropolisation of the population, especially before 1980. This would affect the first part of the hypothesis, but much less the second part which is tested by comparing distances from one election to the next for the same party. Here the test is the most conclusive in the case of the PQ. During the sequence of elections when this party was ascending, from 1970 to 1981, it regularly extended its support away from Montreal. The test is also quite conclusive in the case of the UN, which won the elections from 1944 to 1956 and was able to extend its support towards Montreal, albeit with a slight backward movement in 1952, an election which also corresponds to a slightly lower percentage of the vote for the UN. As for the PLQ, the party support was expanding towards Montreal during the quiet revolution (the two elections of 1960 and 1962). In 1966, when it lost by a small margin to the UN, it expanded its vote outside of Montreal and, subsequently, during the Bourassa era from 1970 to 1976, it first regrouped towards Montreal in 1970, and then gained ground outside the metropolitan area in 1973 when it won almost all of the seats in the national assembly. Further analysis is needed in order to explain satisfactorily this pattern which does not quite fit our hypothesis. An analysis by Lemieux (1988) of the regional pattern in the liberal vote during the 1980s, which notes strong liberal support along the southern border of Quebec, may help shed some light on the process.

Finally, there remains the recent case of ADQ. It is usually thought that ADQ is a pure product of rural Quebec, especially of the regions around Quebec City. Indeed these regions strongly supported ADQ in 2003 and even more so in 2007. But computing average distances reminds us that when this party was founded in the 1990s, it was rooted to a certain extent in the far suburbs of Montreal, one of the key leaders coming from Ville Laval. This accounts for the short distance associated to the 1998 election, when ADQ first gathered significant support. Then, from 2003 to 2007, the support given ADQ moves as expected, towards Montreal. The original hypothesis has to be qualified to take into account the fact that in the 1940s and 1950s, the UN was clearly originating in rural Quebec while, in the 1990s and 2000s, ADQ originates both in rural areas and in distant suburbs, including those of Montreal.

This exercise in electoral geography illustrates aspects of the territorial dynamics of societal change in Quebec. Social, cultural, and political changes in the Province feed on the sustained interactions between behaviours, attitudes and values originating in non-metropolitan Quebec, polarised by "orthogenetic" Quebec City, and those being brought into the Province through a gateway metropolis, "heterogenetic" Montreal. At times, the metropolitan influences may dominate, such as during the quiet revolution of the 1960s. At other times, the non-metropolitan influences may gain ground, as may have been the case during the last two decades. These territorial dynamics contribute markedly to the formation of a specific culture and society in Quebec. Without the metropolitan intake, the Province of Quebec might be rather parochial. Without the non-metropolitan input, it might be like the other metropolitan-centered regions of Canada, constantly in danger of being americanized.

Conclusion

In this paper, the notion of spatial interaction has been mobilized in order to shed some light on aspects of societal change in Quebec and Canada. This key geographical notion need not be reduced to gravity formulations. Indeed, if it is conjoined with the notion of social action, it may help identifying spatial processes that are at the hearth of societal change. Firstly, the idea of Canada as an east-west field of interaction is explored, focussing on the differentiating role of provinces and the integrating role of metropolises within this field. Secondly, the historical destinies of Quebec City and Montreal are interpreted in light of these roles. It is suggested that the differentiating role of provinces account in part for the shrinking *umlands* of Quebec City, which becomes a provincial capital at Confederation, and of Montreal, which looses its status of metropolis of Canada, to become the metropolis of Quebec in the 1970s, in the wake of the quiet revolution. Thirdly, the divergent orthogenetic and heterogenetic roles of cities, grounded as they are in proximate spatial interaction for the first one, and long distance interaction for the second one, are called upon in order to interpret recent social change in the province.

This interpretation suggests that the affirmation of Quebec's culture and identity, influenced as it is by the intensifying constructive tension between Montreal and Quebec City, may deepen the differentiation between Quebec and the rest of Canada while, paradoxically, it may also contribute to differentiate Canada from the United States, a contribution implicitly acknowledged by the Canadian government when it recognised, by a vote of Parliament in November 2006, Quebec as a nation. The motion read as follows: "That this House recognize that the Québécois form a nation within a united Canada." One has to notice that this formulation, while quite different, reminds us of the answer humorist Yvon Deschamps has given to the question: "What does Quebec want?" According to Deschamps, Quebeckers simply want "An independent Quebec within a strong Canada".

References

Becker, H. S. / M. M. McCall (eds.), 1990, *Symbolic Interaction and Cultural Study*, Chicago: The University of Chicago Press.
Bunge, W., 1966, *Theoretical Geography*, Lund, Sweden: C.W.K. Gleerup.
Castells, M., 1989, *The Informational City. Information Technology, Economic Restructuring and the Urban-Regional Process*, Cambridge, Mass.: Basil Blackwell.
Clibbon, P. B., 1972, "Evolution and present patterns of the Ecumene of Southern Quebec", in: F. Grenier (ed.) *Québec*, Toronto: University of Toronto Press, 13-30.
Cutler, F. / R. W. Jenkins, 2000, "Where One Lives and What One Thinks: Implications of Rural-Urban Opinion Cleavages for Canadian Federalism" Paper presented at the conference on "The Transformation of Canadian Political Culture and the State of the Federation", Institute of Intergovernmental Affairs, Queen's University, Kingston, Ontario, October 13-14. [Visited on January 11, 2007: http://www.politics.ubc.ca/fileadmin/template/main/images/departments/poli_sci/Faculty/cutler/Cutler-Jenkins_2000.pdf]
Fotheringham, S. / M. O'kelly, *Spatial Interaction Models: Formulations and Applications*, Boston, Kluwer. 1989
Giddens, A., 1984, *The Constitution of Society. Outline of the Theory of Structuration*, Berkeley and Los Angeles: The University of California Press.

Gunderson, M., 1996, "Regional productivity and income convergence in Canada under increasing economic integration", *Canadian Journal of Regional Science / Revue canadienne des sciences régionales*, 19.1, 1-23.

Harris, R. C., 1987, "Regionalism and the Canadian Archipelago", in: L. D. McCann (ed.), *Heartland and Hinterland: A Geography of Canada*, Scarborough, Ontario: Prentice-Hall Canada, 2nd edition, 533-559.

Innis, H. A., 1956, *Essays in Canadian Economic History*, Toronto: University of Toronto Press.

Lemieux, V., 1988, "Les régions et le vote libéral des années 1980" in: *Recherches sociographiques* 29.1, 45-58

Matthews, R. / J. Campbell Davis, 1986, "The comparative influence of region, status, class, and ethnicity on Canadian attitudes and values", in: R. J. Brym (ed) *Regionalism in Canada*, Toronto: Irwin Publishing, 89-122.

McCallum, J., 1980, *Unequal Beginnings: Agriculture and Economic Development in Quebec and Ontario until 1870*, Toronto: University of Toronto Press.

Polèse, M. / R. Shearmur, 2004, "Culture, language, and the location of higher-order service functions: the case of Montreal and Toronto", *Economic Geography*, 80.4, 329-350.

Raynauld, A. / G. Marion / R. Béland, 1966, *La répartition des revenus selon les groupes ethniques au Canada*, Ottawa: Rapport de recherche préparé pour la Commission royale d'enquête sur le bilinguisme et le biculturalisme.

Redfield, R. / M.B. Singer, 1954, "The cultural role of cities" in: *Economic Development and Cultural Change*, Vol. 3, No. 1, 53-73.

Stone, L. O., 1967, *Urban Development in Canada*, Ottawa: Statistics Canada (formerly Dominion Bureau of Statistics).

Simmons, J. / L. D. McCann, 2006, "The Canadian urban system: growth and transition", in: T. Bunting / P. Filion (eds.), *Canadian Cities in Transition*, third edition, Toronto: Oxford University Press, 40-64.

Ullman, E. L., 1980, *Geography as Spatial Interaction*, posthumously edited by R. R. Boyce (Seattle: University of Washington Press).

Villeneuve, P., 1981, "La ville de Québec comme lieu de continuité," *Cahiers de Géographie du Québec*, Vol. 25, No. 64, 49-60.

----, 1988, "Interaction spatiale et paradoxes culturels au Canada", *Canadian Issues / Thèmes canadiens*, Vol. 9, 47-57.

----, 1990, "Les métropoles canadiennes : ambivalences postmodernes" in: *Études canadiennes / Canadian Studies*, Vol. 29, 47-57.

---- / Y. Jodoin / M. Thériault, 2007, "L'énigme de Québec … ou de ses banlieues? Une analyse de géographie électorale, in: *Cahiers de géographie du Québec*, 51 (144), 375-399.

FORUM

PETER KLAUS

Une certaine latino-américanité de la littérature québécoise[1]

Zusammenfassung

Der Titel dieses Artikels könnte auf den ersten Blick überraschen, vor allem wenn man an Voltaires Bonmot von den „quelques arpents de neige" denkt. Doch zeigt uns die Entwicklung der Literatur Kanadas und vor allem Quebecs seit etwa 1980, dass die Ankunft der „Stimmen von anderswo", sei es aus Haiti, Chile, Brasilien, Mexico oder Uruguay, das Markenzeichen einer neuen schöpferischen Polyphonie geworden ist, zumindest in der Literatur. Dank der Werke eines Émile Ollivier (Haiti), Dany Laferrière (Haiti), Gérard Étienne (Haiti), einer Marilù Mallet (Chile) oder eines Sergio Kokis (Brasilien) wird Quebec und seine Literatur von Strömungen beeinflusst, die das für Quebec so charakteristische Syndrom der Abgeschlossenheit und einer gewissen „provinziellen Einengung" in Frage stellen. Die Schriftsteller, die sich als „Agenten der kulturellen Subversion" betrachten, tragen dazu bei, die Fundamente des „Nationalen" von innen her zu untergraben und das „imaginaire" neuen Horizonten, neuen Welten zu öffnen. Montreal wird so zu einem Schnittpunkt literarischer Strömungen, und es hat sich außerdem in den letzten Jahrzehnten zu einem bedeutenden Zentrum haitianischer Literatur der Diaspora entwickelt. Dank der Migranten und ihrer Werke haben sich Kanada und vor allem Quebec mental und über ihr „imaginaire" den Ländern des Südens genähert.

Abstract

The title of this article might surprise at first sight especially when you think of Voltaire's ironical comparison reducing Canada to "quelques arpents de neige". Yet, the evolution undergone by Canadian literature and particularly by the Québécois literature since the 1980s shows that the arrival of those « voices come from elsewhere », either

---

1 Ce texte a été présenté dans le cadre d'une conférence lors de la Semaine de la Francophonie à l'Universidad de Puerto Rico, San Juan, le 13 mars 2008.

from Haiti or from Chili, Brazil, Mexico, or Uruguay has become the trademark of a new form of polyphonic creation, at least in literature. Thanks to the works written by Émile Ollivier (Haiti), Dany Laferrière (Haiti), Gérard Étienne (Haiti), Marilù Mallet (Chili), and Sergio Kokis (Brazil) Québec and its literature are marked by influences that question the syndrome of isolationism and a certain "provincial narrowness" characteristic of Québec until the years of the Quiet Revolution. With their works the above mentioned writers, who consider themselves "agents of cultural subversion", contribute to undermine from within the bases of the "national" and to open the "imaginaire québécois" to other horizons. Montreal has become a cross-road of different literary trends and an important center of Haitian diasporic literature. Thanks to the migrant writers and their works Canada and above all Quebec have come closer mentally to the "imaginaires" of the South.

Remarques préliminaires

Pour donner un avant-goût, voici une nouvelle auteure qui pourrait servir d'exemple:

Maya Ombasic, une Montréalaise née à Mostar en Bosnie-Herzégovine en 1979, connaît elle-même l'expérience de l'exil, elle qui a vécu aussi bien en Suisse qu'à Cuba. Elle a publié en 2007 un petit recueil de nouvelles intitulé *Chroniques du Lézard*, lézard étant le surnom qu'on donne à Cuba à cause de sa forme géographique et de la mutation constante du lézard qui change périodiquement de peau. Les critiques ont été extrêmement élogieuses. Le but de ces remarques préliminaires n'est pas une analyse de ce livre, mais de simplement relever une thématique évoquée dans ce recueil, étant donné qu'elle se recoupe avec l'intitulé, celle du métissage et du syncrétisme, entre autres. Dans la dernière nouvelle du recueil, « Les Yeux de Yemaya », Soledad, une Québécoise, cherche son père cubain qu'elle n'a jamais connu. Soledad Maya est la fille d'une touriste québécoise et d'un Cubain. À travers la rencontre avec un santero, un prêtre de la Santeria qui avait bien connu son père biologique, Soledad apprend beaucoup de choses sur les croyances populaires et leurs origines africaines. Il s'agit d'une véritable initiation à ce syncrétisme religieux combattu par l'Église catholique tout comme le vaudou en Haïti. Et tout comme dans *Passages*, l'œuvre d'Émile Ollivier, Maya Ombasic tente de rapprocher deux imaginaires, deux cultures; chez Ollivier il y a convergence quelque part, chez la jeune auteure ce sont les regards et les destins croisés.

Une certaine latino-américanité

Il peut paraître en effet incongru de parler de la littérature québécoise comme étant latino-américaine ou bien caribéenne. Ceci surtout à une époque où nous assistons à une continuelle mise en question des frontières nationales en littérature et où certains croient proche l'époque d'une « Weltliteratur » dont rêvait Goethe il y a deux siècles. Goethe, dans ses entretiens avec le fidèle Eckermann, son secrétaire, commentait un jour, autour de 1815, l'impression que lui avait faite la lecture du roman d'un auteur chinois. Vis-à-vis de Eckermann, il exprime son étonnement quant à la proximité inattendue véhiculée par ce roman et c'est là qu'il voit proche l'ère d'une « Weltliteratur » ou « littérature universelle ». Qu'en est-il du rêve de Goethe aujourd'hui? La suite de cet article fera ressortir deux tendances principales:

L'une insistera sur le caractère dit « national » d'une production littéraire et l'autre insistera sur le côté subversif de l'évolution littéraire contemporaine par rapport à l'enfermement national. Les deux tendances coexistent encore au Québec aujourd'hui, comme on a pu le constater lors de la polémique autour de *L'Arpenteur et le Navigateur*, texte controversé de Monique LaRue (1996). En parlant de subversion du national, il faut presque automatiquement évoquer le rôle joué par les écrivains et poètes haïtiens dans la littérature québécoise.

La ou les littératures haïtiennes?

Quand on sait où se produit la littérature haïtienne actuellement, c'est-à-dire en Haïti, bien sûr, mais aussi et surtout à Montréal, aux États-Unis et en France, il serait légitime de se demander si le qualificatif « haïtien » convient à toutes ces productions haïtiennes diverses. Le cas d'Haïti est unique et exemplaire en même temps, sur le plan littéraire: c'est le seul cas – peut-être – d'une littérature qui s'est surtout développée en diaspora ces quarante dernières années, grâce (!) aux dictatures des Duvalier. Les Haïtiens eux-mêmes distinguent une « littérature du dedans » et une (?) « littérature du dehors ». Et les auteurs? Revendiquent-ils tous leur « haïtianité » en tant qu'écrivain? Surtout quand on sait que de nombreuses vocations sont nées en dehors d'Haïti, en « exil ».

Au Québec, un groupe important de poètes et écrivains a commencé à s'impliquer dans la création artistique et littéraire dès la deuxième moitié des années 1960: les Haïtiens. Membres de l'élite dans leur pays d'origine, ils ont fui la dictature de François Duvalier et se sont établis en grande partie à Montréal.

Ils sont peut-être passés inaperçus au début parce qu'ils avaient la même langue que le pays d'accueil, le français. Ils sont passés inaperçus peut-être également parce que l'institution littéraire québécoise n'était pas encore prête à percevoir et à intégrer les « voix venues d'ailleurs ». Cependant, la contribution des poètes haïtiens, surtout dans le domaine de la poésie du Québec des années 1960-70, fut assez importante. La seule évocation des noms de Serge Legagneur, de Jean-Richard Laforest et d'Anthony Phelps nous donne un avant-goût de la contribution significative des Haïtiens de cette génération. Inutile d'ajouter que les poètes cités figurent depuis longtemps dans les anthologies de la poésie québécoise.

Depuis, les écrivains, les nouvellistes et romanciers haïtiens se sont fait entendre. Ils ont eu la notoriété grâce à des œuvres médiatiques et médiatisées telles que le roman de Dany Laferrière *Comment faire l'amour avec un Nègre sans se fatiguer*

(1985). Ils ont récolté des prix littéraires à l'instar d'Émile Ollivier pour son roman *Passages* (1991/1994). La littérature québécoise serait sensiblement plus pauvre sans la contribution de ces auteurs. On a dit plus haut que l'arrivée des Haïtiens en littérature québécoise est d'abord passée presque inaperçue parce qu'ils avaient avec les Québécois le français en partage. Avoir la même langue en partage ne signifie pourtant pas que l'on parle la même langue. Régine Robin évoque dans *La Québécoite* justement le choc culturel ressenti encore plus fortement à cause de, ou malgré la langue qu'on a l'impression de partager. L'héroïne de Flora Balzano dans *Soigne ta chute!* (1991) a vécu une situation semblable. Elle n'arrive pas à se faire accepter, à s'intégrer, à devenir québécoise, et pourtant, elle est francophone. Ce n'est pas seulement une question d'accent. Mark Twain a eu ce bon mot par rapport à l'anglais lors d'un séjour à Londres où il aurait dit à ses interlocuteurs anglais: «Tout ce qui nous sépare, c'est la même langue.» Si chez les écrivains francophones comme Régine Robin et Flora Balzano ce sentiment de l'Altérité, d'être autre, en dépit de la même langue, est déjà tellement présent, ce phénomène devrait être encore plus accentué chez les écrivains haïtiens qui arrivent au Québec avec un fort bagage diglossique et une différence culturelle et ethnique non négligeable.

Dans le cas de René Depestre et son poème «Bref éloge de la langue française», les rapports entre l'écrivain et la langue sont imprégnés d'amour (réciproque), la langue s'abandonne à lui telle une femme qui s'abandonne à son amant, et l'écrivain, grâce à cet amour, la façonne à sa manière.

Dans «Frères d'exil» d'Anthony Phelps, il n'est pas explicitement question de l'outil de l'écrivain, la langue, mais il est question d'un choc culturel certain vécu par l'être exilé.

Frères d'exil[2]

Frères d'exil
compagnons aux pieds poudrés
dans nos regards passe une même vision
les souvenirs en cage derrière la vitre opaque
présent comme une dalle
Nous n'avons plus que gestes de fumée
pour conter le temps des kénépiers en fleurs
car nous entrons dans un domaine étrange
de plus en plus tournant dos au Pays
et le verre et l'acier modifient nos croyances

Nous vivons dans une ville

---

2   Poème cité d'après Joubert, J.-L./J. Lecarme/E. Zabone/B.B. Vercier, 1986, *Les littératures francophones depuis 1945*. Paris : Bordas, 149.

> où la chanson du remouleur
> n'est même pas un souvenir
> où nul se rappelle la flûte triangulaire
> dont les notes aiguës
> montaient et descendaient le long de notre enfance
> Nous vivons dans une ville
> qui jamais ne connut cet homme
> doué du pouvoir de créer des étoiles
> en plein midi
> ville de verre ville d'acier.

Phelps nous décrit le contraste vécu par l'exilé dans son nouveau pays d'accueil, hanté par le souvenir malgré le relatif confort, mais où « le verre et l'acier modifient les croyances ». Le nouveau « langage » est celui des gratte-ciel, du givre et de la neige. Il reste la nostalgie, le bagage culturel de l'origine tel la flûte triangulaire de l'enfance, il reste aussi l'absence d'imagination, de magie et d'émerveillement. La ville de verre et d'acier en est dépourvue. Les forces de la raison n'admettent pas les magiciens qui seraient capables de créer des étoiles en plein midi.

Nous avons remarqué le côté positif, sensuel et érotique des rapports de Depestre avec la langue française et nous avons retenu le contraste vécu par l'exilé venu du Sud et arrivé dans le confort et le froid du Nord. Les deux écrivains et les deux sensibilités haïtiennes nous donnent, du moins je le crois, un avant-goût de ce que les écrivains haïtiens apportent de spécifique à la langue et à la littérature québécoise.

Dans son tout premier recueil de nouvelles *La Plage des songes*, aussi bien que dans son roman *Zombi blues*, Stanley Péan (*1966) se sert d'Haïti comme localisation de l'imaginaire de ses protagonistes. Ceux-ci sont pour la plupart des Haïtiens bien intégrés (à première vue) dans la société du pays d'accueil. Mais souvent il suffit d'un événement imprévu, d'une catastrophe qui perturbe le déroulement de la routine quotidienne, pour plonger ses personnages dans le monde de l'irrationnel, du surnaturel, dans le monde de l'horreur, de la folie, du cauchemar et même de la bestialité. Dans le fond, le basculement du comportement de ses personnages d'un monde rationnel et contrôlé vers un univers peuplé d'angoisses, d'horreurs, de dédoublement de la personnalité, etc. trouve une partie de son explication dans les conséquences des tortures, persécutions et autres sévices qu'ont subis certains protagonistes dans le pays de la dictature des Duvalier, où ils ont été les victimes de l'arbitraire absolu, de l'anarchie politique et du pouvoir des sbires du régime, les tontons macoutes. Il est intéressant de noter que c'est justement un jeune Haïtien qui n'a pas connu personnellement la dictature dans son pays d'origine qui utilise les psychodrames et traumatismes causés par de tels régimes afin d'alimenter son imaginaire et de parfaire les stratégies d'un fantastique littéraire imprégné des horreurs des tristes tropiques. Il est à ce que je sache le seul Haïtien – si l'épithète s'applique encore à lui – qui se soit spécialisé dans le fantastique, un genre cher aux écrivains québécois.

Le réalisme merveilleux des Haïtiens

Mais leur véritable impact, les écrivains haïtiens l'ont eu avec l'introduction du « réalisme merveilleux » dans la littérature québécoise contemporaine. Nous savons que nous devons à Alejo Carpentier les assises littéraires du concept de « réalisme merveilleux » tel qu'il l'a présenté dans le prologue à son roman *El reino de este mundo* (1949). Carpentier se démarque par son concept de « surréalisme européen » qu'il définit comme étant artificiellement stérile et auquel manquerait une certaine authenticité. Il oppose au concept européen entre autres la tradition somme toute singulière et particulière de l'Amérique latine et son enracinement dans un contexte plus large, celui des traditions africaines et amérindiennes. Jacques Stephen Alexis va reprendre le flambeau et définir à sa façon le réalisme merveilleux des Haïtiens. Alexis part d'une définition historico-culturelle et découvre, tout comme Carpentier, trois influences majeures constitutives de la culture haïtienne: l'apport indien taïno chemès, l'apport africain et l'apport occidental et plus particulièrement français (v. Alexis 1956, 252). Ce qui aurait pour résultat l'intégration dynamique du merveilleux dans le réalisme. Le merveilleux ainsi défini peut se lire comme une sorte de réalisme élargi qui inclurait des éléments oniriques, magiques, mythiques et légendaires, éléments intégrés quasi naturellement dans le « quotidien vécu », fait qui distingue le réalisme merveilleux du fantastique.

Comment fonctionne le réalisme merveilleux des Haïtiens? À la suite d'Alexis, René Depestre dans son roman *Hadriana dans tous mes rêves*

> nous entraîne dans un monde où l'invraisemblable des péripéties nous éblouit, il alimente notre imagination de faits qui, selon la perception ordinaire, ne peuvent avoir lieu que dans les contes de fées. [...] Tous ces phénomènes nous plongent dans un récit merveilleux qui défie la logique du réel. (Wainwright 1994, 47)

René Depestre n'est pas le seul à déconcerter le lecteur par l'irruption de faits invraisemblables et qui défient toute logique. Gabriel García Márquez nous l'a démontré dans *Cent ans de solitude*, Gérard Étienne l'a démontré avec son roman *Un Ambassadeur macoute à Montréal* (1979) et a récidivé en 2001 avec son avant-dernier roman *La romance en do mineur de Maître Clo* (2000). A travers la thématique choisie dans les romans présentés, il évoque d'un côté les affres des problèmes identitaires de l'être exilé et de l'autre, il fait partie de ce qu'on pourrait appeler avec Jean-Marc Moura « [l']expatriation culturelle, qui semble presque intrinsèque à l'expression littéraire postcoloniale » (Moura 1999, 144).

Résultats éventuels

Avant de conclure cette partie, je voudrais revenir à une autre conception du réalisme merveilleux et évoquer Émile Ollivier qui dit lors d'un entretien avec Suzanne Giguère:

> J'ai appris à lire la réalité haïtienne et caraïbéenne à travers le réalisme merveilleux. Si on comprend bien l'esthétique du réalisme merveilleux, on est tout proche du baroque. L'écrivain cubain Alejo Carpentier qui a proposé ce terme en littérature est lui-même un écrivain baroque. Je crois fondamentalement que la réalité est baroque. Pour les pays et les sociétés post-esclavagistes, antillaises et, dans une large mesure, latino-américaines, qui ont énormément de difficulté à négocier avec les catégories de l'espace et du temps et de la raison, le rêve et la réalité, l'imaginaire et la fiction, le passé, le présent et l'avenir se fusionnent. (Giguère 2001, 64)

Cette fusion du rêve et de la réalité, de l'imaginaire et de la fiction, Émile Ollivier, ce généreux « schizophrène heureux » nous en fait la démonstration dans le roman *Passages*. La narratrice Brigitte nous familiarise avec cette particularité en disant: « Je viens, monsieur, d'un lieu où l'on croit aux signes et aux songes » (Ollivier 1994, 16). Le réalisme merveilleux se distingue du fantastique par le fait qu'il n'accepte pas seulement le surnaturel comme quelque chose qui va de soi, mais il l'intègre dans la vie des protagonistes. L'intrusion du surnaturel, du merveilleux, est partie intégrante du vécu. Son apparition n'est ni questionnée ni problématisée par les protagonistes. C'est pourquoi les narrateurs de *Passages* nous décrivent les événements singuliers qui marquent le pays après l'arrivée de l'homme mystérieux du nom de « Célhomme » mais ils ne les commentent pas et ils ne les questionnent pas. L'histoire de l'eau qui a déserté Port-à-l'Écu après la mort de Célhomme ne sera pas problématisée, seulement évoquée, sans commentaire. De même que le protagoniste Amédée Hosange qui « de sa vie n'avait cessé de se frotter aux esprits de la plaine, aux dieux délurés, aux prêtresses endiablées » (Ollivier 1994, 21).

On apprend aussi qu'il est apparemment pratique courante de servir Dieu d'une main et les *loas* de l'autre « dans cet univers de soupçon et de méfiance ». Il n'est donc pas étonnant de voir le protagoniste Amédée avoir des visions. Dans ses visions, un ange paraît glaive au poing terrassant un caïman géant, rouge feu et lui dit d'abandonner la poussière du pays qu'il traîne sous ses sandales » (Ollivier 1994, 29-30). Une belle image du syncrétisme religieux, cette association avec Saint Georges ou l'Ange Gabriel. Ni l'apparition de l'ange ni ses prédictions ne sont mises en question tout comme plus tard dans la dernière partie du roman lorsque le narrateur nous explique: « Sur 'La Caminante', toute trace du réel s'était effacée, nous n'étions nulle part » (Ollivier 1994, 153).

Les voyageurs de « La Caminante », malheureux « boat-people » qui désespèrent dans leur pays d'origine et qui rêvent d'un paradis terrestre, se trouvent finalement dans un hors-lieu, ce « nulle part » du texte, dans une sorte d'extra-territorialité et une sorte d'extra-temporalité. Là où les *loas* n'ont plus prise.

À travers ses protagonistes, l'Haïtien « de souche » Amédée, le visionnaire, et Normand, l'Haïtien intellectuel et nord-américain, Émile Ollivier nous fait participer ainsi à ce croisement des deux cultures, des deux imaginaires, de l'enchevêtrement des destinées « métissées ». Émile Ollivier aimait parler de la « créolisation » de la société québécoise qu'il voyait dans la traversée de la culture québécoise par le métissage montréalais (Giguère 2001, 47). Ollivier réussit par ce procédé à faire dialoguer deux concepts narratifs aussi bien que deux concepts culturels et sociaux. Les deux imaginaires – celui du Sud et celui du Nord – se chevauchent et s'influencent, tout comme les deux langues, le français et le créole qui dialoguent dans l'imaginaire d'Ollivier qui nous dit: « Je parlerais d'une acclimatisation de la langue française dans l'espace caraïbéen et québécois » (Giguère 2001, 66-67).

Dans la littérature produite par les écrivains haïtiens du Québec, ce n'est pas seulement l'espace caribéen qui investit l'espace nord-américain voire montréalais. D'après Émile Ollivier, « l'irruption de la Caraïbe des origines; pulsions sauvages de la violence lascive des Tropiques, tout cela vibrait sous le regard médusé des archéo-québécois » (Ollivier 1994, 30-31) serait une des réalités « typiques » du migrant, d'être dans le passage.

Les exemples donnés nous auront peut-être fait comprendre plusieurs choses:

Grâce aux démarches des écrivains haïtiens cités, nous assistons à une sorte de « contamination » de l'imaginaire québécois par l'imaginaire caribéen; nous assistons à une transformation du français traversé par d'autres sensibilités et d'autres imaginaires; nous assistons à une subversion culturelle par ces agents venus d'ailleurs qui sapent notre tranquillité et qui introduisent à travers leurs œuvres des témoignages d'une étrangeté séduisante, oui, mais étrangeté inquiétante également lorsqu'on pense à Gérard Étienne et à Stanley Péan.

Passages, le titre du roman d'Émile Ollivier, ne traduirait donc pas seulement le fait de passer d'un endroit à un autre, de passer d'une culture vers une autre; ce pluriel du titre indique aussi la multiplicité des lieux de rencontres, de traversées et d'interconnections. En dehors de sa qualité d'agent subversif, l'écrivain migrant devient ainsi également un précieux passeur culturel dans la mesure où il contribue à introduire le disparate, à « traduire » l'étrange et l'étrangeté, à décloisonner le national et à le transgresser, au moins en littérature.

Józef Kwaterko nous dit dans ce même contexte:

> Ils [les romans haïtiens du Québec] semblent participer au contraire aux redéfinitions identitaires de la littérature québécoise, pénétrée plus que jamais d'hétérogénéité culturelle,et, plus pleinement encore, à

l'expérience contemporaine de transmigration et d'allers-retours, réels ou imaginaires, qui façonne en profondeur notre vision des choses. (Kwaterko 2002, 58)

Le côté latino-américain de la littérature québécoise

Ce qui pourrait intéresser ici, ce sont les interactions éventuelles entre les différentes sphères de l'imaginaire littéraire évoquées et leurs répercussions sur la littérature québécoise. Ceci dit, le concept de l'« Américanité » revêt ici une toute autre importance. Nous ne sommes plus « enfermés » dans les limites d'une « américanité » qui pour certains n'est que « nord-américaine » ou même seulement « états-unienne ». Au contraire: grâce aux écrivains du Sud, ces voix venues d'ailleurs, l'« Américanité » prend une toute autre dimension, une dimension inclusive et intégrante et non pas exclusive, une « américanité » qui va du Nunavut jusqu'à la Patagonie en passant par la Caraïbe, l'Amérique centrale et le Mexique.

On peut retenir grosso modo deux mouvements:

Le mouvement Nord-Sud des écrivains québécois qui s'intéressent à l'Amérique latine et qui chantent l'Amérique latine dans leurs œuvres ou bien ceux qui sont allés sur place pour mettre en œuvre une sorte de coopération. Pensez aux publications de Lake Sagaris concernant la «Chile-Canada connection».[3] On évoquera plus loin le mouvement Sud-Nord de ces interactions provoqué par d'autres phénomènes comme les guerres civiles, les dictatures ou tout simplement la misère. D'ailleurs, l'infatigable Hugh Hazelton a documenté ce genre d'interaction dans l'anthologie qu'il a publié avec Gary Geddes en 1990.

Hazelton est un des pionniers à documenter et à publier la présence d'une littérature latino-américaine au Canada et au Québec. Et en même temps, il nous révèle le côté latino de certains poètes québécois tels que Paul Chamberland, Claude Beausoleil, etc.

Pour revenir à Hugh Hazelton: il a publié en 1989 un petit recueil intitulé *La présence d'une autre Amérique. Anthologie des écrivains latino-américains du Québec*. Le libellé du sous-titre est peut-être un peu ambitieux, car cette anthologie des écrivains latino-américains ne comporte que 62 (!) pages. Même si ce petit livre n'est pas forcément impressionnant par son volume, il contient déjà tout le palmarès d'un véritable Gotha d'une littérature latino-québécoise.

Rien qu'en énumérant les noms de Tito Alvarado (Chili), Jorge Cancino (Chili), Nelly Davis Vallejos (Chili), Jorge Etcheverry (Chili), Gilberto Flores Patiño (Mexique), Alfredo Lavergne (Chili), Jorge Lizama Pizarro (Chili), Maeve López (Uruguay), Juan-Ramón Mijango Mármol (San Salvador), Salvador Torres Saso (El Salvador) et Yvonne América Truque (Colombie), nous donne l'impression d'un univers latino qui se dessine et qui est assez haut en couleur.

---

3   V. Sagaris 1989 et 1994.

Certains des écrivains dont les noms viennent d'être cités font dorénavant partie de l'institution littéraire canadienne ou québécoise tels que Etcheverry et Flores Patiño, sans oublier Tito Alvarado et Salvador Torres Saso. Certains ont entre temps entamé le retour vers le pays d'origine tout comme certains écrivains haïtiens ont essayé de se refaire leurs racines en Haïti, tels que Antony Phelps. Mais souvent il s'avère que ce retour est impossible comme dans le cas d'Anthony Phelps lui-même. Il a dû constater qu'il était devenu un étranger dans son propre pays. Il a fictionnalisé le désarroi d'un impossible retour dans son dernier roman *La contrainte inachevé* (2006; Montréal: Leméac).

Ce qui est intéressant dans ces mouvements, c'est que ces « retornados » sont entre autres à l'origine d'aventures éditoriales canado-québéco-chiliennes. Actuellement on voit également des créations d'éditions québéco-haïtiennes, comme par exemple *Mémoire d'encrier* de Rodney Saint-Éloi (Montréal / Port-au-Prince).

Certes, le choix de Hazelton dans sa petite anthologie peut paraître quelque peu erratique surtout lorsqu'on découvre parmi ces soi-disant écrivains latino-américains du Québec les noms de Claude Beausoleil, Paul Chamberland, de Hugh Hazelton lui-même et de Janou Saint-Denis. Mais Hazelton a peut-être voulu mettre le doigt sur cette terminologie et ses aberrations en présentant un pot-pourri d'écrivains qui ont tous et toutes des rapports plus ou moins marqués avec l'Amérique latine: certains sont d'origine latino-américaine et vivent au Québec et d'autres ont consacré une partie de leur œuvre à des pays d'Amérique latine. Et c'est là justement que réside le mérite de Hugh Hazelton de créer des rapports et de les documenter. Hazelton, lui-même grand voyageur en Amérique latine, a consacré une bonne partie de sa poésie à cette région des Amériques.

Hugh Hazelton et *Latinocanadá*

Dans l'introduction de son livre *Latinocanadá : Ten Latin American Writers of Canada*, Hazelton parle d'une nouvelle littérature émergente au Canada, celle issue de représentants d'une vingtaine de pays latino-américains. Il remarque que ces écrivains et poètes partagent beaucoup de choses avec le pays d'accueil, dont la colonisation, l'implantation d'une culture européenne dans un environnement indigène, une libération graduelle des modes littéraires eurocentriques et la quête de moyens autonomes d'expression. Il note également le fait que de nombreux auteurs arrivés au Canada suite à la chute d'Allende en 1973 et suite aux dictatures militaires, guerres civiles, etc., venaient de pays dotés d'une tradition littéraire plus longue et plus populaire (concernant la vie artistique) que le Canada. Pourquoi le Canada? Une certaine affinité, un intérêt pour le pays qui se veut officiellement bilingue, mais aussi la facilité d'obtenir un visa. Il s'agit de différentes vagues d'immigration venues des différents pays latino-américains (p. ex. le Chili, El Salvador). Une autre constatation est intéressante et vaut la peine d'être retenue: la littérature latino-canadienne est aussi politisée que celle de la Révolution tranquille au Québec. Les auteurs s'impliquent, créent des théâtres (« Spanish language theater companies »). À Montréal, le dramaturge chilien Rodrigo Gonzalez crée un théâtre pour enfants. Alberto Kurapel, également Chilien, excelle dans ce qu'on appelle le *performance theater* (inspiré du *Living Theater* aux Etats-Unis). Kurapel crée des pièces bilingues espagnol-français. D'autres artistes comme Marilù Mallet et Jorge Fajardo se consacrent à l'art cinématographique, et cela jusqu'à aujourd'hui. Différentes maisons d'éditions latino-américaines voient le jour à Montréal. En 1982 paraît la première anthologie d`écriture latino-américaine au Canada, en 1995 Montréal vit quatre événements de « Spanish-poetry readings ». La vingtaine de nationalités latino-américaines concentrées à Montréal publient dans les années 1980 la première anthologie au Québec *Palabra de poeta*, en 1988, publiée par la Mexican Association of Canada. En 1992 paraît la première anthologie de femmes hispanophones du Canada: *Antologia de la poesia femenina latinoamericana en Canada* (traduction française en 1993).

Plusieurs revues hispanophones voient le jour à Montréal, dont *La Botella Verde, Ruptures. La revue des Trois Amériques*, publiées en quatre langues par le poète haïtien de Montréal Edgar Gousse. Dans d'autres villes, par exemple à Ottawa, les activités éditoriales sont peut-être encore plus importantes qu'à Montréal.

Revenons aux écrivains:

Hugh Hazelton dans son livre *Latinocanadá* nous présente – entre autres – l'écrivain Pablo Urbanyi. Pour ceux qui ne connaîtraient pas Pablo Urbanyi: c'est un écrivain né en Hongrie, d'où il est parti à l'âge de 6 ou 7 ans. Il a grandi en Argentine et il vit actuellement et depuis assez longtemps à Ottawa. Un cas typique d'« écrivain migrant »? Voici la citation: « Although he currently lives in Ottawa, Pablo Urbanyi is one of the most active writers of satirical fiction in Argentina today » (Hazelton 2006, 198). Pablo Urbanyi est l'auteur de nombreux livres, dont plusieurs romans policiers: *L'idée fixe* (Montréal 1998), *Un Revolver pour Mack* (Montréal 1992, traduit de l'espagnol argentin). Depuis, il a reçu plusieurs prix ou a été finaliste: en 2004, Premio Somos pour *Una Epopeya de nuestro tiempo, o como el mondo se convirtiría en una fabula*, un autre prix argentin très prestigieux en 1994 pour *Silver*, traduction anglaise, un événement social à Montréal (Ambassade de Hongrie, 50 ans depuis le départ des refugiés hongrois). Voilà à première vue une attribution « nationale » inattendue qui coïncide quelque peu avec ce qu'on a vu plus haut avec l'apport des écrivains haïtiens. Mais connaissez-vous beaucoup d'écrivains qui marquent leur sphère littéraire d'origine à partir de leur exil, leur nouvelle patrie? Concernant son appartenance, Pablo Urbanyi donnerait probablement la même réponse que l'écrivain haïtiano-parisien Jean-Claude Charles: « J'écris, c'est ma nationalité. »

D'autres exemples

Gloria Escomel, née en Uruguay, s'établit au Québec en 1967, écrit en français, malgré le fait que presque toute son œuvre se situe dans la région du Rio de la Plata.

Sergio Kokis, de Rio de Janeiro, quitte le Brésil de la dictature et s'installe en 1964, d'abord en France et ensuite au Québec. Il vit à Montréal où il est connu comme peintre et où il a publié une douzaine de romans depuis 1994. Son premier roman *Le pavillon des miroirs* a obtenu quatre prix littéraires, fait qui a éveillé la jalousie de certains écrivains québécois « pure laine ». Marilù Mallet, de Santiago de Chile, cinéaste, a publié deux recueils de nouvelles: *Les Compagnons de l'horloge-pointeuse* (Montréal 1981), et *Miami Trip. Nouvelles* (1986). Dans ces nouvelles, Mallet thématise aussi bien les traumatismes vécus par les victimes des différentes dictatures (Chili et Pologne) et leur difficile intégration dans un autre contexte culturel et linguistique. Et elle thématise également l'espoir qui réside dans une éducation plurilingue, telle que vécue par un jeune protagoniste dont les parents sont des réfugiés sud-américains, rescapés d'une dictature

Il faudrait s'arrêter quelques instants sur une petite partie de la production latino-québécoise de ces dernières années. Lorsqu'on jette un premier regard sur la production littéraire de ce qu'on appelle à tort ou à raison « écritures migrantes », on constate grosso modo deux tendances: d'un côté les auteurs font revivre dans leurs œuvres le pays d'origine qu'ils décrivent avec nostalgie et dont ils embellissent souvent le rapport à la réalité. Ils y situent une grande partie de leurs textes (exemples: René Depestre, Émile Ollivier dans ses débuts et Dany Laferrière en grande partie, Stanley Péan, Marilù Mallet). De l'autre côté, on constate que ces auteurs nés non-québécois situent leurs œuvres au Québec même, à Montréal, et thématisent des sujets tels que la violence juvénile dans les grandes métropoles. Certains troublent la tranquillité de la métropole du Nord par l'introduction d'une force subversive venue du Sud. Exemple: Gérard Étienne et les forces néfastes du passé. D'un côté, l'imaginaire de l'écrivain est nourri en grande partie par la mémoire, collective et individuelle et par une certaine nostalgie d'un monde perdu. De l'autre, l'écrivain émigré puise son inspiration sur place, dans le pays d'accueil. Tout comme Marilù Mallet l'a fait dans certaines de ses nouvelles. (*How are you?*, *La mutation*) où les expériences socio-économiques et culturelles des immigrés reflètent une expérience filtrée par ce double patrimoine culturel du vécu des personnages. Deux auteurs latino-québécois ont justement fait ceci:

Maurizio Segura, originaire du Chili, s'est approprié le sujet de la difficile cohabitation multiethnique des jeunes venus de pays comme le Chili, Haïti ou bien le Vietnam. *Côte-des-Nègres* (1998) est un roman que certains qualifient de réaliste, parce qu'il offre un portrait du monde des jeunes immigrants dans la métropole québécoise. C'est aussi « le portrait d'une adolescence livrée à elle-même, car l'héritage qui lui était destiné a été dilapidé, s'est perdu entre terre d'origine et terre d'accueil » (4e de couverture). Le romancier récupère une thématique du déracinement et de la perte identitaire, de l'entre-deux et de nulle part. Il nous fait vivre le désarroi de ces jeunes qui jouent aux durs mais qui sont plutôt à la recherche d'une communauté protectrice, des adolescents qui craignent le rejet et la solitude: une adolescence qui se cherche, qui voudrait enfin arriver quelque part.

Daniel Castillo Durante (Argentin), professeur à l'Université d'Ottawa et écrivain, a obtenu le Prix Trillium 2007, la plus haute distinction littéraire de l'Ontario pour son roman *La Passion des nomades* (Montréal 2006). Un peu sur les traces du grand écrivain Borges, Castillo Durante nous présente un roman quelque peu énigmatique. Juan Carlos Olmos, le consul argentin à Montréal a été abattu par sa maîtresse Ana Stein. À l'annonce de cette nouvelle, son fils Gabriel accourt au Québec afin d'élucider la mort du père haï. Ana Stein, dont il fait la connaissance par hasard et dont il tombe amoureux au point de l'épouser, le tue au même endroit et de la même façon que son père. L'intrigue sert de tremplin aux réflexions des relations père-fils et sur les variantes du schéma œdipien, sur le lien entre crime et passion, et surtout sur le statut de l'immigré au Québec (Ana porte en permanence un bracelet électronique à la cheville) et de son regard sur le pays d'accueil.

Face à ce tableau quasi socio-culturel avec ces existences travaillées par les conséquences du déracinement, l'écrivain Gilberto Flores Patiño dans son roman *Le dernier comte de Cantabria* (1998) procède tout à fait différemment.

D'abord, Gilberto Flores Patiño n'a pas encore coupé les ponts avec son pays d'origine, le Mexique. Dans une interview avec Suzanne Giguère, il met justement l'accent sur la présence du Mexique dans son œuvre et son imaginaire. Son inspiration lui est livrée par sa ville d'origine San Miguel de Allende et son passé colonial. C'est là que se situent une grande partie de ses textes, dont le roman *Le dernier comte de Cantabria*. Conteur né, toute évocation de son passé se transforme en contes où priment le merveilleux, le fantastique, l'onirisme et un perpétuel déchaînement de son imaginaire. (Curieusement, Simon Nodier, le héros du roman d'Anthony Phelps évoqué plus haut, a également vécu entre Montréal et une petite ville de l'État de Guanajato au Mexique, tout comme Gilberto Flores Patiño dans sa vie réelle.)

Dans *Le dernier comte de Cantabria*, son personnage principal Arzate est hanté par la communauté qui habite sa mémoire. Sa mémoire le tourmente parce qu'il se souvient. Et dans ses souvenirs il évoque Borges et une de ses œuvres qui s'intitule *Enquêtes* (en espagnol *Otras inquisiciones*). Cette évocation n'est pas fortuite. Le personnage lit ce livre et il jongle avec le fantastique. Dans certains passages du roman, le lecteur ne saura jamais si telle situation décrite, cette rencontre charnelle avec Angelita a vraiment eu lieu ou si elle est un pur fruit des fantasmes du personnage. Flores Patiño se dit aussi redevable au « réalisme merveilleux ». Il dit dans cette interview : « J'ai connu le merveilleux à travers les mots » ; ce furent surtout les mots du grand-père qui transformèrent tout en un monde de féerie fabuleuse. La complexité narrative du roman amène une multiplication du « je », un dédoublement de la personnalité et une multiplication du « jeu », lorsqu'il évoque le jeu de miroirs dans son texte ou bien un autre jeu: « Près des bords du jeu d'échecs, un homme écrit (moi?) » (Giguère 2001, 170-171). Ces reflets d'une autre réalité, chers par exemple à Maupassant.

Ce roman déconstruit jette d'emblée le doute quant à la perception du lecteur de ce qu'on pourrait appeler la trame du récit. Il n'est certainement pas fortuit que le personnage principal, Arzate soit bibliothécaire, un bibliothécaire qui est entouré et peut-être même dominé par ces fragments de rêves et de réalités que véhiculent les livres. Ce n'est pas un hasard non plus que ce roman illustre dans le cas de son personnage la « puissance obstinée d'une mémoire » (4ᵉ de couverture), une mémoire dont les fragments se heurtent comme autant de miroirs sur la réalité de sa vie de bibliothécaire à San Miguel de Allende. Flores Patiño manie avec génie et adresse les « jeux savants d'ombre et de lumière » (4ᵉ de couverture) qui révèlent les mécanismes de l'oubli et qui mettent un homme en abîme et « lui dictent inconsciemment sa vie » (4ᵉ de couverture). Le travail de la mémoire prend des allures énigmatiques, vu que le narrateur joue avec les identités, avec les personnages et avec la linéarité du récit. Ce n'est que vers la fin que le lecteur croit déceler la « vraie histoire ».

Mais le roman se termine sur cette hésitation du personnage qui ne sait plus si sa rencontre avec Angelita a vraiment eu lieu: « Quand sa mère sera endormie, je la supplierai de me dire si ce fut elle ou un rêve. Si elle est venue, je vais la prier de revenir; s'il s'est agi d'un rêve, j'attendrai qu'il se répète et ne me réveillerai plus jamais » (Flores Patiño 1998, 143).

Conclusion

Ce petit échantillon de ce croisement littéraire et de ces interactions entre les différents imaginaires qui se fraient un chemin dans la littérature québécoise contemporaine tend à prouver que la littérature québécoise contemporaine a effectivement surmonté le syndrome de l'enfermement dont il a été question plus haut. Grâce à l'ouverture vers les Amériques que les Québécois ont entreprise à partir des années 1980 et grâce à l'apport des écrivains originaires des Caraïbes et de l'Amérique latine, la production littéraire du Québec a connu depuis environ 1980 un enrichissement certain par ce métissage des imaginaires. Le résultat en est plus que concluant, et il reste à espérer que la semence de ce croisement des cultures et des imaginaires germera encore longtemps et contribuera à ce que l'on considère le Québec (et le Canada) comme un laboratoire vivant dans le domaine d'une littérature qui fait fi de l'enfermement national.

Bibliographie

Alexis, Jacques Stephen, 1956, « Du réalisme merveilleux des Haïtiens », *Présence africaine. Revue culturelle du monde noir*, numéro spécial (Le 1ᵉʳ Congrès International des Écrivains et Artistes Noirs, Paris-Sorbonne 19-22 septembre 1956), nᵒˢ 8-9-10, 245-271.
Balzano, Flora, 1991, *Soigne ta chute*, Montréal: xyz éditeur.
Carpentier, Alejo, 1949, *El reino de este Mundo*, Mexico.
Depestre, René, 1988, *Hadriana dans tous mes rêves*, Paris: Gallimard.

----, 1990, « Bref éloge de la langue française », *Dires. La revue du Cégep de Saint-Laurent*, 8.1, VII.
Étienne, Gérard, 1974/1989, *Le Nègre crucifié*, Montréal : Nouvelle Optique et Genève.
----, 1979, *Un Ambassadeur macoute à Montréal*, Montréal: Nouvelle Optique.
----, 1983, *Une Femme muette*, Paris: Silex.
----, 1987/1989, *La Reine Soleil levée*, Montréal: Métropolis.
Flores Patiño, Gilberto, 1998, *Le dernier comte de Cantabria*, Montréal : Fidès.
Giguère, Suzanne, 2001, *Passeur culturels. Une littérature en mutation. Entretiens*, Québec : Les Presses de l'Université Laval.
Hazelton, Hugh / Gary Geddes (dirs.), 1990, *Compañeros. An Anthology of Writings about Latin America*, Dunvegan, Ontario: Cormorant Books.
Hazelton, Hugh, 2007, *Latinocanadá. A critical study of ten Latin American Writers of Canada*, Montreal: McGill-Queen's University Press.
Hoffmann, Léon-François, 1991, « Roman haïtien des dix dernières années », *Notre Librairie. Revue du Livre: Afrique, Caraïbes, Océan Indien. Dix ans de littérature 1980-90. II: Caribes-Océan Indien*, 104, 26-36.
Jonassaint, Jean, 1986, *Le pouvoir des mots, les maux du pouvoir. Des romanciers haïtiens de l'exil*, Montréal / Paris: Dérives / Arcantère.
Kamga, Osée, 2001, « Les racines du Nègre », *ICI* (13 au 20 décembre 2001), 45.
Kwaterko, Józef, 2002, « L'imaginaire diasporique chez les romanciers haïtiens du Québec », in: Robert Dion (dir.), *Le Québec et l'ailleurs. Aperçus culturels et littéraires*, Bayreuther Frankophonie Studien / Études francophones de Bayreuth 5, Bremen: Palabres Editions, 43-59.
Laferrière, Dany, 1985, *Comment faire l'amour avec un Nègre sans se fatiguer?* Montréal: vlb éditeur.
Laroche, Maximilien, 1985, « Qu'est-ce que la littérature haïtienne? », *Présence francophone*, 26, 77-91.
Moura, Jean-Marc, 1999, *Littératures francophones et théorie postcoloniale*, Paris: PUF.
Ollivier, Émile, 1991/1994, *Passages,* Montréal: L'Hexagone/Paris: Le Serpent à plumes.
Paratte, Henri-Dominique, 1980, « Gérard Étienne, Un Ambassadeur macoute à Montréal », *Présence francophone*, 20, 188-192.
Péan, Stanley, 1988, *La Plage des songes et autres récits d'exil. Huit nouvelles fantastiques*, Montréal: CIDICHA.
----, 1996, *Zombi Blues*. Montréal: La Courte Échelle.
Phelps, Anthony, 1976, « Frères d'exil », in : *Motifs pour le temps saisonnier. Poèmes*, Paris: P. J. Oswald.
Robin, Régine, 1983, *La Québécoite*, Montréal: xyz éditeur.
Sagaris, Lake, 1989, « The Chile-Canada Connection, or the Future of Fiction », *Canadian Fiction Magazine*, 67/68, 234-235.
----, 1994, « Countries like Drawbridges. Chilean-Canadian Writing Today », *Canadian Literature/ Littérature Canadienne*, 142/143, 12-20.
Simon, Sherry, 1990, « The Geopolitics of Sex, or Signs of Culture in the Quebec Novel », *Essays on Canadian Writing*, 40, 44-49.
Sutherland, Ronald, 1985, « The Caribbean Connexion in Canadian Literature », *Yearbook in English Studies*, XV, 227-238.
Wainwright, Danielle, 1994, « Le réalisme merveilleux chez René Depestre », *Revue Francophone*, 9.2, 45-52.

Helga Elisabeth Bories-Sawala

Accommodements raisonnables, laïcité républicaine ou mosaïque fédérale: les défis de l'interculturalité au Québec, en France et en Allemagne

Zusammenfassung
Anlässlich der politischen Debatte um die « accommodements raisonnables » in Québec untersucht der Beitrag den Umgang mit kulturell und religiös motivierten Konflikten zwischen Minderheiten, speziell Migranten, und der jeweiligen Mehrheitsgesellschaft in Frankreich, Deutschland und Québec. Es erweist sich, dass einerseits die aktuellen Kontexte und konkreten Themen (Kopftuch, Moscheenbau, Kruzifixe) so unterschiedlich sind wie der von gegensätzlichen historischen Erfahrungen geprägte juristische und politische Rahmen, insbesondere das Verhältnis von Staat und Kirche. Andererseits sind sowohl die Konflikte wie die Problemlösungen durchaus vergleichbar. Kulturelle Vielfalt fördert überall die Diskussion um gesellschaftliche Werte und Normen. Verweigerung von Integration und Ausländerfeindlichkeit sind in allen drei Gesellschaften Ausdruck wachsender Prekarität, bleiben aber Minderheitenphänomene. Besonders aber stehen hier wie dort kulturelle Konflikte im Zentrum der medialen Aufmerksamkeit und weniger die eigentlichen Probleme. Diskriminierung am Arbeitsplatz und beim Wohnen, Schulversagen und Ausländerfeindlichkeit sind aber durch eine bloße Anerkennung kultureller Differenz nicht zu lösen.

Abstract
In light of the current political debate in Québec about 'reasonable accommodation', this study examines the treatment of culturally and religiously motivated conflicts between minorities (in particular immigrants) and the respective majorities in France, Germany and Québec. It is found that both the present context and the specific issues (for instance headscarves, the building of mosques, the display of crucifixes) differ substantially between these three societies. The legal and political frameworks, which reflect opposite historical experiences, are just as different, especially the relationship between church and state. By contrast, the arising conflicts as well as the proposed solutions are remarkably similar. Thus, in all three cases, cultural diversity promotes discussion of social norms and values. Reluctance to integrate and xenophobia reflect an increasing feeling of insecurity in some small groups within both immigrant commu-

nities and the majorities. Critically, in all three societies, media attention is focused on cultural conflicts rather than on the genuine problems. However, discrimination by employers and landlords, failure in school, and xenophobia cannot be solved by merely recognising cultural differences.

Les défis auxquels on est confronté en abordant le sujet sont multiples. Tout d'abord, la réflexion sur des sujets encore chauds et débattus avec ferveur sur la scène publique est susceptible d'être utilisée par les uns ou les autres et elle peine souvent à trouver un angle d'approche distancié, car le citoyen-chercheur prend inévitablement parti dans ces processus.

Deuxièmement, la façon de traiter des différences culturelles et sociales liées à l'immigration met en cause, dans chacune des sociétés, une multitude d'acteurs dont les buts, les attitudes et les perceptions sont différents. Les conceptions débattues de façon controversée par les spécialistes des sciences humaines et sociales, les intellectuels, les acteurs sur le terrain ou encore la classe politique sont complexes. Les expériences sur le terrain, les finalités politiques à plus ou moins long terme, les résultats scientifiques, les partis pris idéologiques et les attitudes forgées par la conscience historique ne convergent pas. Il y a notamment un fossé entre l'échange d'idées auquel participent les « milieux éclairés » qui manient aisément les concepts à la mode tels que « multiculturalisme », « interculturalité », « citoyenneté » « communautarisme », et la majorité de la population qui, sans toujours être représentée dans les médias, n'en réagit pas moins, et parfois par des réflexes de rejet, aux défis posés par la présence d'étrangers. La simple prise de parole démocratique, comme cela a été le cas au Québec lors de la récente « crise des accommodements raisonnables » est plutôt l'exception. Les formes par lesquelles les craintes et malaises s'expriment en Europe, en période de crise économique notamment, sont plus inquiétantes: vote d'extrême droite, violences xénophobes, émeutes dans les banlieues.

Bref, étudier comment chacune de nos sociétés « s'accommode » de la diversité est certes très enrichissant pour comprendre pourquoi elle propose telle ou telle solution, en fonction de son passé et des tensions actuelles qui la régissent, mais c'est également s'avancer sur un terrain miné.

Troisièmement, devant la complexité des processus, seule une approche pluridisciplinaire pourra offrir une clé de lecture adéquate. Les cadres juridiques sont une des formes tangibles dans lesquelles une société codifie ses attitudes sur un sujet donné, en fonction des valeurs qui la déterminent, mais il ne faudrait pas isoler ce domaine des autres. Le droit agit fortement sur la société en posant les règles que tout un chacun doit respecter, et les décisions des tribunaux ont à trancher entre des valeurs en cas de concurrence. Mais il n'est est pas moins vrai que la jurisprudence est elle-même le fruit d'évolutions sociétales et ainsi sujette à un processus constant où les convictions non seulement de la classe politique « éclairée », mais également de la majorité silencieuse, le peuple souverain, pèsent de leur poids. Il est donc évident qu'il sera ici question d'« accommodements raisonnables » largement au-delà du sens juridique étroit du terme[1], à l'instar de la commission Bouchard-Taylor et que cette notion recouvrira tout ce qui été débattu sous ce vocable, au Québec et ailleurs.

Enfin, étendre le regard à trois sociétés, alors que chacune d'entre elles présente déjà une réalité suffisamment complexe, n'est-ce pas se compliquer inutilement la tâche en ajoutant à tous ces défis celui de la comparaison ? Car si, bien entendu, les questions qui s'y posent paraissent comparables, les manières de les appréhender ne sont qu'en partie semblables. Le clivage entre les « milieux éclairés » et les « majorités silencieuses » existe dans les trois cas, par exemple, mais ces rapports ne sont pas les mêmes, le rôle des médias est différent, ainsi que l'échiquier des formations politiques en place et la façon dont les tensions se répercutent sur celui-ci. Les défis de l'immigration se posent dans des termes assez différents en Europe et en Amérique du Nord. La composition de l'immigration, son histoire, ainsi que la place que lui attribue la conscience collective dans chacun des trois pays leur sont assez particulières. Par exemple, ce n'est que récemment que la définition de la citoyenneté est passé d'une notion ethnique à une conception civique, avec l'émergence d'une identité nouvelle québécoise outre Atlantique. En revanche, l'opposition entre le droit du sol français et le droit du sang qui régnait jusqu'à très récemment en Allemagne est plutôt ancienne. Autre exemple : le rejet largement répandu du « multiculturalisme » au Québec et en France, tandis que la gauche allemande le prône plutôt comme un modèle à imiter, contre des milieux traditionalistes qui rejettent ce concept, la peur du « communautarisme » se mêlant alors à une xénophobie latente ou explicite.

Même les milieux intellectuels ne s'entendent donc pas facilement au-delà des frontières. Les médias portent souvent un regard sur les situations dans d'autres pays soit pour souligner, parfois de manière hâtive, l'universalité du phénomène, soit pour dénoncer les contrastes (comme la presse allemande à propos de l'interdiction du foulard en France), ou pour les ériger en modèle (à propos du multiculturalisme canadien). Quant à la « majorité silencieuse », elle s'intéresse à peine à ces débats théoriques. Ses attitudes et réactions visent un cadre bien plus concret: le quartier, la ville ou la région, tout au plus - mais plus rarement - le cadre national.

Raison de plus de ne pas entreprendre la comparaison dans le but d'« exporter » des solutions toutes faites. Si elle a une valeur heuristique indéniable – très souvent un regard extérieur fait ressortir des traits profonds passés inaperçus car excessive-

---

1   Cf. Myriam Jézéquel, 2007, dir. *Les accommodements raisonnables: quoi, comment, jusqu'où. Des outils pour tous*. Cowansville, QC ; Yvon Blais, notamment les définitions dans l'introduction (VII-XI). Pour un premier regard comparatif : Yolande Geadah, 2007, *Accommodements raisonnables. Droit à la différence et non différence des droits*. VLB éditeur.

ment familiers – il n'en reste pas moins vrai que chaque société doit trouver et négocier les solutions appropriées à ses réalités.

La principale difficulté tient évidemment en l'espace qui m'est imparti pour traiter d'un sujet qui remplirait aisément un semestre de cours. Je tâcherai néanmoins de prendre le recul nécessaire à la comparaison, tout en illustrant mon propos par quelques exemples concrets, et de trouver des éléments de réponse aux questions suivantes: Quels ont été les enjeux principaux du débat dans les trois cas ? En quels domaines y a-t-il convergence, ou au contraire spécificité nationale ? Et enfin, cette vue d'ensemble de trois sociétés différentes permet-elle une conclusion généralisable ?

Trois rapports, trois situations, une même priorité : combattre les discriminations

Tout d'abord, il convient de signaler l'existence de trois importants rapports mandatés par les gouvernements respectifs, préparés par des commissions sur la base de vastes consultations qui situent assez bien les principaux enjeux et les termes de chacun des trois contextes. Le dernier en date est bien entendu celui de la Commission de consultation sur les pratiques d'accommodement reliées aux différences culturelles sous le titre de « Fonder l'avenir. Le temps de la conciliation » présenté par Gérard Bouchard et Charles Taylor, au Québec. Appelés à « répondre aux expressions de mécontentement qui se sont élevées dans la population sur ce qu'on a appelé les 'accommodements raisonnables' », le rapport retrace les principales étapes du débat, en constatant d'importantes distorsions entre les événements réels et la perception véhiculée par les médias, pour ensuite se consacrer à une analyse du modèle d'intégration socioculturelle mis en place au Québec depuis les années 1970, dont les auteurs constatent qu'il « fonctionne plutôt bien » (113).[2] Après une ample discussion de plusieurs sources de conflits, notamment dans le domaine de la santé et de l'éducation et en comparant la situation du Québec à celle qui prévaut dans plusieurs pays européens, le rapport propose une série de principes et de mesures concrètes qui ont ensuite fait l'objet de débats controversés, tout comme le constat d'un « braquage identitaire » (186) auprès de certains Québécois qu'il explique ainsi: en réveillant « la mémoire du Canadien français colonisé, humilié [...], les demandes d'ajustement religieux ont fait craindre pour l'héritage le plus précieux de la Révolution tranquille, tout spécialement l'égalité hommes-femmes et la laïcité » (Ibid.). « Membres d'une petite nation minoritaire en Amérique, leur culture porte la mémoire vive des humiliations, des oppressions subies et vaincues, des luttes pour la survie, des combats qu'ils ont dû mener seuls, sans jamais pouvoir s'appuyer sur un allié extérieur » (242). C'est ce genre de remarques qui a beaucoup plus retenu l'attention[3] que les appels répétés à ne pas perdre de vue « qu'il ne sert

---

2 «Dans l'ensemble, les rapports interculturels sont bons, relativement harmonieux même» (222).
3 Cf. le débat entre Bernard Descôteaux, Michel David, Jacques Beauchemin, Mathieu Bock-Côté, Daniel Marc Weinstock, Yves Boisvert, Simon Couillard, Paul Cauchon et le Français Jean Baubé-

à rien de parler d'interculturalisme si on ne passe pas à l'action du côté de l'insertion à l'emploi et de la lutte contre la discrimination » (259) et l'affirmation que « quels que soient les choix que notre société fera pour conjuguer les différences culturelles et concevoir un avenir commun, ceux-ci seront en grande partie voués à l'échec si plusieurs conditions ne sont pas réunies », dont voici la première: « Notre société doit lutter contre le sous-emploi, la pauvreté, les inégalités, les conditions de vie inadmissibles, les diverses formes de discrimination » (22).

Avant que la controverse sur les accommodements raisonnables au Québec arrive à son apogée, l'Assemblée nationale française avait clos un débat sur le foulard à l'école publique , qui avait duré 15 ans, en votant à une large majorité (494 contre 36) pour son interdiction.[4] Le rapport de la « Commission de réflexion sur l'application du principe de laïcité dans la République » (rapport Stasi) avait précédé[5] et l'opinion n'en a retenu souvent que son plaidoyer pour une telle loi. Celle-ci avait été revendiquée d'ailleurs par la quasi-totalité du monde enseignant en « désarroi » (57) et elle est justifiée par le souci de protéger la liberté de conscience de tous les citoyens (16), d'affirmer l'égalité entre l'homme et la femme (15) et de s'armer contre les agissements de « groupes organisés qui testent la résistance de la République » (43). Ce qui est passé largement inaperçu, et dans la perception et dans les conséquences politiques qui ont suivi, ce sont les autres éléments de ce texte complexe et nuancé qui fait plus d'une fois référence aux « accommodements raisonnables » québécois, et qui souligne constamment que la laïcité doit avant tout rassembler (50) et assurer le respect de la diversité de la société[6], qu'elle va de pair

---

rot (et bien d'autres) depuis fin mai et la longue réponse de Gérard Bouchard dans *Le Devoir* du 10 juin 2008.

4   Loi n° 2004-228 du 15 mars 2004 encadrant, en application du principe de laïcité, le port de signes ou de tenues manifestant une appartenance religieuse dans les écoles, collèges et lycées publics.

5   Rapport au président de la République, remis le 11 décembre 2003 (La documentation française 2004). Ce rapport avait également été adopté à l'unanimité moins une abstention. Alain Touraine, de longue date hostile à toute mesure coercitive contre le foulard et qui s'est rallié à la (presque) unanimité de la commission Stasi. Il s'en explique ainsi: « Et moi, qui ai constamment dans le passé défendu les jeunes femmes voilées, je veux faire comprendre pourquoi, en signant le rapport de la commission Stasi, j'ai gardé les mêmes idées. (…) Mais, pour prendre position dans une situation concrète, il faut ajouter que nous sommes confrontés à la montée d'un islamisme radical qui attaque ce que j'ai défini comme le noyau de la modernité et qui me semble tout à fait éloigné des projets de beaucoup de femmes voilées. » Et il ajoute: «Je fais l'hypothèse que la loi peut arrêter les mouvements islamistes qui veulent porter atteinte à l'organisation scolaire et hospitalière, mais qu'elle conduira à plus de souplesse, et non à plus de répression, face aux signes personnels d'une foi ou même d'une appartenance.» *Libération* du 7 janvier 2004.

6   « La laïcité d'aujourd'hui est mise au défi de forger l'unité tout en respectant la diversité de la société. Le cadre laïque peut être le lieu de conciliation de cette double exigence. Il doit se donner les moyens de faire coexister sur un même territoire des individus qui ne partagent pas les mêmes convictions, au lieu de les juxtaposer en une mosaïque de communautés fermées sur elles-mêmes et mutuellement exclusives » (Rapport Stasi, 18).

avec la liberté d'expression, y compris religieuse, et serait apte à intégrer en son sein « le plein épanouissement intellectuel de la pensée islamique à l'abri des contraintes du pouvoir » (16). Une longue réflexion historique suivie par des comparaisons internationales soulignent que la laïcité n'est ni immuable ni absolue, qu'elle a su s'« accommoder » aux circonstances, même si la France l'a élevée au rang de principe constitutionnel. Mais surtout, d'importants passages du texte sont consacrés aux difficultés d'intégration des immigrés, aux conditions de vie déplorables et aux discriminations inacceptables, aux regains du racisme anti-maghrébin et de l'antisémitisme, aux violences et tentations extrémistes. Ces constatations sont suivies par des recommandations concrètes pour les combattre. Car « la laïcité n'a de sens et de légitimité que si l'égalité des chances est assurée en tout point du territoire, les diverses histoires qui fondent notre communauté nationale reconnues et les identités multiples respectées » (52). Or, dans l'importante liste des recommandations, c'est surtout l'interdiction du port du foulard par les élèves des écoles publiques qui a été mise en pratique.

L'Allemagne, dont les médias propagent largement « l'image d'une France 'liberticide' » (57), et où le concept de laïcité est inconnu, se retrouve à son tour obsédée par les foulards, mais cette fois sur les têtes des enseignantes (nous y reviendrons). Mais il fallait d'abord trancher deux autres questions. Ayant vécu depuis l'arrêt officiel du recrutement de travailleurs étrangers en 1974 (comme la France) dans l'illusion publiquement proclamée du « nous ne sommes pas un pays d'immigration », l'Allemagne, au tournant du millénaire, a fini par prendre enfin conscience de la réalité de l'immigration, mais aussi du fait que pour des raisons démographiques et de manque de main-d'œuvre hautement qualifiée, son économie avait intérêt à ouvrir de nouveau ses frontières, du moins au compte-gouttes. Les conclusions du rapport de la commission Süssmuth[7] ainsi que de celle ayant pris sa relève[8] et allant dans ce sens furent cependant difficiles à faire passer dans l'arène politique et la très timide loi sur l'immigration ne vit le jour que cinq ans plus tard[9], après de très vives oppositions, comme cela avait été le cas également pour le nouveau code de la nationalité allemande, entré en vigueur en 2000 et facilitant l'accès à la citoyenneté pour les enfants d'origine immigrée en adoptant le principe du droit du sol.

A l'écart de l'attention publique, cependant, l'office gouvernemental sur la migration et l'intégration qui existe depuis 1978 publie régulièrement des rapports sur la situation des étrangers en Allemagne et ne cesse de dénoncer les discriminations qu'ils subissent sur le marché de l'emploi et du logement[10], ainsi que dans la vie

---

7 Rapport présenté le 5 juillet 2001.
8 Commission d'experts pour l'immigration et l'intégration, Rapport publié en octobre 2004.
9 La loi, après un vote contesté du Bundesrat, puis confirmé par la cour constitutionnelle, est entrée en vigueur le 1er janvier 2005.
10 Ces discriminations ont été confirmées par une étude qui avait constaté que lors des candidatures (fictives) en ligne, 41% des personnes portant un nom à consonance turque recevaient une réponse contre 68% pour les noms allemands (v. Planerladen e.V. Dortmund, 2007: *Ungleichbe-*

publique et les loisirs comme le résultat d'une « ségrégation sociale et ethnique »[11]. L'échec scolaire frappe leurs enfants dans des proportions inquiétantes[12] tout comme le chômage et la précarité.[13] Il est difficile de vérifier dans quelle mesure les appels de cet office à pratiquer une « ouverture interculturelle comme tâche transversale »[14] ont été écoutés, car les échelons décisifs se trouvent sur le plan régional voire local. Ceci constitue d'ailleurs une spécificité allemande qu'il conviendra de garder à l'esprit en considérant les étapes du débat dans les trois sociétés.

Au Québec : la « crise des accommodements »

Il est judicieux d'adopter, pour les besoins de la comparaison, le cadre proposé par la commission Bouchard-Taylor, à savoir le quart de siècle allant de 1985 à aujourd'hui. Pour le cas du Québec, les auteurs la découpent en quatre phases : 1. les antécédents (décembre 1985 à avril 2002) comportant seulement 13 cas médiatisés et pour la plupart des « accommodements raisonnables » au sens strict du terme, 2. l'intensification des controverses (de mai 2002 à février 2006) phase pendant laquelle les cas discutés sont accompagnés par le contexte de méfiance et d'insécurité de l'après-11 septembre, 3. la période d'ébullition (de mars 2006 à juin 2007) avec une quarantaine de cas et le terme d'accommodement « désormais utilisé à toutes les sauces » (53) ainsi qu'une récupération politique grandissante du sujet, enfin 4. l'accalmie (depuis juillet 2007) à laquelle aurait contribué la mise en place même de la commission. Si les cas rapportés concernent une grande diversité de domaines, notamment le monde du travail, l'espace public, les écoles et centres de la petite enfance, les hôpitaux, les prisons et même la pratique du sport, il est frappant que la quasi-totalité impliquent des dimensions religieuses. Certains de ces conflits sont très spécifiques au Québec et se prêtent mal à la comparaison, comme la prière dans les conseils municipaux, les « érouv » et « souccahs » à Outremont ou le port du kirpan, qui connaissent des rebondissements depuis une dizaine d'années, mais d'autres trouvent des parallèles outre-Atlantique, notamment le port de signes religieux au travail, en tant qu'agent du service public ou à l'école, ainsi que les régimes alimentaires, les crucifix dans les édifices publics ou l'argument culturel comme facteur atténuant devant le tribunal, ainsi que le refus de soins pour motif religieux.

---

handlung von Migranten auf dem Wohnungsmarkt. Ergebnisse eines Paired Ethnic-Testing bei Internet-Immobilien-Börsen, Dortmund, Deutscher Städtetag, 2007: Integration von Zuwanderern. Erfahrungen und Anregungen aus der Praxis in den Städten, Köln).
11 Rapport de 2006, 120.
12 Rapport de 2007 42-44. Un élève allemand sur quatre, mais moins d'un étranger sur dix arrivent au baccalauréat. Le même écart existe dans le domaine de la formation professionnelle.
13 Les personnes issues de l'immigration gagnent en moyenne un salaire représentant 79% seulement de la moyenne nationale. Leur taux d'activité est très inférieur à la moyenne et celui du chômage deux fois plus élevé. Le risque de pauvreté est de 11,6% en moyenne, mais de 28,2% pour les immigrés (rapport de 2007, 107).
14 Rapport de 2007, 102 et suivantes.

En France : des foulards ...

Nous ne disposons ni pour la France ni pour l'Allemagne d'une telle liste de cas médiatisés.[15] En France, depuis 1989, l'affaire du foulard a largement monopolisé l'attention publique et a été suffisamment commentée sur la scène internationale pour qu'on puisse faire ici l'économie des détails.[16] Mais deux mises au point s'imposent. Primo, l'interdiction du foulard porté par les élèves des écoles publiques (alors que sur la place publique ainsi que dans les universités, les signes religieux sont toujours protégés par le droit à la libre expression) n'a pas autant fait l'unanimité dans l'opinion en 1989 qu'en 2004, lors du vote de la loi. Cinq intellectuels dénoncent dans un appel le « Munich de l'école républicaine » et réclament une interdiction du foulard au nom de l'école comme lieu d'émancipation par rapports aux pressions familiales et communautaires et de l'égalité entre l'homme et la femme.[17] S'y oppose immédiatement un autre manifeste contre le « Vichy de l'intégration des immigrés ». L'interdiction favoriserait l'exclusion et non l'intégration et il faudrait donner du temps à l'islam pour s'adapter au cadre laïque.[18] Qualifié parfois de « nouvelle affaire Dreyfus » le foulard a divisé le monde enseignant et scientifique, les milieux associatifs, les familles et partis politiques. Certes, un large consensus existait pour souhaiter que les foulards disparaissent, mais les voies proposées pour y arriver étaient fortement divergentes. Le ministre Lionel Jospin avait déclaré: « Je suis, moi aussi, contre le voile à l'école, je suis pour le refus du voile. Mon objectif est qu'il n'y ait pas de voile à l'école. Mon seul problème, ce sont les voies par lesquelles on y arrive. »[19] Tandis que le philosophe catholique Guy Coq était catégorique: « Jamais je ne ferai un cours de philosophie avec en face de moi, une jeune tête, un visage, coiffé d'un symbole désormais taché du sang de ces femmes, jeunes ou non, assassinées en Algérie parce qu'elles ne le portaient pas. Je n'accepterai pas ce signe dans ma classe, même si, dans la logique, mon acte devait assumer l'exclusion de nos écoles de centaines de jeunes enfants pris comme otages du fanatisme moderne. Dans la période actuelle [...] accepter le voile islamique dans une classe, c'est se faire complice d'un totalitarisme à prétexte religieux, ou encore d'une 'spiritualité' de l'assassinat. »[20] Si en fin de compte, une écrasante majorité en faveur d'une interdiction a fini par s'affirmer en France, la seconde guerre

---

15 Euroethos, une base de données financée par l'Union européenne et à laquelle participe le ZERP de l'université de Brême est en préparation. Elle doit réunir une documentation sur les décisions juridiques et politique en matière de valeurs culturelles et éthiques dans 8 pays européens. (<http://euroethos.lett.unitn.it/>).

16 V. Helga Bories-Sawala, 2004, « Sacrée laïcité. Eine geschichtsmächtige französische Idee im historischen Abriss » (Sacrée laïcité. Une idée française qui fit l'histoire), *Lendemains*, 113, 11 et sqq.; et « Islam plus Laïcité: die Quadratur des Kreises? » (Islam plus laïcité : la quadrature du cercle ?), Ibid. 57 et sqq. avec de nombreux renvois à d'autres sources.

17 « Profs, ne capitulons pas », *Nouvel Observateur* du 2 novembre 1989.

18 *Politis* du 9 novembre 1989.

19 « Le moment ou jamais. » Entretien avec Lionel Jospin, *Le Débat*, n°58, 1990, 19.

20 Guy Coq, 1995, *Laïcité et République, le lien nécessaire*. Paris: le Félin, 262.

du Golfe et les événements d'Afghanistan, les craintes suscitées par le 11 septembre (moins qu'en Amérique du Nord pourtant), le sentiment d'insécurité face aux émeutes dans les banlieues et le repli communautaire parmi les jeunes y ont certainement contribué, ainsi qu'un flou juridique jugé peu satisfaisant.

Car, et c'est le second élément que je voudrais rappeler, l'exclusion de quatre élèves musulmanes en 1989 a été suivie par une longue période d'hésitations et de jugements contradictoires et accompagnée par des manifestations islamistes intégristes ainsi que des appels à la modération de musulmans plus pondérés. L'attitude du ministre de l'éducation, le socialiste Lionel Jospin, avait été conciliante, misant sur la persuasion et non l'interdiction. L'autorité suprême, le conseil d'État, dans son avis du 24 novembre 1989, avait donné la priorité à la liberté d'expression des élèves et autorisé le port de signes religieux, tant que l'ordre public, la mission d'enseignement et la paix scolaire n'étaient pas menacés. Dès lors, il incombait aux directeurs des établissements de juger de chaque cas individuel, au risque de voir leurs décisions annulées par un tribunal. Une foule de procès s'ensuivit, avec des résultats divergents. L'égalité des citoyens devant la loi s'en accommodait difficilement et la position libérale du Conseil d'État semblait ignorer la teneur symbolique du foulard comme signe d'oppression de la femme, tandis qu'il acceptait d'y voir plus qu'une « pièce d'étoffe » en le protégeant par le principe de la liberté d'expression religieuse. Ce fut un ministre UDF, Bayrou, qui, après avoir continué d'abord sur la même lancée que son prédécesseur socialiste, vira de bord. Sa circulaire de septembre 1994 conseilla aux établissements scolaires d'inscrire dans leurs règlements intérieurs l'interdiction du port de tous les signes « ostentatoires », mais de permettre les signes discrets, comme le fera la loi de 2004, voulue et défendue par Jacques Chirac.

Et derrière le foulard ? Force est de constater que peu d'autres évolutions sociétales liées à l'immigration ont eu les honneurs des devants de la scène publique en France : ni les exemples d'une intégration réussie, comme les succès scolaires des « beurettes », ni les mouvements et projets antiracistes dans les banlieues, ni les nombreux « accommodements » qui se sont faits dans la vie de tous les jours, ni surtout les discriminations autres que symboliques, à l'emploi et au logement, si ce n'est lors des émeutes sanglantes qui ont frappé les banlieues à plusieurs reprises récemment et qui ont rappelé les conditions de vie précaires dénoncées depuis des années par les recherches sociologiques sur le terrain.

Dans la série des affaires débattues récemment, concernant l'« accommodement » des divergences culturelles en France, signalons à titre d'exemple celle qui vient de vivre un rebondissement, à savoir l'annulation d'un mariage entre deux musulmans français pour cause de non-virginité de l'épouse, annulation que le tribunal de grande instance de Lille avait prononcée en avril 2008. Suite à des protestations très vives et malgré l'accord des deux époux, tous deux satisfaits du verdict, la ministre de la justice, Rachida Dati, a fait appel le 22 septembre, non pour sauver ce mariage, mais pour fonder l'annulation sur un motif plus compatible avec le respect de l'égalité homme-femme et de la liberté à disposer de son corps.

... et des mosquées

Contrairement au Québec où ce sujet ne figure pas dans l'énuméré des affaires d'accommodements raisonnables, la construction de mosquées soulève des controverses en France comme en Allemagne. Si dans les deux pays européens, les motifs des réticences se ressemblent, notamment contre la construction de grandes mosquées qui risqueraient de perturber l'équilibre urbanistique et culturel des quartiers concernés, les bases juridiques qui déterminent les décisions des permis de construire sont très différentes. En Allemagne, les édifices religieux appartiennent aux différents cultes et dès lors, les permis de construire sont régis par le seul droit de la construction, régional et local. En France par contre, les biens des Eglises avaient été nationalisés par la Révolution de 1789 et depuis, les édifices appartiennent à l'État, qui veille à leur entretien et les prête aux cultes pour les offices religieux. L'impossibilité de subventionner des cultes ayant été stipulée par la loi de 1905 sur la séparation entre l'Église et l'État, le financement de nouveaux édifices doit désormais être assumé par les communautés elles-mêmes, ce qui n'a pas manqué de poser des questions, pour les deux confessions chrétiennes, dans des zones de forte croissance démographique au XXe siècle, notamment les banlieues. Pour les cultes d'implantation récente, de surcroît pratiqué par une population immigrée et pauvre, une égalité de traitement est, en théorie, difficile à trouver, à moins de revenir sur cette importante concession à la laïcité qui est celle du prêt gratuit. Cependant – aussi pour éviter une dépendance vis-à-vis de capitaux étrangers, notamment de certains pays arabes - des solutions ont été trouvées à de nombreux endroits, en combinant lieux de prière et institutions culturelles (musée d'art, bibliothèque) comme pour la mosquée de Paris (1920) ou la cathédrale d'Evry (1995), ou encore par des baux consentis par des municipalités pour les terrains. Un des plus récents projet de mosquée est celui d'Hérouville ... en Normandie.

En Allemagne : des mosquées ....

La construction de mosquées n'est pas sans provoquer des conflits en Allemagne. La première a été inaugurée à Berlin en 1929, mais il est évident que la forte immigration musulmane et son installation permanente depuis la seconde voire la troisième génération pousse les communautés à réclamer, en Allemagne comme en France, plus de lieux de culte dignes de ce nom. De nombreuses villes s'en sont récemment dotées, sans que les remous que ces processus avaient soulevés localement, notamment quand il s'agissait de grandes mosquées accueillant des milliers de fidèles, soient parvenus à la une des quotidiens nationaux.

A une exception près cependant : les conflits autour de la grande mosquée de Cologne, critiquée par des personnalités insoupçonnables de xénophobie comme la sociologue germano-turque Necla Kalek ou l'essayiste Ralph Giordano qui pensent qu'une telle mosquée, prévue pour 2000 fidèles contribuerait non à l'intégration, mais au contraire, à la ghettoïsation des immigrés, ainsi que par des mouvements populistes de droite qui ont habilement récupéré les réflexes xénophobes d'une partie de la population. Or, le 20 septembre 2008, la tenue d'un congrès contre l'islamisation qui devait réunir des représentants de l'extrême droite européenne à Cologne, a pu être empêchée par les protestations pleines d'imagination de la population, notamment par la tenue d'un festival multicolore affirmant que leur ville tient à ses traditions de tolérance et d'ouverture.

Si de tels événements rares ont des répercussions au niveau national[21], il n'est pas aisé de présenter, même dans les grandes lignes, les débats en Allemagne, car, à la différence du Québec et de la France, beaucoup de ces enjeux sont décidés au niveau régional. Même ceux qui ont été portés devant le tribunal constitutionnel fédéral – et nous allons en citer deux - sont souvent renvoyés, par celui-ci même, à la compétence des *Länder*.

... des foulards ...

C'est ce qui fut décidé concernant la plainte de l'enseignante Fereshta Ludin contre le *Land* du Bade-Wurtemberg, qui avait refusé de l'embaucher devant sa persistance à ne pas ôter son foulard en classe. Un vif débat s'en était suivi dans les milieux enseignants, auprès des associations et des mouvements dont certains arguments rappellent le débat français sur le foulard et ses significations, à la différence près qu'il ne s'agit pas d'élèves, mais d'enseignantes (!). La sentence de la plus haute juridiction allemande[22] est intéressante pour plusieurs raisons. D'une part, elle explique que la seule présomption que le port du foulard nuit à la paix scolaire ne saurait suffire pour conclure à l'incapacité d'une enseignante à assurer sa mission éducative. Contrairement à la croix chrétienne, qui serait à considérer comme un symbole religieux en soi, le foulard pourrait présenter plusieurs significations allant de l'attachement personnel à sa culture d'origine à l'intégrisme contraire aux valeurs occidentales et prônant la soumission de la femme. Seul le comportement de celle qui porte le foulard pourrait déterminer si son message est contraire à la neutralité de l'école. Une attitude de prosélytisme, par exemple, ne serait plus protégée par la liberté d'expression religieuse.[23]

Ayant constaté que les bases juridiques pouvant justifier une interdiction du foulard n'étaient pas réunies, la cour a ensuite renvoyé la balle aux *Länder* en les encourageant à légiférer pour remédier à cette situation[24], le domaine de l'éducation et des cultes étant de leur compétence. Le Bade-Wurtemberg ne s'est pas fait prier et a interdit le port par les enseignants de tout signe politique, religieux ou philosophique pouvant menacer la neutralité de l'État ou la paix scolaire[25], tout en rappelant

---

21 « Heute sind wir alle Kölner » (Aujourd'hui, nous sommes tous citoyens de Cologne), *Frankfurter Rundschau* du 20 septembre 2008.
22 BVerfG, décision du 24 septembre 2003.
23 Art. 33 par. 2 et par. 4 Abs. 1, par. 2 ainsi que 33 par. 3 GG (Loi fondamentale).
24 V. 2. Leitsatz BVerfG, décision du 24 septembre 2003.
25 Gesetz zur Änderung des Schulgesetzes, du 1er avril 2004.

que la constitution du *Land* stipule que l'éducation repose sur les valeurs et traditions chrétiennes et occidentales. Des dispositions analogues sont prises un peu plus tard par la Basse-Saxe et la Sarre.[26] En Hesse, une loi voit le jour, étendant l'interdiction à tous les fonctionnaires de l'État.[27] En Bavière, la différence établie entre les symboles chrétiens – qui restent permis – et le foulard islamique frappé par l'interdiction est encore plus explicite.[28] A Berlin, par contre, une exception pour les symboles chrétiens n'est pas prévue et l'interdiction des signes ostentatoires étendue à tous les fonctionnaires est accompagnée par une loi anti-discriminatoire comportant un plan d'action et une antenne de médiation inter-culturelle.[29] La Rhénanie-Westphalie, Brême et la Thuringe connaissent également des interdictions de foulards, chacune à sa manière, et dans d'autres Länder celles-ci sont à l'étude. En somme, comme pour d'autres sujets, nous sommes en présence d'une multitude de cas de figure qui empêchent de parler de la situation « en Allemagne ».

Pour ce qui est des foulards en dehors du service public, signalons que la jurisprudence allemande, comme en France et au Québec d'ailleurs, a généralement tranché en faveur de la liberté d'expression religieuse et invalidé les licenciements dans plusieurs cas connus.[30] Sans entrer dans les détails, on peut constater que les tribunaux attachent une grande valeur à l'assiduité scolaire et n'admettent les exemptions de cours ou d'activités para-scolaires que très exceptionnellement. Enfin, pour ce qui est de l'invocation de la culture d'origine dans l'appréciation des motifs personnels de crimes (cas de meurtres « pour l'honneur », par exemple) les limites ont désormais été définies de manière extrêmement stricte[31] et des sentences qui en contiendraient sont systématiquement cassées en appel. L'application d'éléments de la charia en matière de droit privé –en principe possible dans certains cas – est également étroitement surveillée par l'opinion publique. Ainsi, dans un cas semblable à celui cité pour la France (v. supra), devant le tollé généralisé, la juge de Francfort a été destituée immédiatement de ses fonctions. En 2006 elle avait refusé l'accélération de la procédure de divorce à une femme marocaine née en Allemagne, en arguant que celle-ci aurait dû savoir qu'en se mariant à un Marocain au Maroc, elle encourait un risque d'être battue, car il s'agissait d'une pratique courante dans cette culture.[32]

---

26 Gesetz zur Änderung des Gesetzes zur Ordnung des Schulwesens im Saarland du 23 juin 2004; Gesetz zur Änderung des Niedersächsischen Schulgesetzes du 29 avril 2004.
27 Gesetz zur Sicherung der staatlichen Neutralität du 18 octobre 2004.
28 Gesetz zur Änderung des Bayerischen Gesetzes über das Erziehungs- und Unterrichtswesen du 23 novembre 2004.
29 Neutralitätsgesetz, Antidiskriminierungs- und Integrationsförderungsmaßnahmen für Berlin, du 20 janvier 2005.
30 Cf. ArbG Frankfurt (24 juin 1992) ArbG Hamburg (3 janvier 1996) BAG (10 octobre 2002), ArbG Dortmund (16 janvier 2003).
31 BGH (28 janvier 2004), BGH (20 février 2002), BGH (2 février 2000), BGH(24 avril 2001).
32 Textarchiv *Berliner Zeitung* du 22 mars 2007.

…et des crucifix

Enfin, revenons à une affaire d'« accommodements raisonnable » qui pour une fois n'implique pas l'immigration mais en dit long sur les rapports entre les cultes et l'État dans une Allemagne qui reconnaît la neutralité de l'État, mais qui ne garantit pas moins aux églises chrétiennes établies une situation privilégiée et aux régions une très grande marge de manœuvre. En même temps, nous voici en présence d'une distance maximale entre les situations française et allemande. Tandis que le parlement du Québec s'est hâté de voter le maintien du crucifix dans la salle du Parlement contre l'avis explicite de la commission Bouchard-Taylor, en France, le retrait des crucifix de tous les édifices publics et notamment des salles de classe avait été réglé dans la décennie suivant la loi de 1905, accompagné, il est vrai, d'un véritable *Kulturkampf*. En Allemagne cependant, cette question fait toujours des vagues et vient de rebondir. Dans sa sentence à propos du cas Fereshta Ludin, la cour constitutionnelle fédérale avait établi une différence de fond entre le crucifix accroché au mur d'une salle de classe qui constituerait un acte d'adhésion au christianisme de la part de l'État, et le simple fait de tolérer qu'une enseignante exprime son appartenance religieuse personnelle, dans le cadre d'un pluralisme religieux. Il a confirmé ainsi indirectement sa sentence de 1995 [33] déclarant explicitement anticonstitutionnelle la disposition de l'État de Bavière selon laquelle les crucifix sont obligatoires dans toutes les salles de classes. La liberté religieuse des élèves de croire ou de ne pas croire et la neutralité de l'État obligerait celui-ci à tolérer la pluralité des convictions, notamment dans le cadre d'une obligation scolaire. Mais rien n'a changé en Bavière. La loi scolaire a été modifiée, tout en maintenant les crucifix obligatoires.[34] Tout au plus, sur demande expresse de parents, des exceptions seraient consenties, mais un tel cas n'est jamais devenu notoire. Le 14 août 2008 encore, le tribunal administratif d'Augsbourg a refusé une demande d'« accommodement raisonnable » de la part d'un enseignant athée qui voulait obtenir le droit de faire classe sans crucifix.[35] Bien évidemment, cet exemple ne concerne que la Bavière, province toujours un peu particulière–elle n'a jamais ratifié la constitution allemande… Mais sait-on que le délit de blasphème[36] existe encore en Allemagne fédérale?

Avant de conclure, il faudrait ajouter qu'en matière d'« accommodements raisonnables » pour la France et l'Allemagne, l'Union européenne joue un rôle de plus en plus important. Malgré le manque de consensus sur les valeurs fondamentales dans le projet de Constitution, et malgré son échec dû au non référendaire français et néerlandais, il existe quatre directives européennes anti-discriminatoires assez ex-

---

33 BVerfGE 93, 1.
34 Art. 7 par. 3 BayEUG.
35 Décision du 14 août 2008.
36 § 166 StGB. Les récentes occasions où il a été invoqué concernaient des prestations théâtrales et humoristiques.

plicites[37] que les États membres sont tenus de traduire dans les juridictions nationales. Ce processus est loin d'être achevé et des conflits persistent, notamment pour savoir comment trancher en cas de conflit de normes juridiques, et il est encore trop tôt pour tirer un bilan sur l'efficacité de la loi générale allemande sur l'égalité de traitement[38], mais la pression exercée par l'Union européenne est susceptible de changer la donne et de faire avancer les choses.

Conclusion

1. Les trois cas de figure analysés présentent des différences indéniables dues notamment à l'histoire. Le Québec et beaucoup plus encore la France se réclament de la laïcité comme valeur fondamentale, pour l'avoir conquise à des moments hautement significatifs: l'un depuis la Révolution tranquille, l'autre par étapes allant de la Révolution de 1789 aux grands débats sur l'école du XXe siècle en passant par la IIIe République et la loi de 1905. Par contre, les Églises chrétiennes en Allemagne sont reconnues comme des piliers de la société, à côté de l'État, en partie pour avoir survécu et constitué une valeur sûre à travers des régimes politiques contrastés depuis deux siècles. Dans la pratique cependant, les situations se ressemblent : les régimes laïques connaissent de nombreuses exceptions petites et grandes et même sans prôner la laïcité, la société allemande n'en est pas moins largement sécularisée.

2. Les trois pays connaissent un certain malaise, plus aigu en Europe qu'au Québec, face à l'immigration et à la présence de cultures minoritaires. Mais les élèves n'aiment en général pas se faire dire « peut faire mieux », trouvent des excuses ou n'écoutent pas, que ce soient les premiers de la classe québécois ou les « cancres » allemands et français. Certains éléments frileux voire xénophobes existent dans toutes les sociétés d'accueil, comme il y a partout certains immigrés qui refusent de s'intégrer. Or, dans tous les cas de figure, ceux-ci sont largement minoritaires et le repli communautaire est surtout le fait des éléments les plus fragilisés.

3. Les immigrés enrichissent les sociétés d'accueil de plusieurs façons : économique démographique et culturelle. Le fait que leur présence oblige celles-ci à réfléchir sur elles-mêmes n'est peut-être pas le moindre de ces avantages. Quelle place accorder à des modes de vie et expressions culturelles en désaccord avec celles de la majorité, qu'ils viennent de minorités autrefois marginalisées, voire criminalisées, de la société ou qu'ils soient liés au phénomène de l'immigration? Y répondre, c'est également réfléchir sur sa propre société, les valeurs qui la constituent, les acquis qui méritent d'être défendus. A titre d'exemple: on a rarement entendu aussi souvent affirmer l'égalité inaliénable entre hommes et femmes que par rapport à la culture musulmane et on croit rêver en voyant des chrétiens-démocrates allemands

---

37 Directives 2000/43/ EG, 2000/78/EG, 2002/73/EG und 2004/113/EG qui préconisent une protection efficace contre toutes discriminations se fondant sur l'origine ethnique, le sexe, la conviction religieuse ou philosophique, un handicap, l'âge ou l'orientation sexuelle.
38 Allgemeines Gleichbehandlungsgesetz (AGG) du 14 août 2006.

ériger l'acceptation de l'homosexualité en critère d'une intégration réussie à la société d'accueil[39]...

4. Les débats qui ont suscité le plus d'émotions ont porté surtout sur des questions symboliques, voire religieuses. Les médias ont certainement contribué à ce regard culturaliste, mais le phénomène est plus ample et affecte également les sciences humaines. Mais si le choc des cultures en cachait un autre? Les trois rapports le soulignent sans ambages : ce sont les inégalités sociales dans le domaine des salaires et du logement, les discriminations à l'emploi et dans la vie publique, les conditions de vie précaires, l'échec scolaire et la xénophobie inacceptable qui sont la véritable origine de ces conflits déguisés comme « culturels » et ce n'est pas par des « accommodements » symboliques qu'on les résoudra.

5. Reprocher au rapport Bouchard-Taylor, comme certains le font au Québec, de ne pas résoudre la « question nationale », c'est se tromper de débat. C'est aussi ne pas reconnaître son pari risqué mais réussi de conjuguer une large consultation démocratique avec une pensée scientifique rigoureuse à propos de la question cruciale du vivre-ensemble entre minorités et majorités, question qui dépasse comme nous venons de le voir, le seul cadre national. Prendre le parti de subordonner tous les sujets sociétaux au seul critère de l'indépendance ou non du Québec est certes une attitude politique licite. Elle pourrait, cependant, à force de trop isoler cet objectif, le manquer. Se constituer en « société distincte » ne saurait être acquis une bonne fois pour toutes, mais suppose un débat toujours renouvelé sur les valeurs qui la définissent et sur la gestion des conflits qui la traversent – que le Québec continue à faire parti de la fédération canadienne ou non. La culture politique du Québec présente de bons atouts pour réussir un tel pari.

---

39 À l'instar des Pays-Bas qui montrent aux candidats à l'immigration un DVD sur les modes de vie qui les attendent, le gouvernement chrétien-démocrate du Bade-Wurtemberg avait introduit en 2006 un questionnaire contenant des questions sur l'homosexualité pour les candidats à la citoyenneté. L'actuel test en vigueur depuis le 1er septembre 2008 dans toute l'Allemagne se réfère non à des attitudes, mais à des connaissances. La bonne réponse à 2 questions sur 310 consiste à savoir (non à approuver) que la vie en couple pour partenaires du même sexe est légale en Allemagne, de nombreuses autres questions soulignent l'égalité des sexes devant la loi.

Besprechungen/Reviews/Comptes rendus

Sammelrezension: Michael Byers, *Intent for a Nation: What is Canada For?* Vancouver/Toronto: Douglas & McIntyre, 2007;
  Roy Rempel, *Dreamland: How Canada's Pretend Foreign Policy Has Undermined Sovereignty*, Montreal / Kingston: McGill-Queen's University Press, 2006;
  Patrick James / Nelson Michaud / Marc J. O'Reilly (eds.), *Handbook of Canadian Foreign Policy*, Lanham, MD: Lexington Books, 2006;
  Steven Kendall Holloway, *Canadian Foreign Policy: Defining the National Interest*. Peterborough: Broadview Press, 2006;
  Duane Bratt / Christopher J. Kukucha (eds.), *Readings in Canadian Foreign Policy. Classic Debates and New Ideas*, Don Mills, ON: Oxford University Press 2006;
  Fen O. Hampson/Brian Tomlin/Norman Hillmer, *Canadian International Policies - Agendas, Alternatives, and Politics*, Don Mills, ON: Oxford University Press 2008;
  John Kirton, *Canadian Foreign Policy in a Changing World*, Scarborough: Nelson-Thomson 2007 (*David Bosold*)
Patrick James / Mark Kasoff (eds.), *Canadian Studies in the New Millennium*, Toronto, Buffalo, London: University of Toronto Press, 2008 (*Martin Thunert*)
Rosmarin Heidenreich, *Paysages de désir. J. R. Léveillé : réflexions critiques*, Ottawa: L'Interligne, 2005 (*Fritz Peter Kirsch*)
Gilles Dupuis / Klaus-Dieter Ertler (éds.), *À la carte. Le roman québécois (2000-2005)*, Frankfurt am Main usw.: Peter Lang, 2007 (*Fritz Peter Kirsch*)

Sammelrezension
Michael Byers, *Intent for a Nation: What is Canada For?* Vancouver/Toronto: Douglas & McIntyre, 2007 (248 pp., ISBN 9781553652502, cloth, C$ 32.95; 256pp., ISBN 9781553653813, pb., C$ 22.95);
Roy Rempel, *Dreamland: How Canada's Pretend Foreign Policy Has Undermined Sovereignty*, Montreal / Kingston: McGill-Queen's University Press, 2006 (189 pp., ISBN 9781553391197; cloth, C$ 60.00; ISBN 9781553391180; pb., C$ 29.95);
Patrick James / Nelson Michaud / Marc J. O'Reilly (eds.), *Handbook of Canadian Foreign Policy*, Lanham, MD: Lexington Books, 2006 (608 pp.; ISBN 9780739106945, cloth, US$ 125.00; ISBN 9780739114933; pb., US$ 47.95);
Steven Kendall Holloway, *Canadian Foreign Policy: Defining the National Interest*. Peterborough: Broadview Press, 2006 (276 pp.; ISBN 9781551118161; pb.; C$ 42.95);
Duane Bratt / Christopher J. Kukucha (eds.), *Readings in Canadian Foreign Policy. Classic Debates and New Ideas*, Don Mills, ON: Oxford University Press, 2006 (416 pp.; ISBN 9780195423693; pb.; C$ 65.95);
Fen O. Hampson / Brian Tomlin / Norman Hillmer, *Canadian International Policies - Agendas, Alternatives, and*

Politics, Don Mills, ON: Oxford University Press, 2008 (432 pp.; ISBN 9780195421095; pb.; C$ 66.95);
John Kirton, Canadian Foreign Policy in a Changing World, Scarborough: Nelson-Thomson, 2007 (562 pp.; ISBN 9780176252076; pb.; C$ 80.95).

Die Mittelmacht in der Identitätskrise: Zur akademischen Debatte in der kanadischen Außenpolitikanalyse

Der Kalte Krieg schien Anfang der 1990er Jahre beendet. Zumindest was die Einschätzung der kanadischen Außenpolitik anbelangte. Angesichts eines Zeitgeists, der von Friedensdividenden und dem Ende der Geschichte träumte, war der damalige akademische Diskurs merkwürdig nüchtern. Das bisherige Koordinatensystem der kanadischen Außenpolitik schien noch weitgehend intakt. Kontinuität stand im Vordergrund. Die damaligen Werke finden sich noch heute auf den *reading lists* der Außenpolitikseminare an kanadischen Universitäten. Keatings „Canada and World Order" (Keating ²2001 [1993]), Nossals „The Politics of Canadian Foreign Policy" (Nossal ³1997 [1985, ²1989] und Coopers "Canadian foreign policy: old habits and new directions" (Cooper 1997) sind damit gewissermaßen schon zu – zugegebenermaßen noch recht jungen – Klassikern geworden. Dass sie mittlerweile auf den ersten Blick – dazu später mehr – etwas antiquiert wirken, liegt daran, dass sich die Welt verändert hat (oder verändert zu haben scheint). Dies ist zwar mittlerweile für sich genommen bereits ein Klischee, jedoch scheint eine Neubewertung kanadischer Außenpolitik angesichts jüngerer geschichtlicher Ereignisse – Kosovo-, Afghanistan- und Irakkrieg sowie 11. September 2001 – vonnöten. Nicht verwunderlich ist es daher, dass in den vergangenen drei Jahren eine Fülle an neuen Werken zur kanadischen Außenpolitik erschienen ist. Dabei ist festzustellen, dass der im Großen und Ganzen bestehende Konsens der 1990er Jahre passé ist. In den Lehrbüchern betont man den Wandel, man relativiert alte Gewissheiten hier, kreiert Metatheorien da und öffnet sich bislang vernachlässigten Themenfeldern. Dass drei der fünf Lehrbücher explizit auf Ergebnisse der *Gender Studies* eingehen, ist vielleicht das augenfälligste Beispiel. Es werden jedoch nicht nur weitere methodologische Zugänge präsentiert, sondern auch grundsätzliche normative Positionen verhandelt. In der Regel mit einem irgendwie halbherzigen Nachsatz, dass diese und jene Aspekte auch von den neuen Theorien erfasst werden müssten. Mitunter aber auch nicht.

Moralische Supermacht oder verlässlicher Partner?

Dies zeigen insbesondere die Bände von Michael Byers und Roy Rempel. Sicher liegt das in deren Fall auch daran, dass im Hinblick auf den Adressatenkreis eine größere Breitenwirkung anstrebt wird – wer mehr Leserinnen und Leser anziehen möchte, muss kernigere Botschaften vertreten. Und was böte sich hier besser an als ein Beitrag zum kanadischen *soul searching*? Zwar hat dies schon immer dafür gesorgt, dass die Stimmen über Kanadas Rolle und Platz in der Welt, die über den universitären Buchmarkt hinaus gehört werden wollten, nie vollständig verstummt sind. Jüngere Vorläufer wie Andrew Cohens "While Canada Slept" (2003), Jennifer Welshs "At Home in the World" (2004) oder Axworthys "Navigating A New World" (2003) belegen das. Während das dortige Lamento sich jedoch vor allem darauf konzentriert, *ob* das Mittelmacht-Label hilfreich sei oder hinderlich sei oder *wie* Kanadas liberaler Internationalismus im 21. Jahrhundert definiert werden sollte oder muss – und damit die Frage nach den Mitteln (finanziellen als auch politischen) und weniger jene nach dem Ziel als solchem aufgeworfen wird – sind die Positionen hier fundamental verschieden. Der ad acta gelegte Kalte Krieg ist zurück, zumindest unter den Außenpolitikanalysten (und, welch Ironie der Geschichte, nun auch im tagespolitischen Diskurs angesichts der Lage im Kaukasus). Im Mittelpunkt der akademischen Auseinandersetzung steht ein Streit, der alle Generationen der Theoretiker und Praktiker der Außenpolitik im vergangenen Jahrhundert geprägt hat. Konkret geht es hier um die Neujustierung von Idealismus und Realismus in der Außenpolitik. Und, damit einhergehend, um die Frage nach nationalen Werten und internationalen Normen bzw. nationalem Interesse und klassischen Formen der Macht(projektion) als richtungsweisendem Element außenpolitischer Entscheidungen. Während die eine Seite nach dem fragt, *was* außenpolitisch möglich ist, setzt die andere Seite Einflussmöglichkeiten als gegeben voraus und beschäftigt sich direkt mit der Frage, *wie* Kanada und die Welt aussehen sollten. Am deutlichsten wird dieser Unterschied bei den bereits erwähnten Bänden von Rempel bzw. Byers, die Lichtjahre in ihrer Einschätzung trennen, welche globale Rolle Kanada zukommt und wie die letzte Dekade seiner Außenpolitik zu bewerten ist. Bei Byers klingt es euphorisch:

„It's time for Canadians to recognize our considerable strengths and past successes in promoting change at the international level […]. […] [Canada] has done so not just in support of its own interests, but also for countries and people everywhere. This latter point is of key importance, for when Canada acts on behalf of the international community, it not only does good, it also bolsters its reputation […]" (Byers 2007, 240)

Für Rempel ist die an Werten ausgerichtete Außenpolitik hingegen ein Zeichen fehlender Stärke:

„A position based on presumed moral superiority does nothing to advance the interests of the Canadian people. […] It is [also] inevitably hypocritical. No state is a bastion of moral virtue. […] This approach to international policy has been irresponsible. It has squandered limited diplomatic capital and failed to advance the real interests of the Canadian people" (Rempel 2006, 23-24).

Selbstverständlich schießen die zwei Autoren in vielem über das Ziel hinaus; nicht weiter verwunderlich bei Untertiteln wie „a relentlessly optimistic manifesto for Canada's role in the world" (Byers) oder „How Canada's pretend foreign policy has undermined sovereignty".[1] Theoretischen Debatten geben sich die beiden Autoren nicht hin und relativierenden Grautönen im Farbenspektrum außenpolitischer Bewertungen entsagen sie ebenso. Das kann angesichts der Radikalität ihrer Ideen auch nicht anders sein. Wer der *Responsibility to Protect* (R2P) zur Geltung verhelfen will, indem er aus Afghanistan abziehen will, um die Truppen anschließend nach Darfur zu verlegen (Byers), gehört sicher nicht zum *mainstream*. Diesem kann man sich schließlich aber auch nicht mit selbstgerechten Bemerkungen wieder annähern, indem man seinen Landsleuten rät, das Fahrrad zur Arbeit zu nehmen und die persönliche CO_2-Bilanz durch Klimaschutzzertifikate für die monatlichen Flüge nach London klimaneutral zu gestalten. Hingegen vertritt sicher auch nicht jener die Mehrheitsmeinung, der die Kernbestandteile der liberalen Außenpolitik der 1990er Jahre wie die Ottawa-Konvention, den Internationalen Strafgerichtshof und das Kyoto-Protokoll als mehr oder minder irrelevant einstuft (Rempel). Die grundsätzlichen Fragen in der derzeitigen Außenpolitikanalyse – und der kanadischen im Besonderen – lassen sich damit jedoch umso schärfer herauskristallisieren: wie lässt sich der außenpolitische Einfluss eines Landes bewerten bzw. bestimmen? Welche Rolle spielen dabei die in den außenpolitischen Theorien als „materielle Faktoren" bezeichneten Instrumentarien wie ein starkes Militär, wirtschaftliche Prosperität und die geographische Lage? Und welche hingegen jene ideellen Faktoren, die Joseph Nye „soft power" nennt: Prestige, Werte und die Vorbildfunktion für andere Staaten? Die in diesem Sinne kompromisslosen Plädoyers für die eine oder andere Sicht sind damit am ehesten als gedruckte

---

[1] Etwas pointierter haben die beiden Autoren ihre Standpunkte in Kurzessays dargelegt (Byers 2007b, Rempel 2006b).

"Begrenzungspfähle" zu sehen, die das Feld für die theoretisch unterfütterten Zwischenpositionen der weiteren Autorinnen und Autoren abstecken.

Ein amerikanischer Blick auf die kanadische Außenpolitik

Das „Handbook on Foreign Policy" ist dabei im Hinblick auf den beachtlichen Umfang von über 600 Seiten merkwürdig selektiv. Und zwar bewusst: „This volume [...] does not examine every important issue in Canadian foreign policy; instead, it tries to highlight both well-known and understudied topics" (James / Michaud / O'Reilly 2006, 3). Dadurch, dass nur sieben der 23 Autoren in Kanada arbeiten und der Großteil aus den Vereinigten Staaten stammt und den dortigen *academic mainstream* repräsentiert, sind jedoch nur die Themen relativ exotisch. Die Untersuchung der Gender-Dimension in der kanadischen Marine (Kapitel 19) enthält sicher einige interessante Zahlen. Ein Satz wie „incorporating women in combat units into the Canadian armed forces is a move to catch the military up to other sectors of society that already have begun integrating women into their professions" (James 2007, 480) klingt jedoch zu Beginn des 21. Jahrhunderts sehr angestaubt. Eine solche Erkenntnis scheint etwa so revolutionär wie die Tatsache, dass Frauen zwischenzeitlich das Wahlrecht besitzen. Das gesamte Werk ist streng auf eine positivistische Methodologie und – in der Hauptsache – neorealistische Zugänge[2] beschränkt. Kanadische Außenpolitik verharrt hier in der metatheoretischen Zwangsjacke der Kausalität in Form des *policy cycle* und zu untersuchender Variablen, die die Stichhaltigkeit der Theorie testen. Aus dieser Sicht liegt das Scheitern der kanadischen Außenpolitik darin begründet, dass es nicht zu einer Konvergenz der außenpolitischen Entscheidungen in den USA und Kanada kommt. Kanadas niedrige Militärausgaben verhindern bis heute die notwendige Interoperabilität der beiden Streitkräfte (Kapitel 3) oder führten vor dem Irakkrieg in die Sackgasse, weil die Regierung nicht auf die Linie der USA und Großbritanniens einschwenkte: „Canada's national interest seemed to call for exactly that kind of policy" (Kapitel 14, S. 354). Selbst in Kapitel 16, welches den bilateralen Beziehungen zu den USA gewidmet ist, wird zwar ausführlichst auf Wahrnehmungsunterschiede und die „Natur" der jeweiligen Spitzenpolitiker eingegangen. Aber auch hier verweigert man sich dem akademischen Mehrwert reflexiver Theorieansätze wie der sozialkonstruktivistischen Außenpolitikanalyse. Angesichts eines solchen Instrumentariums zu dem Schluss zu kommen, dass „[...] policy analysts are surely correct that the nature of personal interaction and the ideological and party orientations of each government figure strongly in the dialogue (Doran 2006, 403), ist insofern erwartbar, zugleich aber auch enttäuschend. Ist es doch implizit auch das Eingeständnis, dass die Lektüre eines Zeitungsartikels, verfasst von eben diesen Analysten, eine kurzweiligere und zugleich bessere Alternative zu Artikeln wie dem vorliegenden ist.

Dass die besagte theoretische Eindimensionalität neben dem bisweilen begrenzten Erkenntnisgewinn ein weiteres Manko besitzt, ist ärgerlich, aber nicht weiter überraschend. Die fehlende Selbstreflexion führt leider immer wieder in die Falle der normativen Grundannahmen, die bei einem Groß-

---

2 Diese hauptsächlich in den USA vorherrschende Theorieströmung der Internationalen Beziehungen leitet das außenpolitische Verhalten von Staaten aus den Strukturen des internationalen Systems ab. Dabei wird nicht nur ein über Gebühr verengter Machtbegriff verwendet, der sich vor allem auf quantifizierbare Größen wie Zahl und Ausstattung der Streitkräfte oder das Durchschnittseinkommen stützt. Ebenso wird außenpolitisches Handeln als objektiver Systemzwang abgeleitet, durch dessen „Entschlüsselung" nicht nur die Theorie in Bezug auf vergangene Entscheidungen „ge- testet" werden kann, sondern diese auch zur Extrapolation hinsichtlich zukünftigen Handelns des betreffenden Staates dienen.

teil der Beiträge als objektive Tatsachen ausgegeben werden. Das Resümee der Herausgeber ist hier am illustrativsten: „The Harper government needs to avoid such bureaucratic ‚merry-go-rounds' if Canada wants to regain its level of influence in a world dominated by the United States […]. If Harper treats foreign policy seriously, then perhaps Canada might recover some of its lost global influence" (James / Michaud / O'Reilly 2006, 522-23). Mindestens genauso bemerkenswert ist auch eine der Schlussfolgerungen aus Kapitel 4 über die kanadischen Streitkräfte: Als Leser eine Frage wie „[…] in an increasingly dangerous world, does Canada believe that military forces are necessary?" (Richter 2006, 70) nicht als rhetorisch verstehen zu wollen, würde der Autor sicher als Beleidigung auffassen. Abschließend bleibt festzuhalten, dass das Werk abgesehen von wenigen Highlights wie Kapitel 2 (zur Rolle von Premierminister, PMO und PCO), 6 (zur Rolle Kanadas in ‚La Francophonie') und 20 (zur Rolle der Zivilgesellschaft im außenpolitischen Prozess) nicht nur außergewöhnlich einseitig ist, sondern zugleich unerklärliche Redundanzen aufweist (Kapitel 3 und 17 behandeln beide die Rolle der Streitkräfte) und zugleich lange im „Trockendock" des Verlags gelegen haben muss. Davon zeugen zahlreiche Kapitel, die auf dem politischen Stand von 2004 beruhen und in den zwei Jahren bis zur Veröffentlichung nicht mehr aktualisiert wurden.

Im Namen des – breit gefassten – nationalen Interesses

Nur auf den ersten Blick ähnlich einseitig – und von der Tendenz in Rempels Richtung gehend – ist Steven Holloways Lehrbuch. Seine *National Interest Perspective*, kurz NIP, genannte Analyse ist nur scheinbar simplistisch. Sie ist vielmehr eine theoretische Synthese, die die Untersuchungsparameter klar benennt und – angesichts älterer Studien des „nationalen Interesses" – überraschenderweise nicht nur die globalen Faktoren und deren Einschätzung, sondern auch den nationalen außenpolitischen Diskurs berücksichtigt. Ausgehend von drei Grundannahmen über die Beschaffenheit des internationalen Systems sieht Holloway fünf außenpolitische Grundprinzipien, die das nationale Interesse eines jeden Staates bestimmen. Dadurch, dass diese jedoch anderen kulturellen, geographischen und historischen Gegebenheiten unterliegen, lässt sich die Varianz in der jeweiligen Außenpolitik eines Staates erwähnen. Die fünf erwähnten Kategorien umfassen neben der territorialen Integrität des Staates (1): weitestgehende Autonomie (2), staatliche Kohäsion (3), wirtschaftliches Wohlergehen (4) und schließlich Statusdenken bzw. außenpolitisches Prestige (5) (Holloway 2006, 14).

Anhand dieser Kriterien skizziert Holloway die historischen Entwicklungen seit 1867 bzw. Ende des Zweiten Weltkrieges und legt dabei den Schwerpunkt auf die Sicherheitspolitik (insgesamt 5 der 12 Kapitel) und die Autonomie (3 Kapitel) kanadischer Außenpolitik – hier zu verstehen als Nichtbeeinflussung durch die USA – (3 Kapitel), bevor er sich dem Dauerbrenner der nationalen Einheit des Landes sowie der kanadischen Handelspolitik und den Versuchen der Projektion kanadischer Identität widmet. Obgleich nicht einmal halb so umfangreich wie das Handbuch, ist das zusätzlich mit zahlreichen informativen Schaubildern, Landkarten und Glossar bestückte Lehrbuch der sicher gelungenste Überblick für einen ersten Einblick in die kanadische Außenpolitik. Dem selbst gesteckten Anspruch wird es jedenfalls gerecht: „the NIP provides a forum for debating the fundamental objectives of our country's foreign policy" (Holloway 2006, 249). Besonders positiv fällt dabei ins Gewicht, dass die den theoretischen Schulen zugrunde liegenden Kategorien dazu verwendet werden, ein möglichst umfassendes Bild der kanadischen Außenpolitik zu entwerfen. Diese Komplementarität ist selten, stellen die meisten Autorinnen und Autoren mittlerweile doch weniger den spezifischen Mehrwert einer bestimmten Theorie als deren komparativen Vorteil im Vergleich zu anderen Theorien heraus. Bedauerlich ist in diesem Zusammenhang lediglich, dass die Essenz der verschiedenen Sichtweisen in insgesamt nur fünf Fallstudien zu finden ist. Insbesondere die Fallstudie „Canada in Afghanistan" (Holloway 2006, 69-71) illustriert hier beispielhaft die Vielschichtigkeit internationaler Politik, die strategischen Optionen für Kanada und die unterschiedlichen Sichtweisen und Lösungsansätze internationaler, aber eben auch verschiedenster kanadischer Akteure.

Vasall, Mittelmacht oder ‚Principal Power'?

Aus Sicht der inhaltlichen und theoretischen Herangehensweise weist John Kirtons „Canadian Foreign Policy in a Changing World" die größten Ähnlichkeiten mit Holloways Band auf. Während dessen NIP eine Synthese verschiedener Theorien der Internationalen Beziehungen darstellt, exerziert Kirton hier eine Analyse anhand dreier Theoriemodelle[3], die er bereits 1983 in einem Aufsatz mit David Dewitt (siehe hierzu Kapitel 2 im Band von Bratt/Kukucha) entwickelte. Demnach ist die kanadische Außenpolitik nur dann vollständig zu verstehen, wenn historische Ereignisse mit den theoretischen Prämissen der drei Theorien abgeglichen werden. Im Zentrum steht das Verständnis Kanadas als einer Mittelmacht, die mittels multilateraler Strategien und anderer Verbündeter internationale Entscheidungen – und damit auch das Verhalten einer Supermacht – beeinflussen kann (liberale Theorie, Kapitel 3 und 4). Einer Mindermeinung zufolge ist ein solcher Einfluss nicht nachweisbar, vielmehr ist der US-amerikanische Einfluss auf allen Feldern so groß, dass eine eigenständige Außenpolitik nicht mehr möglich ist (Dependenztheorie, Kapitel 5). Schließlich – und nach Meinung Kirtons am häufigsten zutreffend – ist eine Perspektive, die beim Blick auf vergangene diplomatische Verhandlungen einen Einfluss aufzeigt, der unter „normalen" Umständen nicht möglich gewesen wäre (z.B. Kanadas Rolle in der Suez-Krise 1956, aber auch das Landminenverbot von 1997 sowie generell in der G8). In solchen Fällen müsse von Kanada als „principal power" gesprochen werden (Komplexer Neorealismus, Kapitel 6). Wie im Handbuch werden im weiteren Verlauf des Lehrbuchs die drei Theorien „getestet": anhand der historischen Faktenlage (Teil 2, „Historical Evidence"), des außenpolitischen Prozesses (Teil 3) sowie regionaler Überblicke (Teil 4) und veränderter Bedingungen des Regierens jenseits des Nationalstaats (Teil 5, „Global Governance"). Kirton stellt mit seinem Band unter Beweis, dass er über einen langen Erfahrungsschatz verfügt. Die Kapitel sind durchweg von einer Detailgenauigkeit, die sonst nur von Tomlin et al. erreicht wird. Ein fast hundertseitiger 25-teiliger Appendix mit Zeitleiste bietet darüber hinausgehende Informationen (und bereits mehr als das gesamte Handbuch von James et al.). Es weist jedoch auch Schwächen auf. Am augenfälligsten ist sicher die dem didaktischen Konzept geschuldete „Überinterpretation" im Lichte der jeweiligen Theorie. Unfreiwillig wird der Eindruck vermittelt, dass die Premierminister von St. Laurent bis Harper und die Außenminister von Pearson bis MacKay ihre Entscheidungen danach richteten, welche der durch die Theorien vorgegebenen Optionen ihnen am besten für ihr Land erschienen. Darüber hinaus vermag Kirton es nicht, den Widerspruch zwischen der Globalisierung und Global Governance – die für ihn Indikatoren eines Bedeutungsverlustes des Staates sind – bei zunehmendem globalen Einfluss eines Staates – Kanada – überzeugend aufzulösen. Dennoch muss auch Kirton zu Gute gehalten werden, dass er unterschiedliche Einschätzungen der Außenpolitik vorstellt und in einem Unterkapitel weitere Verzerrungen in der

---

3 Diese nennt er „liberal internationalist", „peripheral dependence" und „complex neo-realist" (vgl. Kirton 2007, 47-88).

kanadischen Außenpolitikanalyse thematisiert[4].

Eine Geschichte der Geschichte der kanadischen Außenpolitikanalyse

Eine Vielzahl an Zugängen bietet auch der Sammelband von Bratt / Kukucha. Während die Einseitigkeit der theoretischen Ausrichtung des Handbuchs jedoch zu inhaltlicher Armut führt – vor allem hinsichtlich des Umfangs, der mehr erwarten lässt –, ist das Potpourri aus sechs Einführungskapiteln zur Außenpolitikanalyse eher verwirrend. Der Hauptgrund ist maßgeblich im Gesamtkonzept des Buches zu sehen, das als gedruckter „Reader" der beiden Herausgeber zwar Anspruch auf – vor allem – theoretische Vollständigkeit erheben kann, dies jedoch auf Kosten eines fehlenden roten Fadens, der das Werk durchzieht. Am augenscheinlichsten wird dies am Beispiel der Entstehungsgeschichte der einzelnen Beiträge. Von insgesamt 23 wurden 16 bereits vorab veröffentlicht – der älteste bereits 1968, zahlreiche in den 1980er Jahren und die neuesten 2003. Viele zählen – vollkommen zu Recht – zu den Klassikern, wie Clarksons Analyse der außenpolitischen Optionen Kanadas (Kapitel 3, zuerst veröffentlicht 1968) oder der Theorievergleich von Dewitt und Kirton (Kapitel 2, zuerst veröffentlicht 1983). Dadurch, dass hier mit Hilfe unterschiedlicher Theorien Bestandsaufnahmen kanadischer Außenpolitik zu unterschiedlichen Zeitpunkten in der Geschichte erfolgen und dabei selbstverständlich unterschiedliche Ergebnisse produzieren, müssen diese zwangsläufig bei den meisten Lesern zu Verwirrung führen. Der Versuch, hier eine Abmilderung in Form von zwei „Updates" durch Autoren zweier älterer Beiträge zu schaffen, um den Bezug zur Gegenwart herzustellen, wirkt dabei nicht zusätzlich erhellend, sondern halbherzig. Nicht minder konzeptionell unausgegoren erscheint hier die Aufteilung der empirischen Kapitel in innenpolitische und auswärtige Determinanten der Außenpolitik sowie die Themenfelder Sicherheit, Handel und Wirtschaft sowie, drittens, gesellschaftlichen Faktoren. Der Grund hierfür ist wiederum in den unterschiedlichen Veröffentlichungszeitpunkten der Fallstudien als auch deren inhaltlicher Breite zu suchen. Der Teil zu Handel und Außenwirtschaft behandelt lediglich Kanadas Rolle in der G8 (Kapitel 18) sowie WTO (Kapitel 19) und das Zustandekommen des bilaterale Freihandelsabkommen zwischen Kanada und den USA (Kapitel 17) – wobei ebendieser Beitrag wiederum ein Auszug von Kapitel 5 im ebenfalls neu erschienenen Band „Canada's International Policies" ist. Diese institutionell geprägten Studien mögen für vergleichende multilaterale Studien ein Gewinn sein. Interessierte, die sich mehr Informationen zu Kanadas Energiesektor und dessen Exporten oder zu den Auswirkungen der NAFTA erhoffen, gehen dagegen leer aus. Mag man hier noch die von den Herausgebern vorgebrachte Entschuldigung akzeptieren, dass exemplarisches Lernen Platz für inhaltliche Lücken lasse, so endet diese Geduld spätestens mit dem letzten Teil des Buches: „Social considerations". Ein Kapitel zu Kanadas Klimaschutzpolitik von 1999 (!) ist nahezu unbrauchbar und ein Kapitel zu Kanadas Afrikapolitik nach den – sehr erhellenden, aber ebenfalls veralteten – Ausführungen des prominentesten kanadischen Entwicklungspolitikexperten Cranford Pratt schlicht: überflüssig. Einziger Lichtblick sind die ebenfalls erheblich früher veröffentlichten Kapitel zu den innerstaatlichen Determinanten und Prozessen der Außenpolitik und der daran beteiligten Gruppen. Nossal (Kapitel 9) und Pratt (Kapitel 10, beide zuerst 1983 veröffentlicht) kommen darin zum gleichen Ergebnis: dass der Einfluss von gesellschaftlichen Gruppen auf die Außenpolitik schwach bis nicht-existent ist. Pratt verortet die Gründe dafür in der Un-

---

[4] So etwa die Tatsache, dass bis vor kurzer Zeit der Gender-Dimension in der Außenpolitikanalyse keine Beachtung geschenkt wurde oder dass der Großteil der Literatur auf englisch verfasst wird und in der Hauptsache von Akademikern aus Ostkanada stammt (Kirton 2007, 14-17).

vereinbarkeit der Ziele zwischen diesen Gruppen (als „counter-consensus") auf der einen und den Regierenden auf der anderen Seite. Nossal betont hingegen, dass das demokratische System der Zivilgesellschaft über dessen Partizipationsmöglichkeiten erlaube, für die Bevölkerungsmehrheit gänzlich inakzeptable außenpolitische Optionen von vorneherein zu verhindern. Damit würde den Regierenden zugleich aber insofern Handlungsspielraum eingeräumt, als diese nun die Wahl zwischen für die Bevölkerung politisch akzeptablen Optionen besäßen. Mit Blick auf die heutige Situation ergeben sich zwar Probleme hinsichtlich der Anwendung dieser Ergebnisse, schließlich sind Konsultationen mit gesellschaftlichen Gruppen in der Außenpolitikformulierung seit der Mulroney Ära ein erklärtes Ziel der Regierung und des Ministeriums (vgl. Clark 1985, Foreword; Government of Canada 1986, 40). Damit wird jedoch der Blick frei für den Wandel im Außenpolitikprozess, der in den vergangenen zwanzig Jahren stattgefunden hat.

Alles im Fluss: Wandel in der kanadischen Außenpolitik

Der außenpolitische Wandel ist Ausgangspunkt für die Bestandsaufnahme in „Canada's International Policies", dem aktuellsten Band zur kanadischen Außenpolitik. Ausgehend von John Kingdons Modell der multiplen Politikstränge (S. 22-28) identifizieren Tomlin et al. Zeitpunkte in der kanadischen Außenpolitik, in denen bisherige außenpolitische Handlungsweisen nicht mehr praktikabel sind und neue Probleme auf die Agenda gelangen. Diese können kurzfristiger – etwa ein Terroranschlag wie der 11. September 2001 – oder langfristiger Natur sein – so zum Beispiel der Klimawandel (1. Strang). Eine solche Änderung der außenpolitischen Agenda wird durch einen Selektionsprozess neuer außenpolitischer Optionen und Ideen ermöglicht, die erfolgreich in der außenpolitischen Community zirkuliert werden (Strang 2). Entscheidend für den Erfolg neuer Ideen – und damit den außenpolitischen Wandel – ist jedoch der institutionalisierte politische Bereich, der von Wahlkampfstrategien, parteipolitischen Überlegungen und Konsensfindungsprozessen geprägt ist (Strang 3). Nach Ansicht der drei Autoren bedarf der Wandel schließlich wirkmächtiger Fürsprecher (policy entrepreneur) und des richtigen Zeitpunkts (policy window). Dies klingt kompliziert und ist es zu Beginn auch, vor allem die anfängliche theoretische Trockenübung. Angesichts der (als Positivum zu verbuchenden) Schlichtheit in der Übertragung auf die einzelnen außenpolitischen Themenfelder weicht die anfängliche Unübersichtlichkeit zunehmend neuen Einsichten. Die fünf Kapitel zur Investitions-, Handels-, Verteidigungs-, Entwicklungs- und Human Security-Politik skizzieren in einem ersten Teil die drei Politikstränge, der darauffolgende Teil führt diese anschließend in einem Gesamtnarrativ unter dem Vorzeichen außenpolitischer Evolution zusammen. Damit gelingt es den Autoren etwa am Beispiel der Human Security Agenda aufzuzeigen, dass die – erfolgreichen – Versuche Kanadas, durch Initiativen wie dem Ottawa-Vertrag zum Verbot von Antipersonenminen, die Einrichtung des International Strafgerichtshofs in Den Haag oder die „Responsibility to Protect"-Doktrin (R2P) das humanitäre Völkerrecht zu stärken, auf ein Konglomerat verschiedenster politischer Prozesse auf nationaler Ebene und internationaler Ebene zurückzuführen sind. Den einfachen Erklärungen des Handbuchs wird hier eine echte Mehrebenenanalyse entgegengestellt. Demnach wäre die Human Security Agenda ohne die Affinität des langjährigen Außenministers Lloyd Axworthy (1996-2000) zu zivilgesellschaftlichen Gruppen und neuartigen Konsultationsforen wie dem von ihm geschaffenen Canadian Centre for Foreign Policy Development (CCFPD) nicht möglich gewesen (S. 208). Die Einflussmöglichkeiten dieser Gruppen waren jedoch nicht nur von Axworthys Unterstützung abhängig, sondern wurden letztlich von den enormen Einschnitten in die personellen und finanziellen Kapazitäten des Außenministeriums im Zuge der Haushaltskonsolidierung ermöglicht (S. 221). Darüber hinaus gelang es im Rahmen der inter-ministeriellen Auseinandersetzungen zwischen DND und DFAIT Axworthys Vorgänger, André Ouellet, den Handlungsspielraum zu erweitern und somit das Landminenverbot trotz der Widerstände im Verteidigungsministerium als Linie der Regierung durchzusetzen (S. 231-32). Erleichtert wurde die Akzeptanz der neuen außenpolitischen Agenda schließlich durch den Anklang, den die Ziele in der Bevölkerung fanden (S. 250-51, 260), und die Veränderung des globalen Diskurses, der in den 1990er Jahren zur Etablierung des „erweiterten Sicherheitsbegriffs" führte, als dessen prominentestes Beispiel sicher das *Human Security* Konzept gelten kann (S. 221). Den Abschluss von „Canada's International Policies" bilden schließlich sechs von Studierenden geschriebene Fallstudien zur Landminenkonvention, den kanadisch-chinesischen Beziehungen und dem Spannungsfeld zwischen kanadischen Handelsinteressen und seiner Politik der kulturellen Diversität. Weitere Beiträge zur Aufhebung des Patentrechts von Medikamenten im Rahmen der Entwicklungshilfe, die bilateralen Auseinandersetzungen mit den USA über den Devils Lake sowie Kanadas Positionen zum Kyoto-Protokoll komplementieren das Bild und bieten weitergehende Analysen vernachlässigter Themenbereiche.

Was nun? Die Suche nach einer zukunftsfähigen Vision für Kanadas Außenpolitik

Kanadas zukünftiger außenpolitischer Kurs ist offen wie nie zuvor. Zumindest die Frage nach dem *wie* – der Form des außenpolitischen Handelns. Der bisherige Konsens über den Erfolg der Mittelmacht ist nicht mehr existent. Ein „weiter so" ist schlicht nicht mehr möglich. Nicht nur in den Lehrbüchern wird die Zukunftsfähigkeit der bisherigen Instrumentarien einer Mittelmacht – Vermittlerfunktion, multilaterales Handeln, Einfluss durch Mitgliedschaft in internationalen Organisationen – in Frage gestellt. Auch in der Politik ist das der Fall. Premierminister Harper sieht Kanada angesichts seines Ressourcenreichtums bereits als neue Energie-Supermacht – aber ein Blick auf die Produktionskapazitäten enttarnt diese Ansicht als Wunschdenken (Hester 2007, 1 und 10). Auch ausländische Beobachter konstatieren seit den 1990er Jahren – entgegen der Ansicht von Autoren wie Byers oder Axworthy – einen zunehmend geringeren Einfluss Kanadas auf internationaler Ebene (Greenhill 2005). Dies zeigt, dass sowohl der auf Nischenaußenpolitik und größere Nähe zu den USA setzende Kurs im Namen des – wiederentdeckten? – nationalen Interesse, wie ihn Rempel, James et al. und zu Teilen Holloway vertreten, nicht weit führen wird. Schließlich erwartet die Bevölkerung zumindest auf symbolischer Ebene eine stärkere Abgrenzung. Zugleich ist aber auch eine hyper-idealistische kanadische Außenpolitik à la Byers nicht tragfähig. Sie untergräbt mit ihrer starken Orientierung an vermeintlich universalen Werten die bisherigen Stärken der kanadischen Diplomatie, den institutionalisierten Multilateralismus – z.B. in und durch die Vereinten Nationen – und glorifiziert eine Form der internationalen Verrechtlichung – siehe Ottawa-Konvention und internationaler Strafgerichtshof –, deren Errungenschaften in der Theorie besser zur Geltung kommen als im politischen Alltag. Somit wird auch die Auseinandersetzung zwischen Idealisten und Realisten weitergehen. Und über den Erfolg entscheiden wird maßgeblich die Art und Weise der Kommunikation innerhalb der bestehenden Spielregeln des außenpolitischen Betriebs. Am besten erkannt haben dies Tomlin, Hillmer und Hampson, die mit *Canada's International Policies* das überzeugendste gegenwärtige Standardwerk zur kanadischen Außenpolitik verfasst haben. Aber auch sie greifen in einem Punkt noch zu kurz. Zwar zeichnen sie detailliert und überzeugend nach, wie sich der außenpolitische Prozess verändert hat. Außenpolitische Ideen und Expertise werden zunehmend außerhalb der ministeriellen Bürokratie entwickelt. Dies spart zwar finanzielle Ressourcen, höhlt aber zugleich bisherige demokratische Prozesse aus. Der Einfluss des Parlaments ist so „erfolgreich" zurückgedrängt worden (Rempel 2003) und die Regierungen sehen sich aufgrund der Partikularinteressen, die durch ein derartiges „Outsourcing" der politischen Programmentwicklungskapazität in die Kapillaren des politischen Prozesses gelangen, gezwungen, ihre bisherige Strategie des New Public Management in den Ministerien zu überdenken (Bakvis 2000). Erkannt hatten dies bereits Black und Smith (1993) in ihrer damaligen Bestandsaufnahme der Literatur zur kanadischen Außenpolitik. Sie fragten bereits damals, wo die Beiträge blieben, die den Lesern aufzeigten, welche „epistemic communities" mit ihrem Wissen die Sichtweisen der Handelnden prägen würden. Tomlin et al. haben bereits luzide aufgezeigt, welche unterschiedlichen Perzeptionen und Formen des Wissens über die Welt im allgemeinen und Kanada im besonderen die kanadische Außenpolitik prägen. Auf der Frage nach den Ursprüngen dieses Wissens sind wir jedoch noch nicht weiter gekommen als vor 15 Jahren. Schade eigentlich. Aber es kann eigentlich nur besser werden.

David Bosold

Literatur

Axworthy, Lloyd, 2003, *Navigating A New World. Canada's Global Future*, Toronto: Alfred A. Knopf.

Black, David R./Heather A. Smith, 1993, "Notable Exceptions? New and Arrested Directions in Canadian Foreign Policy Literature", *Canadian Journal of Political Science/Revue canadienne de science politique*, 26.4, 745-774.

Byers, Michael, 2007b, "Celebration for a Nation", *Ottawa Citizen*, 16. Juni 2007.

Clark, Joe, 1985, *Competitiveness and Security: Directions for Canada's International Relations*, Ottawa: Ministry of Supply and Services.

Cohen, Andrew, 2003, *While Canada Slept. How we lost our place in the world*, Toronto: McClelland & Stewart.

Cooper, Andrew F., 1997, *Canadian Foreign Policy. Old Habits and New Directions*, Scarborough, ON: Prentice Hall.

Greenhill, Robert, 2005, *Making A Difference? External Views on Canada's International Impact. The Interim Report of the External Voices Project*. Toronto: Canadian Institute of International Affairs.

Government of Canada, 1986, *Canada's International Relations. Response of the Government of Canada to the Report of the Special Joint Committee of the Senate and the House of Commons*, Ottawa: Ministry of Supply and Services.

Hester, Annette, 2007, *Canada as the 'emerging energy superpower': testing the case*, Calgary: Canadian Defence & Foreign Affairs Institute.

Keating, Tom, 2002, *Canada and World Order. The Multilateralist Tradition in Canadian Foreign Policy*, 2. Aufl., Don Mills, ON: Oxford University Press.

Nossal, Kim Richard, 1997, *The Politics of Canadian Foreign Policy*, 3. Aufl., Scarborough, ON: Prentice Hall.

Rempel, Roy, 2006b, "Forget 'values', foreign policy should pursue the national interest", *The Globe and Mail*, 30. März 2006.

Rempel, Roy, 2003, *The Chatter Box: An Insider's Account of the Increasing Irrelevance of Parliament in the Making of Foreign Policy*, Toronto: Breakout.

Welsh, Jennifer, 2004, *At home in the world. Canada's global vision for the 21st century*, Toronto: Harper Collins.

Patrick James / Mark Kasoff (eds.), *Canadian Studies in the New Millennium*, Toronto, Buffalo, London: University of Toronto Press, 2008 (vii + 310 pp.; ISBN 978-0-8020-9468-1; pb, C$ 35.00).

Dieses Buch ist für die akademische Lehre in den Vereinigten Staaten von Amerika konzipiert, wo sich die Kanadastudien einer wachsenden Beliebtheit erfreuen. Die

10 Beiträge dieses sehr gelungenen Einführungstextes nehmen somit stets Bezug auf die USA, um den dortigen Studierenden die Besonderheiten Kanadas zu erläutern. Die Einzelkapitel beschäftigen sich mit Geographie und Wirtschaft Kanadas, der kanadischen Geschichte im nordamerikanischen Kontext, dem Regierungssystem und der Außenpolitik, den Ureinwohnern und Frauenthemen, Quebec, kanadischer Hoch- und Populärkultur. Ein resümierendes Abschlusskapitel der beiden amerikanischen Herausgeber skizziert Trends und Zukunftsaussichten der Kanadastudien in den USA.

Die Lernziele des Buches werden im Einleitungskapitel explizit formuliert. Es geht um die Schaffung von Grundkenntnissen in der Breite, nicht um vertiefte Kenntnisse in einem Teilbereich der Kanadastudien. Ohne es explizit zu formulieren, bereitet *Canadian Studies in the New Millennium* einen Grundkanon der nicht primär literatur- und sprachwissenschaftlich ausgerichteten Kanadastudien – zumindest für die US-amerikanische Kanadaforschung.

Das Buch mag für viele deutschsprachige Kanadisten zu oberflächlich sein, allerdings eignet es sich trotz der amerikanischen Ausrichtung hervorragend zur Heranführung von Nicht-Kanadisten an die Kanada-Materie und auch und gerade somit für Kanada-Module in B.A.-Studiengängen. Die Mehrheit der Autoren lehrt an US-amerikanischen Kanadazentren, einige Autoren stammen aus Kanada oder Europa.

Handwerklich ist das Buch hervorragend lektoriert und indexiert. Jedes abgeschlossene Kapitel enthält eine ausführliche Bibliographie und einen Anmerkungsapparat.

Für einen multidizplinären Einführungskurs in die Kanadastudien, der seinen Schwerpunkt nicht primär auf die Literatur- und Sprachwissenschaft hat, scheint das Buch derzeit nicht nur auf dem amerikanischen Markt konkurrenzlos zu sein.

Martin Thunert

Rosmarin Heidenreich, *Paysages de désir. J. R. Léveillé : réflexions critiques*, Ottawa: L'Interligne, 2005 (135 pp.; ISBN 978-2923274065; pb.; C$ 17.95.

Die in dieser Sammlung vereinten Studien der am *Collègue universitaire de Saint-Boniface* (Winnipeg, Manitoba) tätigen Literaturwissenschaftlerin sind bis auf einen Aufsatz und ein Interview schon während der beiden Jahrzehnte von 1985 bis 2004 veröffentlicht worden. Durch die Konzentration der Analysen auf einen prominenten Schriftsteller, sein Werk und sein literarisch-kulturpolitisches Umfeld gewinnt das Buch jedoch den Charakter einer reich differenzierten und zugleich abgerundeten Monographie, in der die Auseinandersetzung der Verfasserin mit der Literaturgeschichte des frankokanadischen Westens eine vorläufige Krönung findet.

In einer Zeit, in der die Kulturen Québecs und Akadiens im Rahmen der Romanistik in den deutschsprachigen Ländern erst nach und nach durch Gesamtdarstellungen universitäre Aufmerksamkeit auf sich ziehen, ist das literarische Leben der westlichen Provinzen Kanadas, von Ontario bis Britisch Kolumbien, immer noch wenig bekannt. In der *Kanadischen Literaturgeschichte* des Metzler Verlages (2005) wird J. R. Léveillé nur eine knappe Notiz gewidmet, der zufolge er in seinen Gedichten „von der Urbanität Montréals, New Yorks, Paris' und Winnipegs" spricht (S. 370). Dass es sich tatsächlich bei diesem Lyriker, Erzähler und Essayisten um eine zentrale Persönlichkeit in einer nach der Mitte des 20. Jahrhunderts aufblühenden literarischen Landschaft handelt, muss sich bei den Kanadisten des deutschen Sprachraums erst herumsprechen. Jenseits des Atlantiks ist die Aufmerksamkeit der québecer Fachwelt für die Literatur des Westens noch geringer. Die 2007 von Michel Biron, François Dumont und Elisabeth Nardout-Lafarge veröffentlichte *Histoire de la littérature québécoise* widmet der Literatur Akadiens und Ontarios ein Kapitel (S. 568-572), ohne sich weiter nach Sonnenuntergang vorzuwagen. Léveillé kommt im Register nicht vor.

Dabei gibt es bei diesem Autor eine Menge zu entdecken: sechs Romane, einige Lyrikbände, experimentelle Arbeiten auf dem Gebiet der Intermedialität, zahlreiche Essays, darunter auch Studien und Sammelbände zur Literatur Westkanadas. Rosmarin Heidenreich lässt dieses Opus nicht einfach Revue passieren, sondern bringt Annäherungen über einzelne Texte zur Sprache, stets auf der Suche nach fundamentalen Tendenzen, die es erlauben, Weltbild und sprachliche Strategie dieses vielschichtigen Autors auf einen Nenner zu bringen, bzw. in seiner literarisch-kulturellen Lebenswelt zu verorten. Denn mit J. R. Léveillé und einigen seiner unmittelbaren Zeitgenossen ist tatsächlich so etwas wie ein Bruch in der Geschichte des frankophonen Literaturschaffens westlich von Québec erfolgt. In seinen theoretischen Arbeiten beweist der Autor, dass er mit der Geschichte des Westens und vor allem der Provinz Manitoba vertraut ist, von der Tragödie der Métis in der Zeit des Louis Riel bis zur Zerstörung des frankophonen Schulwesens Anfang des 20. Jahrhunderts. Er präsentiert in Büchern wie *Anthologie de la poésie franco-manitobaine* (1990) oder *Parade ou les autres* (2005) die gesamte Entwicklung der Literatur des Westens seit ihren bescheidenen Anfängen bis zur Gründung eines frankophonen Verlagswesens im Winnipeg/Saint-Boniface der 70er Jahre und dem darauf folgenden Aufschwung des kulturellen Lebens. Aber in seinem eigenen Schaffen als Dichter und Erzähler ist von diesem regionalistischen Engagement nichts zu spüren. Hier herrscht allenthalben ein postmoderner Diskurs, der den Text fragmentiert, mit intertextuellen Spielen durchsetzt und den Leser nur zu leicht durch freies Komponieren mit heteroklitem Material verwirrt.

Aus alledem ergibt sich, dass das vorliegende Buch ein doppeltes Ziel verfolgt: Es soll einerseits einen außerhalb von Manitoba und den anderen kanadischen Provinzen des Westens (zu Unrecht) wenig bekannten Autor ins Rampenlicht des Interesses einer kanadischen und möglichst auch internationalen Öffentlichkeit rücken. Andererseits hat es aber auch den Charakter einer Anleitung, welche die Integration schwieriger Texte ins Repertoire eines engeren, westkanadischen Leserkreises, dessen Erwartungshorizont zum Teil von heimatverbundener Thematik und leicht lesbarer Darbietung geprägt ist, erleichtern soll. Den genannten Zielsetzungen entspricht wohl auch der Aufbau des Buches, das mit Interpretationen einzelner Texte einsetzt, im Mittelteil ein detailliertes Panorama der frankophonen Literatur Manitobas liefert (drei Kapitel!) und danach noch einmal einen der Romane Léveillés (*Plage*, 1984) präsentiert – diesmal in englischer Sprache –, um mit einem ausführlichen Interview des Schriftstellers durch die Autorin und bibliographischen Angaben zu Primär- und Sekundärliteratur zu enden.

Ein solches Ziel, Neugier zu wecken und Freude an der Lektüre zu vermitteln, lässt sich nur in dem Maße erreichen, als sich die Vermittlung auf starke persönliche Motivation und gründliche Auseinandersetzung mit den Texten stützen kann. In diesem Sinne setzt Heidenreich alles daran, jene Aspekte zu beleuchten, die sich zum Mosaik einer attraktiven literarischen Gesamterscheinung zusammensetzen lassen. Da ist die zivilisationskritische Komponente, die Léveillés virtuoses Komponieren mit Elementen der Medien- und Werbesprache motiviert. Da ist sein intertextueller Spieltrieb, der ihn ständig treibt, literarisches Erbe aus Amerika und Europa verfremdend und neuen Sinn stiftend in seine *écriture* einzubauen. Da ist aber auch und vielleicht vor allem ein durch einen weiten Bildungshorizont und philosophische Ambitionen gestützter Drang, sein ganzes Schaffen in den Dienst des literarischen Ausdrucks von Glücksempfindungen zu stellen. Damit ist nicht nur die sinnliche Komponente gemeint, zu der sich Léveillé freilich ausdrücklich bekennt, wenn er sich (z. B. im Interview am Ende des Bandes) als Dichter der Erotik outet, sondern ein Zustand der geistigen Wachheit und Disponibilität, der keineswegs ausschließlich an die Gegenwart eines geliebten Menschen gebunden ist. Offenheit für die Geschenke des Zufalls, illusionsloses Annehmen der Conditio humana (nicht zuletzt im Hinblick auf die Verdüsterung seiner Kindheit durch ein schweres Asthmaleiden) und Freude am Schreiben gehen eine wahrhaft festliche Verbindung ein, durch welche J. R. Léveillé unter den anderen Avantgardisten des frankophonen Manitoba, welche Heidenreich im Mittelteil ihres Buches ausführlich präsentiert, eine Sonderstellung einnimmt. Solche von Heiterkeit geprägte Schaffensfreude ist auch ein kulturpolitisches Programm, wenn es sich um einen Schriftsteller aus den Reihen einer in ihrer Existenz bedrohten Sprachminderheit handelt. Diesen Elan fühlbar zu machen, ist der Autorin an mehreren Stellen ihres Buches gelungen, was nicht das geringste Verdienst der vorliegenden Studie darstellt.

Fritz Peter Kirsch

Gilles Dupuis / Klaus-Dieter Ertler (éds.), *À la carte. Le roman québécois (2000-2005)*, Frankfurt am Main, Berlin, Bern, Bruxelles, New York, Oxford, Wien: Peter Lang, 2007, (493 pp.; ISBN 9783631553404; € 53,00)

Der Appell der beiden Herausgeber weckte offenbar ein kräftiges Echo in der Fachwelt: 24 Forschende und Lehrende, die sich mit der québecer Literatur befassen, haben nach eigenem Gutdünken einen während der ersten fünf Jahre des neuen Jahrtausends erschienenen Roman gewählt und im Rahmen von jeweils rund 20 Druckseiten analysiert. Auf vollständige Erfassung der Romanproduktion in dem genannten Zeitraum wurde kein Wert gelegt, schon eher auf die Einhaltung des zeitlichen Rahmens der Publikationsdaten, allerdings mit kleinem Toleranzspielraum diesseits und jenseits der Periode von 2000 bis 2005. Auf diese Weise kommen Autor(inn)en aus verschiedenen Generationen zusammen. Neben Nelly Arcan, die 2001 mit *Putain* debütierte und in dem vorliegenden Band mit ihrem zweiten Roman *Folle* von 2004 vertreten ist, finden sich Autor(inn)en wie Nicole Brossard und Jacques Poulain, deren Produktion schon vor längerer Zeit begonnen hat, so dass die präsentierten Texte bereits in die Kategorie Alterswerk fallen. Rund die Hälfte der Beiträger(innen) kann kanadischen Universitäten zugeordnet werden, die andere Hälfte besteht aus Europäern aus Österreich, Deutschland, Rumänien und Norwegen (die beiden letztgenannten Länder werden von je einer Person repräsentiert).

Wie in der Einleitung klargestellt wird, geht es den Herausgebern um die Erstellung des vom Titel versprochenen Menüs, das dem geneigten Leser einen Überblick über die Romanproduktion Québecs in der Gegenwart liefern soll. Auf dem Buchdeckel wird der kulinarische Ansatz noch hervorgehoben durch die Reproduktion eines Stilllebens, das der frankokanadische Maler Marc-Aurèle de Foy Suzor-Côté Anfang des 20. Jahrhunderts geschaffen und mit *Le Déjeuner du célibataire* betitelt hat. Damit wird auf die Freiheit angespielt, die den Beiträgern zugestanden wurde und die natürlich auch für den Leser gilt. Statt sich einem grob charakterisierenden Motto zu unterwerfen, wie dies an einem vergleichbaren, von Wolfgang Asholt herausgegebenen Band zum französischen Roman der achtziger Jahre zu beobachten ist (*Intertextualität und Subversivität. Studien zur Romanliteratur der achtziger Jahre in Frankreich*, Heidelberg 1994) breitet sich das Romanmaterial gleichsam als appetitanregendes Nebeneinander vor dem Blick des literarischen Gourmets aus, um ihn zu attraktiven Leseabenteuern zu inspirieren. Solche Verbindung von Literatur und Buffet kann bei dem Literaturwissenschafter, der es gewohnt ist, Dichtung nicht als Konsumartikel zu betrachten, sondern als Arbeit an Sprache und Kultur, Unbehagen hervorrufen. Hingegen fällt es leichter, für ein solches Konzept Verständnis aufzubringen, wenn der apologetische Zug des gesamten Projekts bewusst wird: Québecs Literatur stand so lange im Schatten der großen Produktionen Frankreichs und Anglo-Nordamerikas, dass ein munteres Auftrumpfen mit nahrhafter Dichtung aus guter und zeitgemäßer Küche seine Berechtigung haben mag. Speziell der Romanist aus den deutschsprachigen Ländern wird sich an das alte Bild des Buches als Speise erinnern, auch wenn sich Dantes Dictum vom Brot der Engel kaum auf die zu Beginn des 21. Jahrhunderts doch recht unfromm wirkende Literatur aus Französisch-Kanada anwenden lässt.

Anregend wirkt die in diesem Band dargebotene Vielfalt einer blühenden, zu Unrecht international wenig bekannten Romanproduktion zweifellos. Da es sich um Momentaufnahmen handelt, stellt literarhistorische Perspektivierung kein besonderes Anliegen dar, was dem gesamten Projekt nicht angekreidet werden kann, in manchen Fällen aber zu Verkürzungen führt. Hier nur ein besonders frappantes Beispiel: In ihrer Analyse von Michel Delisles *Dée* betont Catherine Mavrikakis die pessimistische Beurteilung des Einzugs von Québec in die Moderne während und nach der *Révolution tranquille*, so wie sie sich in der vorwiegend negativen Darstellung der Relation von Kindern und Erwachsenen bei dem behandelten Autor manifestiert. Hier hätte sich die Gelegenheit geboten, über das Nachwirken einer thematischen Konstante nachzudenken, die schon bei Marie-Claire Blais, André Langevin oder René Ducharme eine entscheidende Rolle spielt und auf kulturhistorische Besonderheiten der Familienthematik in der québecer Literatur seit dem 19. Jahrhundert verweist. Die Lektüre macht Lust, solche kurz geratenen Fäden weiterzuspinnen, was ja der Intention der Herausgeber durchaus entspricht.

Nicht nur die zeitliche Beschränkung, auch die Frage der räumlichen Abgrenzungen macht Appetit auf Mehr. Es ist geradezu faszinierend, zu beobachten, wie wenig scharf gezogen die Ränder des wissenschaftlichen Untersuchungsgegenstandes „Literatur Québecs" wirken, ohne dass das immer wieder hereinwirkende Draußen selbst konsequent in die Analyse einbezogen wird. Denn nur wenige Beiträge begnügen sich mit der Beleuchtung eines Textes im Rahmen der Gesamtproduktion des Autors/der Autorin bzw. im Kontext des québecer Literaturbetriebs. Meist landen die Interpretationen früher oder später beim Problemkreis des Frankreichbezugs der québecer Literatur oder bei den nicht minder aktuellen Fragen nach der „américanité" oder der Positionierung der „littérature migrante". Inter- und transkulturelle Bezüge werden immer wieder angedeutet, ohne dass es die ganze Anlage des Bandes erlaubt, ihnen mit Nachdruck auf den Grund zu gehen. Der eine oder andere Beitrag bleibt stecken in der klischeehaften Gegensätzlichkeit einer identitär-nationalistischen Tradition eines sich dem „repliement" verpflichtenden Québec und heutigen Öffnungstendenzen im Sinne der globalen Hybridisierung. Man fragt sich, ob es den Beiträger(inne)n in allen Fällen bewusst war oder wurde, wie problematisch ihr speisekartenhaftes Nebeneinander die immer noch einzelsprachlich eher, im günstigsten Falle, auf zwei Gründernationen und ihre kulturelle Nachbarschaft hin orientierte Literaturgeschichtsschreibung im heutigen Kanada erscheinen lässt. In einem Fall hat das Flimmern des theoretischen Konzepts zur Einbeziehung eines Aufsatzes geführt, der eigentlich in einen anderen Sammelband von literarischen Essays zu integrieren gewesen wäre. Gemeint ist hier der (ausgezeichnete) Beitrag von François Paré über die Akadierin France Daigle, der sich bemüht, die literarische Existenz der frankophonen Minderheiten außerhalb Québecs zu betonen, aber gerade dadurch die Stimmigkeit des Bandes stört.

Der Mitherausgeber Klaus-Dieter Ertler hat sich offensichtlich von den vielfältigen Anregungen seines Sammelbandes zum Weiterdenken anregen lassen, wenn er im letzten Band der *Zeitschrift für Kanada-Studien* (28. Jahrgang 2008/ Heft 2, 67-89) sozusagen als sein eigener Rezensent ein

Panorama mit dem Titel „Das literarische System der Provinz Québec: Der Roman von 2000 bis 2006" entwirft und in einer Fußnote desselben Aufsatzes das Projekt einer weiteren Sammlung von Romananalysen für die Jahre 2006-2010 erwähnt. Am Puls der literarischen Entwicklung Québecs zu bleiben ist sicher sinnvoll und wichtig. Es ist aber zu hoffen, dass durch solche kulturimmanenten Initiativen der wahrscheinlich unvermeidliche Übergang zu einer Literaturgeschichte interkultureller Prägung nicht verzögert wird. Damit ist nicht eine Neuauflage der eher schematischen Paarungsversuche zwischen Anglophonie und Frankophonie gemeint, wie sie einst Ronald Sutherland (*Second Image*, 1971), Clément Moisan (*Poésie des frontières*, 1979) und Philipp Stratford (*All the Polarities*, 1986) vorgeschlagen haben, sondern die wechselseitige Beleuchtung literarischer Texte innerhalb eines sich in der Geschichte konstituierenden Areals kultureller Abhängigkeiten und Austauschmöglichkeiten. In dem Maße als ein québecer Roman nicht mehr isoliert bzw. unter dem Aspekt des Eindringens „fremder" Einflüsse betrachtet wird, sondern inmitten einer literarischen Landschaft, in der die Strukturen der hereinwirkenden Referenzkulturen, ob sie nun von derselben Sprache getragen werden oder nicht, ebenso deutlich gemacht werden wie jene, die für die literarische Arbeit innerhalb Québecs maßgeblich sind, sollte es auch möglich sein, das atlantische Akadien, Louisiana oder die Frankophonie Westkanadas sowohl unter dem Aspekt ihrer Abhängigkeit wie auch jenem ihrer Eigenständigkeit, als Literaturen in französischer Sprache im Kontext Nordamerika, zu behandeln.

Literatur Québecs heute, das ist die Literatur einer multikulturellen Gesellschaft im Werden, der keine Eigenstaatlichkeit die einheitsstiftende Klammer liefert, während das sprachliche Vehikel Französisch einem beträchtlichen Assimilationsdruck seitens der auf kontinentaler Ebene dominierenden Konkurrenzsprache ausgesetzt ist. Sprache und Kultur einer Mehrheit, die zugleich eine Minderheit ist – solche Fälle machen Probleme, nicht zuletzt weil sie letztlich auch die „Normalität" der Mehrheitskulturen in Frage stellen. Das vorliegende Buch klammert diese Probleme aus und setzt voll auf die Freude am Text, wie sie der Philologe als Interpret bei sich selber aufkommen lässt, in der Hoffnung, damit die intensivere Teilhabe des Lesers gewinnen zu können. Dass sich diese Freude meldet, kann der Rezensent nach der Lektüre aller Analysen, von denen ihn keine einzige gelangweilt hat und jede für sich das hohe Niveau der québecer Romanproduktion demonstriert, getrost bestätigen.

Fritz Peter Kirsch

Verzeichnis der Autor(inn)en und Rezensent(inn)en

Die Autor(inn)en

Bories-Sawala, Helga E., Dr. habil., Bremer Institut für Kanada- und Québec-Studien, Universität Bremen, Fachbereich 10, Postfach 33 04 40, D-28334 Bremen. sawala@uni-bremen.de

Kammel, Armin, Dr., c/o VÖIG, Schubertring 9-11/2/2/33, 1010 Wien, Österreich. armin911_at@yahoo.de

Klaus, Peter G., Dr., Freie Universität Berlin, Institut für Romanistische Philologie, Habelschwerdter Allee45, D-14195 Berlin. klauspet@zedat.fu-berlin.de

Krampe, Christian J., M.A., Zentrum für Kanadastudien (ZKS), Universität Trier, 54286 Trier. mail@cjkrampe.de

Mensel, Isabelle, Universität Bonn, Institut VII/Romanistik, Am Hof 1, 53113 Bonn. imensel@uni-bonn.de

Richter, Miriam, Am Hallenbad 22, 41352 Kleinenbroich. m.v.richter@web.de

Stange, Marion, M.A:, John F. Kennedy-Institut, Abteilung Geschichte, SFB 700 – Teilprojekt B3, Binger Straße 40 14197 Berlin. stange@jfki.fu-berlin.de

Villeneuve, Paul, Prof. Dr. em., Centre de recherche en aménagement et développement, Université Laval, Québec, G1K 7P4. paul.villeneuve@crad.ulaval.ca

Die Rezensent(inn)en

Bosold, David, Deutsche Gesellschaft für Auswärtige Politik e.V., Rauchstraße 17/18, 10787 Berlin. bosold@dgap.org

Kirsch, Fritz Peter, Univ.- Prof. (i.R.) Dr., Universitätscampus AAKH, Hof 8, Spitalgasse 2, A-1090 Wien. Fritz.Peter.Kirsch@univie.ac.at

Thunert, Martin, PD Dr., Heidelberg Center for American Studies, Universität Heidelberg, Engelhorn Palais, Hauptstraße 120, 69117 Heidelberg. martin.thunert@web.de

Hinweise für Autor(inn)en

Die Zusendung von Aufsätzen, Miszellen sowie Literaturberichten ist erwünscht. Beim Verfassen der Texte sind die "Redaktionellen Hinweise", die auf Anforderung von den Sektionsleiter(inne)n zugesandt werden, zu berücksichtigen.

Bitte lassen Sie Ihre Beiträge der zuständigen Schriftleitung über das jeweilige Mitglied des wissenschaftlichen Beirats zukommen. Jeder Autor bzw. jede Autorin ist für den Inhalt des jeweiligen Beitrags verantwortlich. Alle Beiträge sind in einem Ausdruck sowie auf Diskette einzureichen.

Die Vergabe von Rezensionen erfolgt über die jeweiligen Fachvertreter; bitte richten Sie Rezensionsvorschläge an diese. Rezensionsexemplare sind der zuständigen Schriftleitung, Prof. Dr. Peter Dörrenbächer, zuzusenden.

Veröffentlichungssprachen der *Zeitschrift für Kanada-Studien* sind deutsch, englisch und französisch. Grundsätzlich sollen die Artikel in der Muttersprache der Autoren bzw. Autorinnen veröffentlicht werden. Abweichungen von diesem Grundsatz liegen in der Eigenverantwortung der Autor(inn)en.

Notes for Contributors

Contributions in the form of essays, reviews, or miscellaneous articles are welcome. Contributors should follow the editorial guidelines ("Style Sheet"), which are available on request from the editors.

Contributions should be sent to the managing editors via the respective members of the academic committee. Authors are responsible for the contents of their contributions. All contributions should be sent in one print-out as well as on disk.

The works to be reviewed are chosen by the individual members of the academic committee; any suggestions for reviews are welcome and should be directed to them. Review copies should be sent to the managing editor responsible: Prof. Dr. Peter Dörrenbächer.

The *Zeitschrift für Kanada-Studien* publishes articles in German, English, and French. In general, articles should be written in the contributors' native language. Contributors are responsible for any departures from this general rule.

Avis aux auteurs

Nous acceptons les collaborations sous forme d'articles, de notes et de comptes rendus. Les auteurs sont priés de tenir compte des règles de rédaction qui leur seront envoyées sur demande par les directeurs de la publication.

Nous demandons aux auteurs d'envoyer leurs collaborations au membre respectif du comité académique, qui les fera parvenir à la direction. Les auteurs sont entièrement responsables du contenu de leurs articles. Nous demandons une copie et un exemplaire sur disque de toute collaboration.

Les membres du comité académique choisissent les œuvres qui feront l'objet d'un compte rendu; nous vous prions de leur adresser vos suggestions et d'envoyer les exemplaires de service de presse au directeur responsable, Prof. Dr. Peter Dörrenbächer.

Le *Zeitschrift für Kanada-Studien* publie des articles en allemand, en français et en anglais. Généralement, les articles doivent être écrits dans la langue maternelle de l'auteur. Les auteurs sont entièrement responsables de toute déviation de cette règle.

Beiträge zur Kanadistik Band 13   Schriftenreihe der Gesellschaft für Kanada-Studien

Dirk Hoerder

To Know Our Many Selves Changing Across Time and Space

From the Study of Canada to Canadian Studies

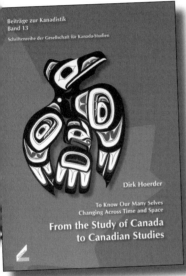

In the early 1970s, the Commission on Canadian Studies prepared its report under the title "To Know Ourselves." Taking a perspective from outside of Canada and a focus on issues of diversity of the 1990s – "our many selves" – the present study argues that rather than place the beginning of Canadian Studies in the 1960s and 70s, the Study of Canada evolved in three major phases of innovation since the 1840s.

While around 1900, Country Studies in Europe began from self-images propagated by "high culture," Canadian Studies, in contrast, began from the analytical social sciences and in the 1960s became a self-study to counter the still predominant colonial contexts. However, it neglected Canada's own colonized Native peoples. Thus decolonization approaches and nationhood perspectives clashed with or engaged each other.

Band **13**
Dirk Hoerder
From the Study of Canada
to Canadian Studies
347 pages, ISBN 978-3-89639-495-8
€ 19,80

Band **12**
Dirk Hoerder and Konrad Gross (Eds.
Twenty-Five Years Gesellschaft für
Kanada-Studien
256 pages, ISBN 978-3-89639-417-0
€ 24,80

Wißner-Verlag
Im Tal 12
86179 Augsburg, Germany
www.wissner.com

Beiträge zur Kanadistik Schriftenreihe der Gesellschaft für Kanada-Studien

Band 11
Hartmut Lutz
Approaches: Essays in Native North American Studies and Literatures
282 Seiten, ISBN 978-3-89639-340-1
24.80 EUR

Band 10
Armando E. Jannetta
Ethnopoetics of the Minority Voice: An Introduction to the Politics of Dialogism and Difference in Métis Literature
179 Seiten, ISBN 978-3-89639-238-1
24.00 EUR

Band 9
Christina Strobel
Reconsidering Conventions: Jane Rule's Writing and Sexual Identity in North American Feminist Theory and Fiction
346 Seiten, ISBN 978-3-89639-164-3
24.00 EUR

Band 7
Christina Strobel, Doris Eibl (Hrsg.)
Selbst und Andere/s: Von Begegnungen und Grenzziehungen
184 Seiten, ISBN 978-3-89639-124-7
16.00 EUR

Band 6
Birgit Mertz-Baumgartner
"Monologues québécois" oder Geschichten eines "Monsieur qui parle tout seul": Standortbestimmung einer Gattung am Rande
218 Seiten, ISBN 978-3-89639-063-9
24.00 EUR

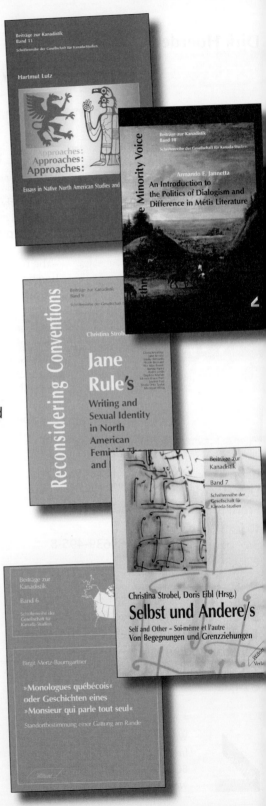